The Deadly Deals

Rites of Passage of a Master Spy

Based on a True Spy Story

Dr. Julio Antonio del Marmol

The Cuban Lightning

© Copyright 2017 Dr. Julio Antonio del Marmol.

All rights reserved. No part of this publication may be reproduced, stored in a retrieval system, or transmitted, in any form or by any means, electronic, mechanical, photocopying, recording, or otherwise, without the written prior permission of the author.

ISBN: 978-1-68588-016-3 (sc)
ISBN: 978-1-68588-015-6 (hc)
ISBN: 978-1-68588-017-0 (e)

Because of the dynamic nature of the Internet, any web addresses or links contained in this book may have changed since publication and may no longer be valid.

Any people depicted in stock imagery provided by Thinkstock are models, and such images are being used for illustrative purposes only.

Certain stock imagery © Thinkstock.

Cuban Lightning Publications, Int rev. 10/31/2017

Introduction

At the age of twelve, the author, Julio Antonio del Marmol, found that his destiny had taken him through extraordinary circumstances that happen only a few times in history during widespread social chaos—like those seen in the deranged turmoil of the Cuban Revolution in 1959. The supreme leader, Fidel Castro, nominated this young boy to be the Commander-in-Chief of the new army for the future.

As Fidel Castro went through his own changes of heart at the start of this tumultuous time, the youth went through his own conflict as he watched his childhood friends abandon the island, discontented with the complete disruption of democratic establishment and the institution of Marxist ideology by the new leaders. Julio Antonio del Marmol, the Young Commander, sadly remained behind and daily observed the freedom of the Cuban people evaporate as promise after promise was broken. In spite of the commitment to equality for all without distinction based on political or religious belief, the Castro brothers and Che Guevara ruthlessly hunted down and exterminated all opposition. His admiration towards the leaders turned into disappointment and frustration, as he watched the Castros' forces execute their enemies and commit the most horrendous crimes humanity had ever seen in their ambition to maintain power.

He concluded that this is not what the Cuban people had fought their revolution for and decided, before sharing these horrible experiences with anyone, including his father, to abandon the country as his friends had done. When he did share these intentions with his uncle, he received the most shocking surprise: his relative was a veteran master spy. His uncle proposed that he be trained to be the next in line, and Julio Antonio del Marmol became the youngest spy in modern history at the age of thirteen.

In this story, the reader will find seemingly unbelievable and undoubtedly controversial details about the blueprints to create communist revolutions, spread corruption, and commit assassinations so outrageous that nobody ever could create this as a fiction. We are transported back to 1961, in which the young master spy foils the insurance fraud for the La Coubre explosion, attempts to warn the Americans about the planned decoys to thwart their planned invasion of Cuba, and continues his deadly dance with the G-2's Piñeiro. He also discovers that Che is playing a double game against his Soviet masters and the Chinese communists, playing one group against the other, and is shocked at the connection he forms with Guevara's illegitimate daughter.

The author tells the story not merely as a narrator; he was an active participant in these events as part of his first steps in his life as a thirteen-year-old spy, as he tried to retrieve what he felt to be important documents for his friends in his intelligence network. He perceived the relevance and import of what he had obtained. Readers will draw their own conclusions and put the facts together. Only when the author's friends reviewed the data did he realize the sheer magnitude of what he had accomplished as he exposed in this one act what really lies behind the deadly deals.

The Cuban Lightning

Volume IV of Rites of Passage of a Master Spy

Acknowledgements

I am a very lucky man because I have a great group of people by my side that I not only consider my friends but also who are the most capable, sacrificing professionals equal to the ones I've risked my life with over the past 50 years in their dedication and values. This group has made possible the publication of this book. To them, with all my heart today, I give the best of my love, gratitude, and sincerest thanks to every one of these fantastic warriors. In order of seniority, I would especially like to thank O'Brien: a great friend, a great individual with extraordinary values, thank you for your contributions you have made in many different ways to this project, as well being loyally by my side and watching my back for almost all of my career. I know for a fact you have never done that before for anyone. To my right arm and great friend, Tad Atkinson: for your dedication to every detail in research and many hours of hard work with me, never hesitating to sacrifice even your personal and private family time in order to make this happen. To Steve Weese: thank you for the many pieces of computer and graphic work as well professional enhancement of photos to improve the quality of the book. To Carlos Mota: my thanks for your dedication and multiple contributions and sacrifices you have made in order to make this happen. To Gervasin Neto: for your constant loyalty and many hours standing on your feet or hiding between cars in order to maintain our security with your group of people you've coordinated to watch our backs, continually keeping us informed of any suspicious activity that occurs in our surroundings. To Chopin: for your great companionship, loyalty, and support for the last 50 years with me in our fight for freedom and that beautiful, generous letter you wrote in behalf of the project. To our editor, Jen Poiry-Prough: who managed to make this book as easy to read, using her magic touch to polishing this piece of coal and bring to you, the readers, what I consider to be a very rare diamond. It makes all of us very proud to be involved in this project. Your professionalism, vast knowledge, and dedication, has made this book a great piece for future generations. To all of you, my friends who remain in the shadows, who contributed in one way or another in making this book and help me to bring the truth to the public, you have given the best of yourselves, putting forth your best effort to educate future generations. God bless you all. I embrace you as the Christian warriors that you all are.

Dr. Julio Antonio del Marmol

Prologue: A Lesson to Remember

My birthday started promisingly: a beautiful, sunny day in the early hours of May. We still lived in the same villa in the small town of Guane in the province Pinar del Rio in which I was born. It was the ninth anniversary of the morning I was delivered into the hands of the good and lovely midwife, Majito. She had in turn received me into the world under stressful circumstances from my Mima's womb.

I woke up in my bed to find before me both women, Majito and Mima, smiling broadly with a large birthday cake with nine lit candles. Surrounding them were my brothers and sisters, who all joined in singing "Happy Birthday." I felt that this should be a wonderful day, given this joyous start to it. Half-awake, urged by multiple voices, I blew out my candles. I said, "It looks like a yummy cake!"

Everyone yelled at the top of their lungs, "Happy Birthday, Julio Antonio!"

Mima was grinning mischievously. She said, "Hurry up and get dressed, so you can open all your presents." She raised a finger. "But you have a small present on the terrace that I want you to attend to first."

Majito looked at Mima, her grin exactly matching Mima's, which was a very unusual expression for both of them. I didn't give it too much importance, as I was busy rubbing the sleep out of my eyes. I joyfully assumed that the present on the terrace might be the precious *kikiriki*[1] I had asked Mima to buy for me earlier while we were at a pet store, and I eagerly jumped out of bed. Everyone else left my room and headed towards the dining room where the cake was to be cut.

I ran into the bathroom, washed my face, and dressed hurriedly. Mima, however, was waiting for me outside my room. She took me by the hand and said, "Come with me. I want to show you what's on the terrace first."

I smiled and nodded. "OK, Mima."

"Don't worry about it. They won't cut the cake until you come back. But I think your stomach should be empty when you see this."

I felt a little apprehensive as we walked out onto the terrace. She pointed at the impeccable tile floor of the terrace, pink with flecks of gray and shining in the early morning sun. I followed the direction of her gesture in confusion.

I looked back at her and saw in her hands a small piece of toilet paper. She handed it to me. I looked again at the terrace and noticed a trail of chicken feces by the stairs leading to the patio. Down there on the patio were the fruit trees, pig corrals, and pens in which other animals were kept. Suddenly, from one of the planters lining the terrace, my small bantam hen jumped down, followed by

---

[1] A bantam rooster

six tiny chicks. Mima looked at them with an unhappy face.

"There you are!" she said to them. "I was wondering where you were hiding."

I looked into the planter in which Mima had so carefully kept her herb gardens and saw that the hen had been scratching in the dirt. It was an utter mess.

I hurriedly apologized and moved towards the hen. I opened the gate and attempted to herd the hen and her chicks into the yard. The hen, however, thought I was threatening her chicks and hissed menacingly at me. Unless the chicks walked in front of her, she didn't allow me to come close. Any time I drew near in my attempts to shoo them through the gate, she would turn, her frill fluffed out intimidatingly, and courageously advance on me with hisses and angry clucks. She came right up and pecked at my pants leg, forcing me to skip back a little. Mima watched all of this with a smirk on her face, a little unhappy at what had happened but a trifle amused at the sight.

My frustration grew at my pet's lack of cooperation. I noticed Mima's expression and remembered my father's main rule: no animals allowed near the living area of our house. I tried to hurry the poultry through the gate. Finally, I managed to remove my pets from the terrace. I turned and apologized. "I'm sorry, Mima. Somebody—and it wasn't me—left the gate open."

Mima nodded understandingly. She pointed at the mess left by the chicken on the terrace tile. "You know what you have to do. Go ahead."

I said nothing but grimaced in disgust. I knew I had to do it. It was my pet, after all, and it was my responsibility. I took the toilet paper and got down on my knees. I put the toilet paper over the pile, but as I started to pick it up in the paper, my finger rubbed along the remains still on the tile. It smelled so bad, and the combination of that and my revulsion of touching the residue made me retch, and I held my hand to my mouth to avoid vomiting. I dropped the toilet paper, and the disgusting substance it contained spattered over the tile, making an even greater mess than before.

Mima watched me gag and said, "Now you know why I wanted you to do this on an empty stomach."

Majito, my emergency mother and salvation, approached us from the other side of the terrace. She watched pityingly at what was going on and looked at my mother, silently asking for permission to help out. Perhaps because it was my birthday, Mima looked a little guilty. She nodded her permission and turned to me with a stern expression. "I will allow Majito to help you and do it for you today, but only because it's your birthday. Next time if you're not capable of preventing this from happening or cleaning up after your pet, don't think I'll ever buy another one to jump in the planters and destroy our hard work. These are the herbs I put in your food! These pets should be in a cage, not running around on the patio, much less in the house. Next time, remember, if I find this has happened again, your pet will end up in the pressure cooker in one of those delicious Sunday macaronis I prepare for your father on the weekends."

Majito knelt down beside me and was cleaning the remainder of the excrement, pitying my unhappy expression which formed at Mima's last words. She pursed her lips into a sympathetic pout and compassionately patted my hair with her left hand. "It's OK, don't worry about it. Mima is just a little upset. But you have to be responsible and not let that bird wander around here on the terrace. Put it where it belongs, in the cage."

Mima said, "OK, that's good enough. Majito can take care of the rest. Go wash your hands and go to the dining room. Your brothers and sisters are waiting for you to cut the cake."

Like I had been hit by lightning, I jumped up and ran to the bathroom before Mima could change her mind. I washed my hands desperately, continually smelling my fingers until that horrific odor was gone. As I walked back to the dining room, I felt that this day was not turning out as pleasantly as I had initially anticipated after all.

Very late in the afternoon, Mima asked me to go to the little store a few blocks from our house to bring a glass bottle of milk, a loaf of bread, and some chicken eggs. She wanted to make a special dessert for my birthday, *torrejas*[2].

On my way home, I saw that the sun was nearly down and it was already fairly dark. I tried to rush home, as I wasn't fond of being alone in the dark that much. In the distance, I saw with horror the short, plump black man named Tatun, dragging his right leg as he came in my direction. He always had that strange limp.

He bore a very heavy, black braided beard and he wore his long hair in dreadlocks. His teeth were stained by tobacco, and he had the worst body odor I had yet encountered—until a few years later when I met Che Guevara. He stunk worse than the chicken feces I had

---

[2] A slice of bread soaked in milk or wine with honey and spices. After being dipped in egg, it is fried in a pan with olive oil.

cleaned up earlier that day. I got goosebumps.

That revolting individual lived alone by the bank of the Cuyaguateje River—the bogeyman of town, feared by all the children and disliked by the adults. There he practiced the African religion of Santeria. He was for a long time my greatest terror and nightmare after the stories Majito and Mima had told me from my infancy.

As I always did when I saw this man, I ran to conceal myself. According to everyone in town, this man had been in jail repeatedly for different crimes. Though they could never prove it, this man had been suspected in the disappearance of many young children. The story was that he killed the children to cut out their hearts as offerings during his morbid rituals or to sell to the other members of his cult for the same purpose.

I clutched the loaf of bread and bottle of milk against my chest with my right hand and held onto the basket of eggs with my left. I darted into a long corridor that led to one of the office doors of the *escogida de tabaco*[3]. It was of typical Spanish construction—the roofs of the various buildings created overhangs to protect pedestrians from the rain.

I walked to the end of the corridor and virtually glued myself against the wall, hoping he would pass by the mouth and I could hide, unseen, in the growing darkness. I took a deep breath. I had no doubt in my mind that this was the most unpleasant birthday I had ever had. I asked myself why on this precise day I had to have an encounter with Tatun, the one character I didn't simply fear—he made me panic. My hands started to sweat, and my heart

---

[3] Warehouse where tobacco is sorted by quality of leaves.

pounded like a train locomotive. As if this weren't enough, the darkness in the corridor was deepening. Although this was in my favor, as it concealed me from the man in the street outside, darkness was my second greatest fear after Tatun.

    I was not able to control it, and I started to hyperventilate. I swallowed, clenched my jaws, and closed my eyes, wishing to be buried in the earth where no one could see me. I prayed with all my heart that Tatun would walk by without spotting me.

    I heard his shuffling drag as he came down the stairs to the sidewalk. The sound drew closer. I got goosebumps again. The nails on his shoes made a strange metallic clink against the concrete sidewalk as he dragged his handicapped leg. Clink, drag. Clink, drag. The sound was eerie. Suddenly the sound stopped, right at the mouth of the corridor. Until this moment, my eyes had been squeezed shut, but at the cessation of sound, I opened them, turned my head, and looked toward the mouth of the corridor.

    I could see his silhouette at the mouth in the twilight. He leaned against the wall, and I could see a hand reach into his tattered coat and pull something out. It was a rag. He mopped his face with it, evidently taking a breather after his long walk.

    Completely petrified, I held my breath. If he discovered me there, I had no way to escape. I lifted the basket of eggs over my head in preparation to defend myself.

    Tatun, however, remained at the mouth in his same position. He looked in my direction, but apparently he could not see me. My dark clothes blended with the darkness of the corridor. Nevertheless, my heart stopped when he looked inside. He pulled something else out of his pocket. I took a deep breath as quietly as I could. I wondered why I had to endure this horrible moment on my birthday, dealing with my two worst fears at the same time. At least I was beginning to feel less fearful about the darkness, since it was presently my ally. Tatun represented the greater immediate threat.

Tatun lit a match—the object he had taken from his pocket. I very slowly and cautiously crouched down. Unfortunately, I did not calculate my nearness to the wall. The bottle of milk clinked against it. In the silence of the corridor, the echo sounded more like glass breaking. Luckily, the bottom was the portion that struck the wall, and so it did not break, but it caught Tatun's attention. Instead of lighting the cigar stub in his mouth, he held the match up and into the corridor to see what was inside.

He yelled authoritatively and in irritation, "What the Devil are you doing in here, kid? Get out of that corner and come over here right now!"

The match he held in his hand was burning faster that he was prepared for, and he burned his fingers. He grunted in pain and threw the match in my direction.

I gathered myself slowly, petrified in my panic. At the same time, he lit another match. I tucked the loaf of bread inside my shirt as I stood, held the bottle of milk in one hand and the basket of eggs in the other, and slowly started to walk towards him, timidly, taking short steps.

He snapped, "Hurry up! Come over here! Let's see what you've got there! Give it to me!" He held his left hand out towards me as his right hand held the match. I held out the basket of eggs. He shook his head angrily. "No, give me the bottle of milk you have in your other hand."

The Deadly Deals

That insult of my generosity enraged me. I had offered the eggs, knowing that Mima had more on our patio. My indignation filled me, and the courage of the tiny hen defending her small chicks flashed through my mind. In spite of the great difference in our size, she had no problem attacking me. I grasped the bottle by its neck and raised it high over my head like a club. I was ready to break it over his head, and my eyes bulged in anger. I yelled, "I'm not going to give you anything, but you're going to get it if you try to take anything from me, you bullying old cripple!"

Tatun's eyes widened in astonishment. I lifted the basket of eggs as if I were ready to use it as a weapon as well. He stepped back as he realized I was ready to punish him for his abuse. Without lessening my aggressive attitude, I advanced more rapidly towards him. He backed against the wall. His eyes were no longer combative or demanding; they were filled with insecurity and fear, the same fear I had long held him in. Now he tasted a flavor of it as he realized my intentions. He continued to back away, lifting his hands to protect his face and head. He did not interfere with me as I freely passed in front of him, leaving the corridor I had for so long hidden in, no longer running as I once had so often. I could feel my heart pounding like a military band clear down in the heels of my shoes.

Walking at a natural pace for me, I began to head back home, thinking that I had already taken longer than normal and Mima might be worried. This time, however, I was filled with pride and dignity, feeling invincible after what had happened. I swore to myself that I would never again allow anyone to frighten me into a panic like Tatun had done for so long to me. Even if it happened again in the future, I would at least not show that fear to anyone.

Instead, I would confront it as I did on this day.

I realized, many years later, that this was the day I learned that fear is a normal and logical feeling in every one of us. With courage, however, every single one of us is capable to not only conquer it, but also control and destroy it. On that day I had done just that, and from that day on I never left a space in my heart in which fear could incubate and control me once more. I had sworn on the evening of my ninth birthday in 1956: never again.

The Deadly Deals

Chapter 1: The Deadly Trap

Only those willing to take the risk to lose everything will find the satisfaction of sweet success that can bring joy, peace, and plentiful happiness into their lives.
Dr. Julio Antonio del Marmol

To try and change my mood and distract myself from the recent horrible events I had encountered—including my narrow escape from the Belgian embassy and the deaths of Ambassador Abdul Marcalt and his assistant Sonia—and in order to finally eat a decent meal, I drove to the Capri Restaurant Cabaret. I arrived at the fancy restaurant and tossed my keys to the valet in charge of the parking area. He received me with courtesy, saying, "Welcome to the Capri. You're coming at precisely the time to enjoy not only the most delicious food in Havana but also the best show of the night!"

I smiled. He recognized me from my previous visits to that beautiful place. After that, the maître d' took me to a table with the greatest courtesy. "Here is the best table in the house." He put his hands to his forehead. "With my telepathy, I knew you were coming here tonight, and using my psychic powers, I made sure to keep this table free, because I knew you were going to come to our last show."

"Thank you, Captain," I said with another smile. "I hope you can use your telepathic connection to make the evening a little more pleasant for me. I had a dog day today, and up until now the night has been very similar. Maybe you can change things for me."

After he got me settled and introduced the waiter, he replied, "I hope, my young Commander, that the rest of the evening will be different for you and will bring many great moments to take away your sadness. I will leave you in good hands. Roberto will take the best care of you." He excused himself and left to attend to a recently arrived couple.

Roberto was a man in his forties with a round face and a pleasant smile. He explained to me that I had an hour and a half to order and eat, because the lights would turn off at the beginning of the show. He didn't want me to be eating in the dim light. "Order as soon as you can, please, so that we'll have time to cook your food and serve it appropriately to you. You'll also have the time and tranquility to eat in peace before the show starts."

Roberto left the menu and when he returned a few minutes later, I had already made my selection. "I would like the filet mignon with shrimp and green wine sauce, with rosemary and capers."

He smiled and said, "A very good choice! That's the chef's special today. Would you like soup or salad?"

"Both, please," I answered. "For the soup, lobster bisque, and for the salad, please add avocado and bell pepper. And plenty of olives—I love olives!"

Roberto said, "Of course. And to drink, what you prefer?"

"Vegetable juice with a twist of lime and a pinch of salt and pepper."

"Very well," he replied with a big grin. "Anything else?"

"No," I answered, "you've already brought to me what I was going to ask for—ice water. My hunger is like a lion left in a cage for a week with only a few bones in it."

He smiled and left to place the order in the kitchen. Soon after, he returned with a silver tray with all of my order. On the side was a bowl with a variety of different kinds of olives, in case I wanted to add more to my salad. I looked at him in satisfaction and said, "Excellent service! I love that filet mignon so medium rare—nice and bloody!"

He looked at me in gratitude and pleasure, and replied, "Thank you very much. Since you told me you love olives, I told the chef to prepare an extra plate so that you would be completely satisfied."

"Thank you again. My hunger increased while you went to the kitchen to the point that it now like a castaway alone on the island who's already eaten both lion and bones and is waiting to eat something more!"

He smiled and laughed. "I hope this satisfies you. If it doesn't, let me know right away and I'll bring you another order."

"Thank you very much, Roberto," I replied.

He left to attend to other customers. I ate with great appetite the exquisite meal. It was almost midnight by this time.

I looked around when I was finished, and saw that the people around me were from the old middle class that was less often seen in Cuba. The rich had already disappeared, and increasingly the new class had been taking over as they squeezed what was left of the middle class out: the army officers, ministers, and directors of different national consolidations of industries created by the government composed this new class. These bureaucratic parasites had been created by the socialist Revolution: the Cuban Agrarian Reform, the Urban Reform, and the Consolidateds, which were the various companies that came into the hands of the government and renamed under a single term.

Of course, the people were unaware of what more was coming, some of them naively thinking that this was going to help Cuba's economic prosperity. The new Revolutionary government said that these reforms were by the people, for the people. But the reality was that it was by the government, for the government, and no one else mattered.

I sat at my table and tried to convince myself that even though things hadn't been going our way lately, everything could still be changed, if only we could open the eyes of people like my father. Even fanatics like him could be persuaded if only they could see the path the Castro brothers and Che were taking the beautiful island of Cuba and the Revolution: straight to a Marxist totalitarian regime.

I asked myself how it was possible for all the leaders of the Revolution to criticize the people who enjoyed privileges at places like the Capri and yet visit them without any shame, enjoying such exquisite food and the same privileges they had been criticizing so strongly. To listen to them, it was immoral for some people to enjoy such sumptuous extravagance while others were starving and lacking the most basic necessities. Clearly, they practiced the philosophy that others should do as the leaders told them, and not how the leaders themselves behaved.

I looked around and saw some familiar faces—

ministers, Commanders of the Revolution—and I could see how these previously skinny individuals now were corpulent, with flushed faces and pink cheeks, only two years after the victory of the Revolution. I shook my head and smiled, thinking how we would consider some act horrible until we did it ourselves. The biggest difference that I could see between the old fat cats and these new ones is that the previous ones worked very hard and paid in sweat for these privileges, while the new fat cats hadn't worked a single day in their lives for one tiny mouse.

I finished eating, and Roberto came to bus my table. He brought me my dessert—a small flan with coconut marmalade on top—along with the bill. I paid the bill to get it over with before the lights were turned town, leaving him the generous tip I felt he had earned. He thanked me and inquired whether I wanted anything else, informing me that if I did, I needed to order within the next fifteen minutes before the kitchen stopped taking food orders. I thought about it for a few seconds and said, "You know what? Yes, bring me a Jupiña, so I can take the sweet taste of the flan out of my mouth."

A few minutes later, Roberto returned with my bottle of soda pop and a glass of ice. When I asked how much, he answered, "Please—with the tip you gave me, I could buy half of the Jupiña factory." He raised his arm high in his polite refusal. "It's on me—please, enjoy your show."

"Thank you very much," I replied.

A short while later, the lights started to dim gradually down to full blackout, and darkness claimed the room. A loud fanfare played, and the curtains began to open. The presenter came out into a spotlight and announced the first act, which were two noted Cuban comedians. Their act was so hilarious that I forgot my troubles for a moment as I laughed so hard that my eyes filled with tears.

After the comedians, a magician came onstage. His illusions impressed the entire crowd, including me.

After the magician, the emcee came out to another fanfare and announced, "And now, Benny Moré." He opened his act with the famous song, "Santa Isabel de las Lajas." The great black singer was internationally famous for his music and charisma—he was a true personality, who was at ease whether performing or interacting with his public. After a few songs and jokes, Benny had the audience wrapped around his finger. He even made some satirical remarks about the Revolution, and even the big wigs sitting in the audience didn't dare raise a voice to reprimand him.

"So," he said, "a lady Cuban exile has returned to repatriate herself, two years later. She goes to the store to get some groceries. She asks the clerk, 'Could you please give me a six pack of Coca-Cola?' He says, 'No, ma'am, it's now called Son. The Revolution renamed Coca-Cola to Son.' 'OK,' she says, 'and please give me some Palmolive.' He says, 'I'm sorry, miss, it's not Palmolive anymore. The name now is Batey.' 'OK,' she says in resignation. 'Could you also please give me a box of Fab detergent?' 'I'm sorry,' he says, 'it's not Fab anymore. The Revolution has renamed it Sol.' The lady is a little disturbed by all these changes and walks out of the market with her bag of groceries. Just outside the store are a couple of bums lounging around. One of them says, 'Mamacita! What do you call that thing you have behind your back?' She turns herself around and touched herself there. 'Well, it used to be called an ass—I don't know what the Revolution calls it today!'"

The Deadly Deals

A joke like this didn't sit well with the government, and it was only a couple of years later the government accused Benny of possessing marijuana. He was sentenced to a forced labor camp on the extreme Occidental side of the island called Guanacabibes. He was known to be a heavy drinker and was already beginning to experience health issues from his liver. The forced labor aggravated his cirrhosis, eventually causing his death.

Now, however, all of this entertainment raised my spirits, and by the time I left the Capri, I not only was satisfied in terms of my physical hunger, but I felt renewed in my heart and energy to continue my fight against the government. Many Cuban actors and comedians either had to leave the country, wound up in political prison, or were executed as Counterrevolutionaries for making less pointed comments than Benny had just made.

It was very late when I left, but since I was not very tired, I decided to drive back to my home in Pinar del Rio. I drove through the city, and I saw the large sign for the bakery La Gran Via, which prompted me to stop to purchase some fine pastries for my mother. She loved such treats so very much, and I wanted to please her. I noticed a car following me a few blocks behind. Even though I didn't need gas, I decided to pull into a fuel station and have the car checked and serviced. I wanted to be certain that I didn't have a tail, since I was going to be driving for a few hours on an isolated interprovincial highway.

After I pulled in, I asked them to make sure my windshields were cleaned and to check the oil and fill the gas tank. The car behind me continued on, and I tried to put my mind at ease by reminding myself that no one knew where I was going or where I had just come from. It was very easily a mere coincidence, and I needed to remain calm.

I realized that what I had endured at Che's safe house meant that I had to move very carefully. The next attempt on my life could come not just from one of my enemies; I was so deeply placed that the attempt could come from the hand of a friend, mistaking me for an enemy.

I moved the travel bags from the front seat to the back, and I picked up the machine gun. I made sure it was loaded and cocked but put the safety on. I threw a shirt over it. I went to the trunk and did the same with the M-3, making certain that weapon was also ready to fire. Instead of replacing it in the trunk, however, I put it on top of the travel bags in the back seat. I removed a couple of shirts from one bag and used them to cover the M-3 as well. The attendant informed me that the car had been nearly a quart of oil low and that he had topped it off. I paid the attendant and continued on towards the pastry shop.

I purchased some pastries, and as I left the shop with a large box in my hands, I saw a dark bottle green 1959 Buick La Sabre with several men inside. I could not, in the darkness, see any of their faces, and the hair on the back of my neck raised as I noted the slow pace at which they crept by the shop. For a moment, I thought they were going to pull in, but they continued slowly past. My danger sense was triggered, and I started to walk faster. I opened the door of the Mercedes and at once deposited the box of pastries on top of the machine gun in the front seat. I pulled out my pistol, cocked it, and put it in my lap. I stayed there for several minutes without starting the car.

1959 Buick La Sabre

I waited for five minutes. The car did not return, and I saw no one else around. I smiled, telling myself that I was getting paranoid. I was beginning to automatically consider each person passing by to be an enemy who wanted to harm me. I rearranged the passenger side so that the pastries were near the door and the machine gun close to me, just in case it was needed. It would be easy for me to grab it with my right hand should an emergency arise.

I started the engine of the car but still waited for a few moments to make sure that car hadn't turned around the block and was returning. The coast was clear, and I thought that it might perhaps have been drunks leaving a bar, driving so slowly so that they wouldn't catch the attention of any police. I leaned back slightly in my seat.

I could not resist the temptation any longer, and I opened the box to take one of the sugared napoleons I had ordered. I put it on a napkin, closed the box once more, and replaced it where I had arranged it earlier. I drove out of the parking lot, eating that delicious napoleon in one hand.

I drove down to 23rd Street, crossing L Street, in the direction of the Malecón. I wanted to breathe the ocean air for a bit before leaving the capital. Driving along slowly, I had nearly entered the Malecón when I felt an impact to the rear of my car.

The first thing that crossed my mind was that a drunk that late at night had not seen me and rear-ended me. I glanced in my rear-view mirror, and saw the same green Buick. The impact caused me to drop the pastry to grab the wheel with both hands. The napoleon rolled on top of my pants and then onto the floor. My pistol also fell to the floor.

I felt the power of the car behind me. They hadn't just hit me—they were pushing me towards the cross traffic traveling along the Malecón. The traffic was light, owing to the hour, and some cars slammed on their brakes to avoid hitting me. The people behind me apparently didn't care, and continued to push me towards the old retaining wall along the Malecón. I tried to accelerate, but my pistol had slid beneath the petal and blocked it from going down much further.

I whipped the wheel around to hop up onto the sidewalk. I crashed against the side of the wall. The only thing I could do was to turn my wheel to the right, but this did not stop the Buick. They continued pushing me, and I could see the smoke rising from their tires, since I had completely slammed on my brakes. As I turned the wheel, they continued their push to my rear, and the resulting mutual slide brought them to my rear quarter.

I was completely at their mercy. They pushed my car onto the sidewalk, thrusting me against the wall of the Malecón so hard that a piece of the wall fell onto the hood of my car.

The Buick reversed five or ten feet and then powered forward again into my car. They did this several times in their attempts to pound me through the wall. It was clear they wanted to push me over the cliff and onto the reefs below. I could see the cracks appearing in the old wall, and each successive impact caused the separation to grow greater. I could now see the water crashing below through the cracks in the wall.

Another car arrived on the scene—a 1957 Oldsmobile. This one, however, had a specially designed bumper, like the kind police would use to push vehicles. This car approached at a very high speed and hit me in the front door so hard that it bent inwards, hitting my arm with the armrest. It took me completely by surprise, knowing how reinforced a Mercedes door was. I realized that I had to get out of there, and I leaned down to the floor to clear my pistol from behind the accelerator pedal. It was stuck, and I pulled the pedal up to give myself more room. I jiggled the jammed weapon back and forth, and finally it came free.

With each blow from one of the two cars, a piece of the masonry from the wall broke free and fell onto my car. I started to panic, as my view of the ocean through the wall increased now with each slam.

1957 Oldsmobile

The wall would collapse at any moment. So far, I had heard no shots—they must be wanting to make my death appear accidental, as they had with Abdul's. Out of the corner of my eye, I saw the machine gun lying on the floor in the far corner where the jarring impacts had thrown it. I tried to reach it, but the next impact threw me headfirst into the steering wheel. I nearly lost my grasp on the pistol. I felt something warm running down the left side of my head and my vision grew blurry. I tried to get up as soon as I could.

The Oldsmobile approached at a high rate of speed to hit me once more. I raised my pistol and shot at the tire, even though my vision was doubled at the moment. Since I could see four tires, I decided to roll with it and shoot all

The Deadly Deals

four of them.

The driver lost control as two of my shots hit home, flattening both front tires. He slammed into the Buick, which was also approaching rapidly. I continued firing my pistol through the back window until my ammunition was spent. The Oldsmobile, instead of hitting my front quarter, skidded and smashed into the Buick, glancing slightly against my car and moving me forward slightly.

Between the sudden hit on the front of the Buick and the way my car slid, instead of administering a coup de grace and shoving me through the wall, the Buick completely missed me, and itself broke completely through the wall. It flew right through, sparks flying, its engine suddenly revving as the tires no longer had a surface to grab. It continued its flight, arcing gracefully downwards and crashing on the rocks below. I could see through the sparks on the rocks as the car hit.

I started the Mercedes again, as the impacts had shut the engine off. I remembered that my father's mechanic had always told me to start an engine and hit it in reverse, as that gear was the hardest to break of any of them. I jumped for joy as the motor started, and I jammed the gearshift in reverse and stomped on the accelerator pedal.

The Oldsmobile was now behind me, and I struck it so hard that it slid off the wide sidewalk and right into oncoming traffic. A few cars slammed on their brakes to avoid hitting both the Oldsmobile and my rapidly accelerating car as I pulled out of there in full reverse. As I left that place, pieces of brick and mortar fell off of my hood and clattered onto the pavement. I turned the wheel to the left and stomped on the accelerator so hard that smoke rose from my squealing tires as they gripped the pavement. Still in reverse, I zig-zagged erratically as I sped backwards away in my anxious frenzy to get away from there. I nearly died, and it was the reliability of this car that saved my life. This was the evening I fell in love with the lady Mercedes; had it been any other car, I would most certainly have been killed.

In spite of that beating, my Mercedes had maintained its functionality like a professional boxer. I thanked God for it, even though the car was a complete disaster. The windows were broken in, the windshield was cracked, the doors jammed shut, and the body of both sides and the trunk were completely smashed.

On my way out of the capital, I pulled into the Shell gas station on that sole road from Havana to Pinar del Rio to assess the damage. The young, skinny mulatto who had taken care of me previously clapped both hands to his head in astonishment when he saw me enter the station.

"Oh, my God!" he exclaimed in surprise. "Your car! What happened to you, my friend?"

He walked around the Mercedes, checking the damages. He continually shook his head as he walked and then said to me jokingly, "What did you do to my car, man? This is why you can't loan your car to anyone—I will never, never loan my car to you again."

I smiled and replied, "Please, check to make sure if everything is OK mechanically. I need to make it to Pinar del Rio without any problems."

He saluted me. "OK, Commander." He walked up to me and pointed at my left temple. "You should get that nasty cut on your head checked out. It could get infected."

"What cut?" I asked. My adrenaline rush was so great that I felt nothing, and I had forgotten that impact against

The Deadly Deals

the wheel.

He pulled a small flashlight out of his pocket, turned it on, and pointed it at my forehead. He went over to a servicing bucket and removed the opener to punch open a can of oil, the funnel, and several other utensils used in routine checking and servicing of a car. He pulled out a broken mirror that must have been left over from a previous service call and held it out to me. "Look at yourself in that, man."

He shone the flashlight on my forehead as I raised the mirror to look at myself. I saw partially dried blood coating the left side of my forehead. The attendant handed me a small box with a red cross on it. "Why don't you go to the bathroom and clean that wound while I check your car? You'll find everything you need in the first aid box: Band-Aids, peroxide, antiseptic cream, and anything else that you might require. Wounds to the head are easily infected, so you should take care of that right away, man."

"Thanks," I said. I took the box from him and walked straight to the bathroom. Inside, under the fluorescent lights and in front of a huge mirror above the lavatories, I washed my face and cleaned the wound, applying disinfectant and then bandaging the cut.

My left arm started to hurt, so I removed my shirt. There was a large hematoma just below my shoulder on the arm. It must have been from the massive impact of the Oldsmobile, when the door buckled in and hit me so hard. I checked over my body to look for any other damage, especially my chest and other arm. The only thing I found was a scratch under my left ear, but it was only a superficial injury. There was also a scratch on my left knee. I cleaned these as well, and I realized how lucky I had been. I thanked the Lord for protecting me once more and helping me to get out of this latest attempt on my life with only a few scratches on my body.

The strangest part of the whole thing was that even though I had emptied the entire magazine of my pistol in firing at them, they never returned any fire. I had no complaints about that and was very grateful for it, since between their close proximity and superior numbers, they should have easily put me down had they decided to shoot back.

I thought for a minute that if I hadn't killed one of them, I must have wounded at least one of them. No one had gotten out of the Oldsmobile, and the Buick should have no survivors, given the speed with which they had been running towards me and the rocks below. Even if the impact hadn't killed them, they would soon drown in the ocean, trapped in that car as they would be.

I returned to the attendant and handed the first aid box back to him. He took one look at the bandage on my forehead and said, "That's better, man. That looks good. When you got here, you looked like you had just come from Vietnam or some other war zone."

I smiled and asked, "How much do I owe you?"

"Nothing. Your gas is full, oil is OK, and mechanically—you see how bad this car looks? You could drive all the way to Rome in this car, and as far as I know, Pinar del Rio is only an hour and a half or two from here." He grew serious. "It's really a pity what happened to this beautiful car, though."

"Yes, it's very unfortunate." I handed him twenty pesos. "Keep it for your kindness and good service."

"Thank you very much," he replied.

The Deadly Deals

I shook my head. "I don't know what Che is going to say when he sees this—it's his car."

The young man looked at me in open-mouthed surprise. "You're just kidding, aren't you?"

"No," I replied. "It's not even a week since Che loaned me this car while they repaired my Volga in Pinar del Rio."

He clapped his hand to his forehead. "Oh, my God! What are you going to tell him?"

"The truth: that not fifteen minutes ago, someone tried to kill me, and I managed to survive by a fluke. That's what's left, and I'm lucky to still be alive. The car can be fixed."

The attendant smiled, a little concerned this time. "*Claro, claro, chico.*" He looked at me nervously. "Really? Who would want to kill you, man? Who would want to harm you? No offense, but you're still a kid. I'm sorry that happened to you, my friend." He held out his hand to me. "My name is Casimiro. Nice to meet you, Commandantico. I know you already, but I never told you my name. Your car is done, and you can leave anytime you want. Thank you for your generous tip." He picked up his service bucket. "I'm sorry, but I have some things I need to do," he said as he started to walk away at a fast pace, trying to put a little distance between us. As he walked away, he glanced around periodically in nervous concern.

Before he reached the building, he tripped over something at his feet. He pitched forward and fell to the ground, dropping the bucket. The contents tumbled out, some things rolling all the way to the side. I was by the car and said, "Do you need any help?" I stepped out of the car to move towards him.

He raised both hands, "No, no, no! I'm fine, it's good."

He began to scramble around, reclaiming the contents of his bucket. I didn't insist, and it occurred to me that he must be afraid that my aggressors might be nearby and try something again or that he might at any moment be in the middle of a firefight.

I thought about it and worked at opening the passenger side door. The hinges at the top were still clear, but the dents on the side of the door bent it out of shape, and so it didn't lift up properly. After several tries, I managed to get the door open, and checked the pastries I had gotten for Mima. I had to first remove the machine gun, which was now on top of the pastry box.

When Casimiro saw me pick up the machine gun, he just about had a heart attack. He must have thought I was preparing myself for another confrontation. He pulled himself together, sprung up from the ground, and walked away from me. In his hurry to get away, he left some minor things from the bucket lying on the ground. Still keeping his eyes on me and searching around, he walked straight to the small building.

Suddenly, we heard some loud music, and an old Chevrolet convertible drove very rapidly into the station and screeched to a halt. We heard three explosions in rapid succession, and I thought that Casimiro must have soiled himself at that moment. The reports certainly made me spin to look in that direction, but they were only backfires from the car. Casimiro must have thought that my aggressors had followed me there. He dropped the bucket once more, which slid towards the gas pumps. Once more the contents spread all over the place, this time in an even larger arc. He dove face first towards the floor, completely covering his white overalls in dirt.

The Deadly Deals

The three teenaged couples that got out of the convertible burst out laughing at the sight of Casimiro's discomfort. They were probably used to the startled reaction to the backfires, and little could they possibly imagine what would have caused his extreme response. For that matter, Casimiro was not the only one reacting, as I noticed that I had taken the safety off of the machine gun. I breathed deeply, exhaling slowly to release my tension and avoid my instinctual reaction to shoot them. I realized they were harmless, a bunch of kids who were probably half drunk.

I relaxed and checked the pastries as I had originally intended to do. I saw with pleasure that only a couple of pastries in the corner had been smashed, very likely as a result either of the impacts against the car or from when they had flown to the floor. I left the box on the floor where they belonged. Should I have any further adventures, they certainly could not drop any further than that.

I put the machine gun in the front seat and covered it once more. I walked around the car and entered it the same way I had exited it, through the window. The passenger side door had been hard enough to close, and even if I could open the driver's door, there was no way I would be able to close it from the inside. I said goodbye to Casimiro from the car, started the motor, and slowly started to drive away from the gas station. He waved goodbye to me with a nervous smile as he pumped gas into the Chevrolet. I thought he was probably very happy to see me leave.

Chapter 2: The Alpha Prints for the Kennedy Assassination

The trip to Pinar del Rio was the worst in my life. I had no glass left intact in the car, and the windshield was cracked. The wind from my high velocity became an annoyance to deal with. It rained occasionally during the trip, and I grew soaked from the precipitation. Though the windshield was still in the car, it was broken in several places, which caused it to jam the windshield wipers. In the wind, pieces of glass that still were connected waved like whips.

Nevertheless, I had no major problems, and I was glad to finally arrive home very late the next morning, even soaking wet as I was. I walked into the house, trying very carefully not to make any noise and wake anyone.

I dried myself off with a towel and changed into clean pajamas. I went to bed, and half-asleep, I felt the lips of my mother kissing my hair. I heard her moving around, picking up my wet clothes from the armchair where I had draped them.

It was still very early when I got up a few hours later; no one else was up yet. I got dressed and left so that my mother would not see the condition of that car and be scared even more. I drove to the regiment and reported to

The Deadly Deals

Commander Escalona what had happened to me. They were glad to see me alive, and informed me that the Volga was ready. I left the Mercedes with them to see what they could do to fix it.

Before returning home, I went to the veterinary clinic to check and see how my dog Kimbo was doing. After I saw to it that he was still recovering well and making daily progress after his gunshot wound and the amputation of his leg, I decided to spend a day in school in order to keep Mima happy.

When I arrived at school, my teachers received me with joy and a great deal of respect. The director of the school was a tall, skinny black man in his late 50s named Saul. He was balding on top with a fringe of white hair. He and the good and lovely teacher, Sofia, were both Revolutionaries and *Fidelistas* fanatics.

I explained to them what had been going on and that I had a lot to do with the government working with Che. They were fascinated and encouraging. To my surprise, Saul said, "Don't worry about it. The Revolution needs you laboring with the government. Just give us one day a week, and your grades won't suffer at all." They told me that as long as I picked up the homework that would be assigned to me each week and turned it in the following week, that would suffice for them.

That was the Revolution's way of resolving such things.

I said goodbye to Kinqui, Cisneros, Pablo, and my other friends and returned to my house.

It was about noon, and Mima welcomed me with joy and a kiss, thanking me for the pastries. When she saw me with the books under my arm, her face shone with satisfaction until I explained to her what Saul and Sofia had told me. Her demeanor changed completely as she shook her head and rolled her eyes. "My God, these stupid, fanatic communists are all cut from the same cloth."

"Well, Mima, I can at least assure you that I won't fall behind in my education this way."

"Well," she said in a clearly unconvinced tone, "I don't know about that."

We all sat down to eat at the table, Mima moving back and forth as she brought things to the table from the kitchen. "You have to be careful, OK?" she said. "Strange things have been happening in this town lately."

"What things?"

She crossed herself. "The Devil is loose in this part of the world. I saw in the newspaper this morning a very young mulatta had been found in central park last night, not only raped and killed, but mutilated. They cut off some of her fingers and pulled out one of her eyes." She crossed herself again. "Who could commit such horrendous and outrageous a crime as this? She looked like she was still a kid; I don't think she was even an adolescent yet."

I shook my head. With a half-chewed piece of bread and butter still in my mouth, I said, "Mima, I have lately seen the cruelty of what men can do." With a rueful expression, I shook my head. "It doesn't surprise me anymore." I continued eating in silence, thinking about what she had said. Mima continued frying some green banana chips. After she finished, she brought a large platter in for us and sat down next to me, as was her custom.

My youngest sister and brother, Mima, and I ate the exquisite fricassee of chicken and other delicacies she had made for us. Like a light in the sky, a thought flashed into my mind. I stopped eating, and held up my fork. I put it

The Deadly Deals

down on the table, my body paralyzed as I thought. I asked Mima, "Do you know the name of that young girl who was killed?"

Mima vaguely gestured, confusion on her face. "Yes, yes. They said the name of the victim and the article had a picture of her dead and mutilated and then a picture of her with her mother because she was so unrecognizable." She put her hand to her temple in thought. "Yes, I think she lived by the hospital La Colonia Española."

When Mima said this, I turned white. She noticed and asked, "What is wrong, my son? You just got as pale as the napkin in your hand."

I sprung up from my chair and asked, "Mima, where is the newspaper?"

She pointed towards the living room. "In the magazine rack in there. But for God's sake, what happened? Finish your plate. It will grow cold."

I paid her no attention. I left the table and headed into the living room, paying no heed to the complaints she directed at my back. I looked at the magazine rack until I found the newspaper. I snatched it up and opened it anxiously.

My worst fears were confirmed. The innocent victim who had been raped and mutilated was Marlina. That beautiful mulatta, still so young and tender, could still be called a little girl. She was no longer with us.

Two tears rolled down my cheeks, quickly followed by others. A feeling of frustration and impotence filled my chest, and I wanted to scream and hurt somebody. All I could do, however, was let myself sit down in the rocking chair, my eyes full of tears, and look at the ceiling.

I realized now how the conniving, unscrupulous G-2 had

obtained the information that I was going to be in the Belgian embassy and delivering those negatives that would so compromise the government. For that same cause, Abdul, Sonia, and their driver had been assassinated.

The G-2 never dreamed, however, nor would it ever enter into their brains, how I had come into the embassy in the old lady disguise I had used. At that moment I thanked God, who had inspired me to do it in the way I had. No matter how they had obtained that information, they had nothing to corroborate or prove that I had been inside that embassy. Since they could not prove it to Fidel or the others, they had to try and put me down in an attempt to make it look like an accident.

I realized that my life was in greater danger than ever, and I had to do something to retaliate in order to protect myself from the dark hand of the G-2. I needed to use fire to fight fire and mete out to them the punishment they deserved for this outrageous act and make them pay back, as the Old Testament said, an eye for an eye and a tooth for a tooth. My only alternative was to ultimately end up like Abdul and all the others who opposed this government.

I proposed to myself to be better, and I came up with a plan at once. It flashed through my thoughts, sadness, and frustration. I hadn't even realized or heard that Mima had come in and sat down close to me, leaving her plate at the table in her extreme worry over my sitting in complete silence in the living room and staring at the ceiling. She reached out, took my hand, and asked, "What is wrong, my Julio Antonio? Why are you like this? What has happened now?"

I leaned my head against the back of the rocking chair. I

held both hands against my face. The newspaper was sitting over my legs in my lap. I removed my hands from my face, and it was only then that Mima saw my red face and the tears in my eyes. She stood up and crouched next to me. She massaged my shoulder and murmured, "Oh, my son! What happened, my son?"

I took the newspaper from lap and pointed at the picture of Marlina. "Don't you remember who she is? You have to remember. She was here not too long ago, looking for me. You're the one who opened the door for her. As a matter of fact, she was sitting in this rocking chair." I pointed at the chair in which I now sat.

Mima held the newspaper up and scrutinized the photo for a few seconds. She let the paper drop into my lap once more as she exclaimed in horror, "Oh, my God!" She clapped on hand to her mouth and the other to her forehead. "No, no, no! That cannot be the same girl! That beautiful mulatta!" She crossed herself. "Who could do such a thing? She was such an angel, so sweet, such good manners!" Tears flowed down her cheeks and she hugged me. "I'm sorry, my son, I'm sorry."

After she held me for a while, she separated from me. She shook her head and said, "Who could be the evil person to commit such an outrageous act?"

I raised my head to look at her. I was very close to telling the whole truth to her, but I held my tongue. If I told her, it would not resolve anything and would only accomplish making myself feel better while at the same time inflicting tremendous and unnecessary worry on my mother. My Mima did not deserve that. So I held back my knowledge of who had done the deed.

I said instead, "God will give His judgment to these

miserable murderers, and I assure you they will receive their punishment. This cannot be left unpunished."

She hugged me once more. I thought once more of the plan I had created, which was growing in detail in my mind with each passing second. I knew how I was going to find out who did it and how I would punish that party. From now on, anyone who would attempt to harm anyone I knew in the name of protecting their government would do so at their peril.

I said to Mima, "I'm sorry, but I have to go now and take a shower. I need to get out of my head the knowledge that produced the bad influence in my soul at this horrendous news."

She let me go and said, "Very good idea, my son. Go and take a long, hot shower. It will clear your mind and make you feel better."

I left Mima in the living room, still contemplating in horrified sorrow the picture of the newspaper and weeping over it. I got into the bathroom and took a long shower. I took the opportunity to iron out my plans of punishing those responsible for these atrocities.

After I finished my shower and got dressed, my mother passed by. She noticed the hematoma on my left arm. "You have a Band-Aid on your head, and now you have a bruise on your arm! What happened to you? What is that?" she demanded.

To avoid giving her more worry, I said, "I fell off of my horse before I left for the capital. It's fine. As for the scratch, I ran into one of the bathroom doors at Che's house in Havana, that's all." That was the greatest untruth, since my arm had started to hurt badly.

Mima insisted, "Please stop by the hospital and have it

looked at. That is why your father pays that subscription to the Colonia Española."

"OK, Mima, in a little while I'll go there and have it checked out."

I finished dressing and dialed the number of my uncle in the capital. My aunt answered and informed me that he was not home. I had no idea if it was true or if it was simply imprudent for my uncle to take my phone call until they caught the mole within the organization.

However, this was an emergency, and so I used the emergency code to indicate that my life was in extreme danger. I said to her, "Tell my uncle that the mangoes my grandfather brought from his farm for you guys are completely red and ready to eat. If you don't come immediately, we might have to throw them away."

My aunt said, "Thank you very much. I will tell your uncle as soon as he gets back home. And say hello to everyone in the house."

After we said goodbye, I hung up. I heard someone knocking at the front door, so I went to answer it. My former girlfriend Sandra was standing outside. I greeted her a little coldly, but she seemed overjoyed to see me again.

"It's so good to find you here," she said. "God knows how many times I came looking for you, but your mom and brothers always said the same: you were in Havana and didn't know when you would be back. I almost gave it up, but I decided today to come back once more. And here, God is with me, because I found you!"

I half-smiled politely.

"Can we go someplace and talk?"

"We can talk here," I said.

"No, please, if you have some time, I'd rather go someplace where we can talk without being interrupted."

I nodded. "OK, let's go and get out of here." We walked to the Volga, and I opened the door for her.

"Thank you," she said. "You're a gentleman like always, even when you're mad at me."

I gave her another half-smile.

I drove to one of the cliffs along the river. We could see from there the ranch and the scenery down by the river and the bordering forest. I considered this a safe place to talk without interruption, and Sandra could then tell me what she had on her chest.

While I drove there, I observed her out of the corner of my eye, but resolutely ignored her without looking directly at her. I turned the engine off and turned away from her slightly.

"OK," I said. I turned and looked her straight in the eyes very seriously, my memory on the fact that only she had known about the guayabita bottles Marcel the charcoal man had given me. She must have been the one who turned him in, leading to the torture of him and his wife Fraya.

Sandra reached out to take my hand. As soon as I felt the contact of her hand on mine, I knew I still had feelings for her and heard deeply in my heart a small voice telling me to forgive her. Love is blind, and I clearly had some love for her left in there. All unbidden, I felt chills of satisfaction at her touch, but I kept my feelings hidden, maintaining an icy exterior. I did not remove my hand; neither did I return her touch.

After a few seconds of her leaving her hand on top of mine, and feeling rejection, she slowly slid her hand off of mine. She asked, "What happened between us? Something so beautiful and pure like our love—this is not easy to find in life. Even though we're both so young, I know what we have is real. I feel it in my heart. I see you being so cold and distant in the few months since I last saw you." She put her right hand on her chest. "I never imagined, even for a second, that this would hurt me so much." I saw tears in her eyes. "If you wanted to punish me, you're accomplishing it. This hurts me so deeply, to be treated by you like this. It hurts worse than all the months I haven't seen you." She dried her tears on the back of her hand.

In that moment, I felt in my heart the impulse to hug and kiss her, but I restrained myself. I breathed deeply and controlled myself as I replied, "Do you remember the letter you left with my friends? The one you didn't even have the courtesy and dignity to hand to me personally? The night of Disa's wedding?" I pointed at my temple. "I still have that letter here in my memory. Even though I've saved the actual letter, I don't need it, because I've memorized the contents. Unfortunately, it's very difficult, if not impossible, to serve two masters. In this case, your heart and your love for your friends and family and your political feelings are so radical, full of the injustice that has been perpetrated on a daily basis by some of the people in this Revolutionary government that we all put in power, precisely to end those injustices." I paused and breathed deeply. "When we close our eyes and hearts in the face of those injustices, we not only become accomplices but we also destroy the hearts and lives of many innocent people for the only reason that they have different ideas from what we hold. Simply, that is not fair."

Sandra looked at me with tear-filled eyes and a little guilt. "You have to understand my position. My father is a minister in the government. I can never betray him."

"Nobody has asked you to betray your father," I replied. "That is nothing but a very poor excuse for you. You don't have to betray your father any more than you have to betray your friends and the ones you love."

She looked at me in surprise. "Who did I betray? It's not you, for a fact," she said firmly.

"Well," I replied, "somebody told the G-2 of the contraband guayabita bottles Marcel gave me that day. It cost Marcel and his wife not only arrest, torture, and humiliation, but almost their lives! The G-2 tried to escalate the accusation to their being Counterrevolutionaries and then attempted to implicate me in the theft of Che's portfolio. If I hadn't intervened in time, using my influence with Fidel and Che, the G-2 might have gotten away with putting those poor, innocent people in front of the firing squad. Only you, Sandra, knew this; even my father never saw those bottles. I gave them to my friend Leocadio at the ranch. This is proof that you not only betrayed me, but you also betrayed my friends. You did serious harm to them."

Sandra opened her large and expressive eyes. She shook her head. I could not tell if she was pretending or attempting to justify her act. She raised her right hand and brought it over her heart. "Yes, you have all the reason. I might have made such a stupid indiscretion in a casual conversation with Piñeiro, but it was never my intention to harm anyone, much less you."

I nearly blew a fuse at the mention of Piñeiro's name and her admission that she might have been the one to implicate my friends. A chill ran over my body as I wondered what else Sandra could have told that bloody murderer. I leaned back in my seat and tried to keep myself from screaming at her. I contorted my face as I worked hard to control myself. I put my finger to my temple. "Only a person with a stupid head could have the idea to say something like that to anyone, much less to the Chief of the State Security for the entire country! I don't think you are stupid at all. If you ask me, I think you did it to earn points with Piñeiro or because you were really pissed with me. I cannot comprehend any other reason. Do you work for Piñeiro, for the State Security?"

She reacted immediately. "No, no! I don't work for anyone! I'm in school right now."

I leaned back skeptically. "School for what, Sandra? School for being a spy? Why is Piñeiro around you?"

She was caught completely by surprise. She looked at me questioningly, clearly wondering how I had come up with that. She grew upset herself and demanded, "Where the hell did you get that accusation? I was at a dinner gathering with my father, and Piñeiro was just there as a guest. You came up in a conversation, along with your friends, the charcoals."

"Those 'charcoals' have names," I snapped. "They are Marcel and Fraya."

I looked at her with narrowed eyes. I knew she was lying to me. I never revealed it to her, but every time she lied, there was a very slight involuntary quiver in her upper lip.

I decided not to pressure her any further. For my own security's sake, I needed to make sure I didn't turn her into my enemy. Instead, I decided to put a worm on a hook to see what sort of fish I would catch.

I nodded my head, and then slowly shook it. "What a pity," I said. "It makes it very difficult for me to ever trust you again." I shook my head once more. "What a pity."

She looked repentant, though I could not tell if it was feigned or sincere. "What can I do to make you believe in me again?"

"I'm sorry, but there's nothing you can do to repay the pain and damage you inflicted on my friends and the doubt you put in Piñeiro's mind that now hangs over my head when you told these stupidities to him. He's like a vulture, always looking for a new victim to eat."

I shook my head in discontent. Without saying a word, I started the Volga. We didn't speak the entire drive back. When we reached her house, I didn't lose my chivalry. I got out and opened her door for her.

She looked straight into my eyes and thanked me. She gripped my arm firmly and said, "Remember, I never said anything derogatory about you to Piñeiro."

I smiled and replied, "Can you imagine it? If you did that? Even so, he practically wants to destroy me. From that moment, there have been several attempts on my life. Thank you," I said with a small reverence.

She squeezed my arm even harder. "Be careful with Piñeiro. He has in his head—and I don't know who put it there—that you are the famous spy they've been looking for these past several months, the Lightning. He believes that's the spy who stole Che's attaché from the military compound."

"Ah, ha!" I said. "Now the truth comes to the light," I added with a small smile. "Why are you telling me this now?"

She drew near to me and gave me a tender kiss on the

The Deadly Deals

lips. "Because I love you."

I let her kiss me, but I did not return it. As far as I was concerned, it was like Judas' kiss to Christ.

After she moved back, I said with irony, "Thank you. I just want to know one thing before I leave, if you can find it in your heart to be honest at least once with me. Did Piñeiro put you on my back? Is that true?"

She remained still for a few moments, locked in indecision about how to reply.

I smiled once more in irony. "Never mind. I don't think you have it in you to be honest, anyway."

She squeezed my arm once more and nodded her head silently, her large, expressive eyes holding mine.

"Thank you," I said again. "Just remember—one of these days, I will return to Piñeiro the favor of his great sympathy with me. He will be paid in his own currency of fraternity, only my coin will be a lot bigger than his."

I said goodbye to Sandra with a long face. I could see that she was also very sad, but I ignored it so that she would have some time to reflect on and perhaps repent for what she had been doing. I could not deny a sense of great satisfaction as I drove away, though I don't enjoy seeing people suffer. But I had obtained from Sandra a confession. She also corroborated what I had already imagined: that Piñeiro was behind all of this, and that he had sent her to me in order to gain more information.

I knew that I had in Piñeiro a bad enemy, both ideologically and personally. He had a vendetta against me. That was certain. Perhaps it was because he couldn't stomach how close I was to Fidel and might one day replace him. That thought alone was probably enough to drive him crazy.

I drove to the La Colonia Española, and had a very bad surprise waiting for me when I asked for the jeweler, Mr. Aldames, who had recently been shot point blank in the head by Che's assistant Fausto during an apparent robbery at his store. They informed me he had passed away the previous day while I was in the capital.

I thought that one day Fausto would pay for this crime. It was still a puzzle to me why he had done it. I walked towards the pavilion of the clinic, hoping that I would one day have the answer. As I passed by one of the consulting rooms, I noticed the name on one of the doors was that of the man who was my doctor and had been our family doctor for many years, Dr. Tosca.

Dr. Tosca was a tall, slender man with wavy, black hair. He was one of the classiest men I knew and had practiced medicine in Tampa, Florida, after he had completed medical school in the United States. He had returned to Cuba several years later after marrying an American woman, and he set up a practice in Pinar del Rio.

He greeted me exuberantly, as he had always liked me. He was a pleasant man whose face continually bore a smile. He immediately noticed the bandage on my head. "What happened to you?"

"Oh, I bumped my head on a door," I said, trying to keep my story straight. In truth, the pain had increased in intensity over the past several hours. It had been bothering me all day long, even while I had been talking with Sandra.

"Um, this is more than a bump against a door," he said as he peeled off the Band-Aid and examined the wound. "This is a cut that's going to need a couple of stitches. Has your mother seen this, or did you cover it before she saw it?" He knew how protective my mother was, and must have been wondering why she wasn't there with me.

I looked at him with a mischievous smile. "No, she only saw the bruise on my arm." I unbuttoned my shirt and showed him.

"Oh, that is a nasty one! What did you do, try to open the door with your shoulder?"

"No, I fell off my horse."

"Hmm, you're having a lot of injuries lately."

I shrugged. "You don't even know the half of it! It's no big deal."

"OK, sit down there." He began to stitch my wound up.

"Would you please not tell Mima anything? She's going to insist I get a whole bunch of shots."

"Don't worry about it—I'll tell her I already gave you those shots." He put his finger to his lips. "Shh. It'll be our secret. Just come back in a week and I'll take a look. If it's healing up properly, I'll take the stitches out in a couple of weeks."

He opened a drawer, pulled out a tube, and handed it to me. "Here's some antibiotic cream. Be sure to put some of this on the wound each time you change the dressing." He began to move my arm around to check my range of mobility. "Doesn't look like anything is broken—it's just in the muscles. Does it hurt?"

"Yes, it does," I replied.

He gave me another tube. "Here's a muscle relaxant. It'll help ease the pain while the blood in the muscle breaks up and is eliminated." He pulled out a sling for my arm.

"No, no, no!" I protested. "If I show up at the house wearing that, Mima's screams will be heard clear up to Heaven."

"OK, but don't do anything physical with that arm until

it clears up. No heavy lifting with it. Let the muscle heal."

As I dressed again, he asked how school was going.

"Everything is good. I'm starting to study music and piano. Since my mom and sister both play piano, I want to become a composer."

He clapped a hand to his forehead. "Oh, my—definitely! Now that piano is going to look like it's gotten termites, you're going to use it so hard! It's going to fall apart under you."

"Be careful," I jokingly warned him, "I might become another Beethoven. When you have to pay to hear me play, you'll remember those words about the termites!"

He laughed, "Oh, I have no doubt about that! You achieve anything you set your mind to do, and I know this will happen."

We said our farewells, and I left feeling much better.

It was about 4:00 p.m. when I left the clinic and walked to the parking structure outside. I walked through the garage and noticed a light mint green and white 1958 Chevrolet Impala parked right next to my Volga. My uncle was watching me through the rear-view mirror. Without opening the door or greeting me, he started the engine. He waved his hand at me, indicating that I was to follow him. He slowly started to drive away.

I got into the Volga, feeling a little strange and surprised by my uncle's attitude. However, I followed him closely until we got to a small outdoor farmer's market. The government had not yet taken control of these. It was not until later that even such small businesses as these disappeared, confiscated from private hands without any compensation. After the takeover, this plaza in which we now met would be deserted; at the moment, however, it was bustling with activity.

My uncle parked his car in the lot and double-checked the doors to make sure they were locked. He mixed himself in with the crowd. He walked over and got into my car, a folded newspaper under his arm. "Drive any place you like, just make sure we don't have a tail."

"No problem," I replied. "Hola, how are you doing?" I was a little nonplussed with his reaction and lack of even the briefest of greetings.

"Fine, thank you," he replied. He looked at me nervously. He constantly looked in the interior rear-view mirror, checking to see if we had anyone following us.

"Is everything OK?" I asked.

"Well, a little worried from your call. I hope this really is an emergency." His tone angered me, and I kept my silence. It was clear he wasn't happy that I had called him, but I could see in his face genuine worry and curiosity.

"I'm sorry, but I have to tell you that I have the chief of the G-2, Piñeiro, on my back. This has been going on for a while, but now he's been more openly hostile. Not even a few hours ago, I confirmed that he wants my head, no matter what. Last night, they killed the new contact I established a few weeks ago in the Belgian embassy, and a few hours later they almost killed me on the Havana Malecón. Other than that, I'm still alive—do you think this is a sufficient emergency? I need your help to put into place a retaliation plan against the G-2 that I've developed in these past few hours. I need to send a clear message to these sons of bitches and put psychological fear in their minds so that each time they think to do something like this, they'll think twice. I assure you they won't forget for a long time what I'm going to do to them, and at the same time I want to have some justice for what they did to one of my lady friends."

My uncle unfolded his newspaper. He pointed his index finger at the picture of Marlina's mutilated body. I looked at him in surprise. He shook his head slowly with an expression of disgust on his face. "She was the daughter of our main contact in here with the rebels in the mountains. Of course, she didn't have a clue about what her father was doing. This man, Martin Correa, is the strong arm and military brain behind all the movements our guerrilla forces in the mountains make against the government."

I drove into the parking lot of the Jupiña factory. I looked for a space that would allow us to keep the entire lot under observation. "We can talk here without any problem. I come here all the time for my soda pop supplies, and everyone here, including the owners, are very good friends of my father's."

My uncle scratched his head nervously. With a small, forced smile, he said, "This is a very good place. There's only one entry and one exit, and there are so many cars in the parking lot that nobody will notice us, while we'll be able to see every car that comes and goes."

I scrutinized him closely. I had never seen him like this before. I could not hold it in any longer. "Why are you so nervous?" I burst out. "I've only ever seen you maintain calm and tranquility, even in the worst situations."

He looked directly into my eyes, realizing that his attitude was not helping mine at all and that the level of stress I had been enduring was only exacerbated by his demeanor. Even though my problems were perhaps bigger, I was still appearing relaxed and in control. Especially considering my age, it was shameful to him that it would seem like he needed my support, and not the other way around.

He breathed deeply to pull himself together and lay his head back over the seat to relax himself. "I'm sorry—I'm very, very sorry. There are times when we get so stressed by our own problems that we become selfish and can't see the problems of others or see them as insignificant. Please accept my apologies."

I shook my head and raised my right arm. "No problem. We all have stresses and bad moments. I believe strongly that the hand behind the death of Marlina is the local G-2, obviously under the orders of Piñeiro. I had obtained some photographs from the fisherman Hector on the beach of Las Canas, and Piñeiro was trying to find out who I was going to show the negatives to. They clearly show a Cuban MiG in the act of shooting a civilian boat, killing the entire family. It was evident that they knew, based on the precarious situation I found at the embassy when I wanted to bring them there. They obtained this information from the terrible torture and mutilation of Marlina, the only person who knew it, and it's equally clear that she held out to the point of death. Luckily, I never showed up as they expected I would, as myself. They will never guess in a million years what happened. If they get to know one day that I actually was in that embassy, they still won't know how I did it."

My uncle said, "Well, evidently your training took." He squeezed his chin in thought. He asked, "Marlina knew that you were taking those negatives to the Belgian embassy?"

"Yes, unfortunately," I replied. "She came with me to Las Canas. I regret that tremendously; I should never have brought her, but I did it so that she could identify me to Hector and his family, and to show me where he lives." I shook my head in regret over that mistake. I rubbed my forehead in distress. "She is an innocent victim in our game of espionage."

My uncle saw my pain, and his harsh attitude shattered. He put his hand on my shoulder and said in commiseration, "You cannot blame yourself at all. Sometimes things happen, and there's nothing we can do about it. You should not feel guilty. The guilty ones are those who did those horrible things to Marlina." He wiped his forehead in relief. "Thank you for that information. It took a heavy weight off of my shoulders and removed a worry I had all day long. We thought that this was a retaliation from the G-2 against Mr. Correa through his daughter, sending a message to him. We thought his cover had been blown. In spite of how tragic this is, I can give him the good news that he can sleep in peace, because he is not the G-2's target. Thank you again for that information."

"No problem, you're welcome," I replied. "I need a favor from you. That is related to why I called you. I need to get in touch with the rebels. Since Mr. Correa is our contact here, I need him to bring me to the commanders in the mountains."

He shook his head. "I don't think you should do that. I can do this for you, or somebody else, but you personally contacting the rebels is too risky for you and could expose you too much."

I replied in a firm tone, "This is something I have to coordinate personally with the guerrilla commanders. Precisely for my security, I don't want anybody at all to know I'm behind all we're going to do."

"If that is the way you want it, I will contact Mr. Correa and arrange for you to meet with the commanders."

"Thank you," I replied. He smiled, a little more relaxed this time. I looked at him and said, "There's something that's had me very worried lately."

He rubbed his neck with one hand and looked at me with raised eyebrows. "What is it? What is your worry?"

"Did you and the General receive my information about Che and Fidel's plan to kill the new President of the United States, John Kennedy?"

He nodded emphatically. "Yes, yes—we gave that information at once to U.S. intelligence at the Guantanamo Naval Base."

"What was their reply?"

He shook his head vaguely and shrugged. "They don't take it seriously. They feel like it's a joke in bad taste or the boastful way the Castro government would attempt to intimidate the U.S. But they don't consider them capable financially, much less in terms of manpower, to take on this kind of operation."

"What do you think, personally, about this?"

My uncle shook his head indecisively. He made a sour expression. "Truthfully, in my heart I have to agree with the Agency—I don't see how they have the capacity to handle a sophisticated operation like this outside of Cuba. Even if they did, what would be the purpose in assassinating the President? The Vice President would simply take over."

I removed my beret and put it on top of my knees. I ran my fingers through my long hair. "You're all wrong. Mark my words, they will do this. I am convinced that one way or another, they will execute this plan." I pointed to my eyes. "These eyes have personally observed how many millions of dollars Che has invested into this operation with the green light and blessing of the Castro brothers. I don't think they would let all of that investment go to waste. I don't know to what extent it will be successful, but I assure you that Che and these morons will enact this operation. I don't know how much they will accomplish, but they will go forward with it." I raised my left arm to my forehead. "Did you personally read my report that I gave to Chandee?"

"Yes, yes," he replied. "Using your report as a basis, your conversation with Che, and the documents from Che's portfolio, we made a full report to the intelligence authorities at Guantanamo."

I made an expression of discontent and shook my head in disbelief. "Still, after all this, the intelligence advisers consider this a joke in bad taste."

"No, no, no," he rushed to say, "they consider it that Castro and Che are making a bad joke to distract us—not you. Do you understand?"

I shook my head again. "I understood from the beginning. The joke will be on us once JFK winds up with his head blown off by the bullets of those assassins. Then you and those in the U.S. intelligence will question yourselves about what happened and what you did wrong."

I pointed at my temple as I said, "Remember, Che is not a typical individual. He is a man with a thousand faces. He walks around the world disguised as an innocent hobo, but he's really one of the greatest KGB agents they ever had. Because of this Soviet agent, hundreds if not thousands of innocent people all over the globe have been killed.

"Now he's getting older, and he thinks he wants to leave

this world with a band and cymbals in order to achieve his golden dream: to be remembered by posterity as a major historical figure. What better way than to kill the president of the most powerful nation on Earth? His followers can scream to everyone, even fifty or sixty years after his death, that Ernesto 'Che' Guevara is the architect behind the death of President John F. Kennedy. Especially considering the results they expect from it, that it will change world history for a thousand years to come."

I added emphatically and passionately as I stared my uncle full in the face. "I know him very well. They already have groups infiltrated inside the United States and the unions, and they are expecting widespread civil unrest. Through their people in Hollywood and other propaganda machinery, they will shift the blame to the U.S. government and the CIA for this assassination. It could be the collapse of the establishment and a socialist revolution inside the United States."

My uncle looked at me, surprised by the passion with which I said this. He tried to calm me down. "There is not much we can do here, my nephew. Remember, the USA is another nation, and it's far out of reach of our hands. Besides, those hands are full trying to restore democracy and freedom and bringing back order to Cuba."

I smiled sarcastically. "If this son of a bitch gets away with killing JFK and consolidates his ability to intimidate the rest of the continent, forget about any democracy, freedom, or order for many decades in Cuba. What we have here today is the beginning of a cancer. If we don't check it, it will spread like a plague to all of the Americas and then to the rest of the world, for Heaven knows how long. The USA is the lighthouse for the rest of the world. If this lighthouse collapses, all the other countries, like ships in a dark night with no light to steer by, will inevitably be sunk in the ocean."

My uncle looked at me with a mixture of surprise and admiration. "What do you see in this guy that worries you so much?"

I replied, "The same thing I see in Che's eyes is what I see in the eyes of every leader in this Revolution: they are capable of doing whatever it takes to accomplish their goals without regard to how many lives are lost in the process or what they have to do personally to accomplish it. They are selfish and ambitious, with no thought but for their personal control of the world. It is also same look I see in the old newsreels in the eyes of Adolph Hitler during his speeches to the German people, making them cry in laughter while filling them with fantasies, until he took the entire population to the sour reality that made them cry instead tears of blood and pain as they realized the depth of their betrayal and at the millions of people who were taken to the extermination camps." I shook my head. "Let's pray to God that history does not repeat once more, because only fools ignore the lessons of history and so repeat it."

His eyes widened as he understood my frustration. "Please—what can we do?"

"First, put the terror of Hell into the minds of your contacts in intelligence. This is an undeniable reality. It will happen if we do nothing to stop it. It's no bluff, much less a bad joke. It is a tool of intimidation. This is the way they think. They won't have to maintain what they're doing in absolute secrecy if everyone is too scared to stop them. I have the privilege to see these plans very closely. This is not any joke.

"Second, another elemental thing: follow the money. Follow Jack Ruby, and they will find out who Ruby is buying off and the way he is corrupting authorities and police to become a part of the plan, guided by the dark hand of Che. It is only in this way that they will discover who is involved in this operation and how they are moving the pieces on the chess board. We might then be able to stop it.

"And third, maintain completely open eyes with this individual Lee Harvey Oswald. He has several names and passports; one of them is Alek James Hidell. The reason for this is because he already has three identical doubles, all of whom I have personally met.

"This man speaks some Spanish and perfect Russian. According to Che, he's working on our side with the CIA. They have prepared for him the surprise of his life. If the information I got from Che is true and Oswald works for our intelligence community, his life is in imminent danger. Che says that he's a double agent or mole trying to plant misinformation with the KGB about the U.S. satellites while he was staying in Russia for a period of time. Now, he's trying to infiltrate the plans of Cuban intelligence, his primary goal being to destroy our Revolution through a military invasion of Cuba and destroy any secret operation we could be developing in Latin America.

"Che also said that they've obtained through their double agents inside U.S. intelligence the complete file of Mr. Lee Harvey Oswald. They know he's not only been trained by the CIA but is also educated in the Russian language while he was in the Marine Corps. He's been sent to sophisticated special training in counterespionage since 1958. He was then assigned to the U-2 base in Japan, working directly under the orders of the highest officials in intelligence. He continues to this day his function under the orders of a very influential CIA case worker, Mr. E. Howard Hunt. They work together in training an anti-communist group in Guatemala."

My uncle looked at me, full of worry.

"I think the most important thing you should do," I continued, "is to immediately inform your contacts in intelligence that this information is truthful and valid and that this man Oswald should be alerted and protected. Or at least give him the benefit of knowing the consequences he will have in dealing with Cuban intelligence and that they are prepared for him.

"My question is why, if Che has all this negative information about this supposed agent, they don't arrest him. Others have been put in front of the firing squad for less than that here. I believe they are going to use him as a patsy, and the one who will bring this on him is his friend, Jack Ruby. If it's true that he works with the CIA, Ruby must know it for a fact. He has picked him like you would pick cherries off a tree, preparing a bed for him, directed by Che, and they're just waiting for him to get sleepy and lie down. He has no knowledge of the double game they're playing with him. I would bet my life that he doesn't know that these duplicates of him even exist. If he knew this, he would be so worried that he wouldn't even show up in Cuba anymore."

My uncle leaned forward and asked, "You didn't put this in your last report."

"No," I answered. "I've been waiting. I would like to find out if it's possible to piece together the puzzle and discover what the true purpose is for these doubles. I want to see if any others appear in the game. I also want to know exactly the role Jack Ruby is playing in all of this. On top of being a financier for Che, he brought the second of the doubles I met to the meeting in Santa Clara."

"This is over my head," my uncle said. "I have to get a meeting with the intelligence community and put it before them. Perhaps they can see clearly what is behind all of this. For the time being, keep your head down and be extremely careful. I think that maybe all Piñeiro is doing is a double game by Che and Fidel, and they could be using you, too. Walk like you're on a glass roof or on thin ice. We still don't know who our mole is; we only know that we have one. Even though only a very few people know about you, I think they planted that mole just to get to you."

"Don't worry," I said. "I'll keep my eyes open, but I have a plan to push them back a few steps."

"Very well," he said. "How is your relationship with your father? Is it improving?"

"After he told me to get out of the house when I tried to open his eyes to the truth of what is being planned for Cuba and I spent some time with you, we pretty much don't talk anymore. I communicate with him primarily through my mother. It made her happier that I was out of the house. Maybe it's better this way; he's never at home and is still blind to this government. He is still in love with the Castros and thinks they are the new prophets."

"Be patient and give him some time. He will eventually wake up from his dream to this nightmare. Keep your eyes open, OK? And keep far away from us, unless you have an emergency like this one."

"Are you sure?" I teased him.

He hit me on my shoulder. "I'm sorry again. But until we

detect that mole, for your own security you have to stay far away. Chandee will be back in a few days. You can re-establish your contact with her, and we'll stay in touch with you through her."

"Very well."

"Anything else?"

"Yes. When can Mr. Correa take me to meet the leaders in the mountains?"

"Let's let a few days pass so that Mr. Correa has at least the peace and tranquility to mourn his daughter and put her body to rest. He will get in touch with you."

He pulled a small book out of his pocket and handed it to me. "This is a Spanish-English dictionary. Keep it with you at all times. You never know—in the circles you're moving in, it could save your life to be able to write a small note to someone who can understand you."

"Thank you—this could come in handy. I'll start looking into it."

"I will stay in Pinar del Rio for a few days to be by Correa's side in this horrible time. I will return to the capital after the funeral."

"Very well."

I started the Volga's engine, and we drove out of the parking lot and back to the farmer's market where we had left his car.

"Wait a minute," I said after we had parked the car. I got out and opened the trunk of the Volga. I pulled out a box like the one I would take pastries to Mima in.

My uncle was full of curiosity. "What is that?"

"The red mangoes I said over the phone that I had for you." I winked at him. "Just in case somebody was listening in."

The Deadly Deals

My uncle grinned from ear to ear. "Double thanks to you, my nephew. God bless and protect you. You are becoming a better spy than me—a Master's master, with a PhD in it. I hadn't even thought of that."

He walked to his car with the box in his hand with an expression of satisfaction.

Dr. Julio Antonio del Marmol

Taking Off the Gloves

The man who allows himself to be intimidated by others, no matter how horrible they can be, will never be able to find peace in his journey through life. No matter how many times he moves around, trying to avoid confrontation with those harmful ones, he will always encounter a bigger bully in his path. The only way to rest in harmony and happiness, unfortunately, is by standing for yourself in front of those oppressors and removing the white satin gloves to courageously fight.

Dr. Julio Antonio del Marmol

Chapter 3: The Lightning Disrupts the Fraudulent Claim

I remained in my car and waited after he had left to make sure no one had followed us. I waited for ten minutes, and once I saw that no one was following him, I left and drove towards the ranch.

I went to my hiding place and retrieved the U.S. dollars I needed to send to Ricardo, the man who had helped me sneak into the Belgian embassy in a shipping container. I addressed a manila envelope as Chopin had directed me and sent it off through the local post office.

I then headed toward Raimundo's clinic to check up on Kimbo's progress. I discovered that my dog was doing better and better, and I was able to spend some time with him. I was very pleased with how much recovery he had already made.

It was time to have dinner, so I headed home to appease the hunger signals my stomach had been sending me. I hadn't even finished lunch, and so I had by now worked up a keen appetite.

When I arrived, I had a surprise waiting for me. Kinqui and Pablo were waiting for me on the porch. We greeted each other, and they let me know that they had something important to communicate to me. I had to go to the market to get some supplies for my plan, so I told them to come with me to the market. It was only a few blocks away from my house.

I bought several cartons of fresh duck eggs. While I waited to pay for them, Kinqui came close to me and murmured, "We know who killed your good friend Marlina. Or at least we have a good idea."

I almost let the box of eggs fall out of my hand at that. I turned to him and asked, "What? What are you saying?" I looked at Pablo, who nodded silently in affirmation. I paid the attendant for the eggs and said to them, "Let's go outside."

As soon as we were outside, Kinqui said, "The other day we were behind the bread store where Cisneros works. He told us that he would give us some loaves for free if we came at a certain time through the back window. We were hiding there waiting for him when we saw a G-2 car stop very close by. We immediately thought that somebody had blown the whistle on us. We moved back to hide behind the wooden flats by the garbage cans. You know they can put us in jail for ten years for taking a loaf of bread. I know those guys: Leonel and Danilo. We see these guys all the time, harassing people. They are royal zeros. They looked like they were waiting for somebody, by the way they were looking around and staring into the rear view mirror. We couldn't leave without being spotted, so we stayed where we were. Then we saw Marlina come out with some loaves on her bicycle. They both opened the doors when they saw her, and they held up their badges. She argued with them a little bit, but there was nothing she could do. They started to push her around. They threw the bicycle to the ground, letting the bread roll out. One of them forced her into the back of the car with him. The other guy put the bicycle and bread into the trunk of the car, and then they left. This happened two days ago. Just last night, her mutilated body appeared in the central park."

I asked, "Did they see you?"

"No, they didn't," Kinqui said with a shake of his head. Pablo also shook his head.

"Do you know where these individuals live?"

Kinqui said, "I know where Leonel lives but not Danilo."

Pablo added, "I know where Danilo lives. Why?"

"Don't worry about why," I said. "Let's walk to my Volga."

Pablo asked, "What are you planning to do?"

I looked at him gravely and nodded, my face red in outrage. "It's better I not tell you guys anything so that you're not involved."

They both looked at me a little frightened and perhaps now regretting they had entrusted me with their secret. Neither of them dared to say a word, and they accompanied me to my car.

I followed their directions, and they took me by the houses where the G-2 men lived. After writing down the addresses, I engraved the location of each house into my brain. When my friends saw me writing down the addresses silently, Pablo said, "My friend, if you need any help, whatever you have in mind to do, you can count on me."

Kinqui looked at Pablo incredulously, looked at me apprehensively, and swallowed nervously. Then he nodded and said in a small voice, "Me, too."

I smiled. "Thank you, both you guys. I think I can manage this by myself. But I thank you for the offer and will bear this in my heart and thoughts."

I thought to myself that I had reached the end of my patience and the last stop in my diplomacy. From now on, I was declaring a full-out war against the G-2 or any other governmental agency that wanted to cause any physical harm to those close to me—especially not with the excuse of defending the government. My tolerance had reached its limit as I shook my head.

I softly said aloud, "They will bite my chorizo." I smiled slightly at the irony of it.

Kinqui said, "What did you say?"

"Nothing, just talking to myself."

He smiled and said, "I would give everything in this world to X-ray your brain and find out what you're thinking."

"I don't want to worry you guys with what the devil in my brain is thinking, but I promise you will see the physical results very soon."

They both looked at me uncomprehendingly and looked at each other with raised eyebrows.

I pulled up outside a hardware store and asked them to wait in the car, as I needed to buy a couple of things for my mother. They told me it was no problem.

I went inside and bought several cans of black oil paint, turpentine, and some of the other things I needed for my plan. After I made my purchases, I picked up the bag and took it out to the car. I asked both of them, "Please, don't repeat to anyone what you just told me. Not just for your security, but for mine. If this comes to the ears of the State Security, they will not hesitate to kill both you guys as well as me in order to conceal their crime."

A short while later, I dropped them at their houses

The Deadly Deals

and returned home. Finally, I was able to sit down at the table and get some dinner.

After I ate, I went to my room to begin to prepare the first phase of my plan. I took the duck eggs, a large syringe, and an ice pick. I used the ice pick to poke a tiny hole in one corner of an egg. I drained both yolk and whites into the toilet, flushing after each egg, as I repeated this with each egg in the tray. I put on a pair of rubber gloves. I diluted some paint using turpentine. I stirred the combination around to make the paint thoroughly liquid. I then used the syringe to take some paint and fill an egg. I repeated this until all of the eggs were filled. I took a box of Band-Aids and cut off a corner of the adhesive strip, and then used it to cover the hole in each egg. When I had finished, I had 48 eggs ready to go.

I washed the gloves and cleaned everything up thoroughly. I took everything up to the roof over my room and concealed them in a small box in the reservoir of the water pump we used to create water pressure in the shower.

I changed my clothes, putting on a one-piece gym suit. I selected a black baseball cap with a long visor. I put on a pair of tennis shoes. Once I was ready, I wrapped several eggs in some old socks to protect them and prevent them from making a mess should one break. Then I wrapped them into a towel, dividing them into a couple of different packages. I left the house carrying a gymnastic bag in one hand, in which I had my uniform, beret, and boots. I got into the Volga and drove to the address at which Leonel lived.

I circled the block a couple of times. Through one window, I could see the dining room of their house. I realized that he had just returned home from work to his family and they were having dinner.

I parked a few blocks away in the parking lot of the primary school which held night school classes for adults. If I had to leave in a hurry, I had a quick exit.

I walked to Leonel's house. As I walked, I started to unwrap from my package, one by one, four eggs. I had two in each hand, ready to drop. I looked through the window and saw them inside. I looked around and saw that nobody was nearby. Right by the number of the house, I smashed two eggs, splashing black paint all over the side of the house, almost covering the street number and even reaching to the door. I threw the other two eggs at the car sitting in the driveway, one on the hood and windshield, the other on the back over the trunk and rear windshield.

I double-checked the neighbors' houses, but everyone was either watching television or listening to whatever comedian's show was currently broadcasting on the radio.

Even the furniture on the front porch was splashed with the black paint. I didn't run, but walked along the sidewalk normally. I was not even two hundred feet away when I heard a man's voice scream, "Son of a bitch! Look at what they did to our home, Maria!"

If Leonel had come to the porch five minutes earlier, I might have by pure coincidence thrown an egg right into his face. I thanked God for protecting me once more, since I was already at least half a block away by the time he had come out.

I walked a little faster and turned the corner. I worked hard to get myself away from there as soon as possible without attracting attention to myself. As soon as I reached the Volga, I took off my baseball cap and put on my beret.

The Deadly Deals

My uniform shirt went on over my gymnastic suit.

A short while later, I arrived at the address of the agent Danilo. I followed the same security measures I had at my first target. However, this family were all sitting on the front porch. Apparently, they had finished dinner, and it was their custom to sit on the front smoking cigars or drinking coffee. I was forced to wait in the bushes a couple of blocks away, watching them until they decided to go back inside and go to sleep.

I changed again and removed my shirt and beret. I tucked my long hair under the baseball cap, leaving my car in the local market that was open until the late hours of the evening: they specialized in sandwiches, coquettes, and other late night snacks. I mingled with the crowd, leaving my car there. I walked to Danilo's house. I repeated what I had done before to both car and house. Whenever the eggs hit anything hard, they splashed in a way that looked like a grenade explosion. The best part of the whole thing was that they were completely silent, making even less noise than a gun with a silencer attached.

I returned a few minutes later to the Volga without incident. I once more changed clothes in case somebody had been looking out a window of the neighbor's house and gave my description to the local police. After finishing successfully, I returned home for more eggs.

I left black mourning spots on every house and car of every extremist that supported the government for political reasons that came to my mind: police, G-2, military—they all received the black stain that night.

By the time I returned home, I was very tired. I hadn't slept much the night before, and I went to bed with the great satisfaction that my first phase had been accomplished to perfection. I thought of the faces of those abusers and delinquents first thing in the morning, and I smiled at the certain knowledge that they didn't even know what was coming next. They knew not the significance of the black spots on their houses and cars.

    I got up early the next day. After showering and eating a light breakfast of fruit, I drove around the city to corroborate and see by the light of day the effects of the initial phase of my plan. I saw with satisfaction that it had not only been effective, but so many of the common people enjoyed immensely seeing the houses and cars with the black stains. At every location, as I drove by, a large crowd was gathered. Between the police cars and commotion, the black stains identified the sycophants and abusive agents of the government, and I could see individual people smiling as they enjoyed the proof that someone was doing something to aggravate these petty tyrants. It may even have been something along the lines of something they themselves had wanted to do for a while, but fear of the Revolutionary government had prevented them from acting.

    After I drove by the final locations, I was completely satisfied with my work. I noticed a car was following me a short distance away. I drove towards my house to verify whether my suspicions were valid or unfounded. After I turned down several streets, I saw that I was not wrong. I was being followed.

    A half a block later, the car started to flash its lights on and off, a sign either that I was being asked to stop or being cautioned to some danger. I slowed down and looked carefully through my rear-view mirror. I saw the black Oldsmobile getting closer to me, and I saw that Fausto was

The Deadly Deals

driving with two other guards inside the car.

I pulled over by the sidewalk in front of some stores and stopped. I pulled my pistol and chambered a round. I replaced it in the holster but kept the peace bond off.

They stopped a few steps away from my rear bumper. All three men got out of the car, and I did likewise. Fausto had a huge smile on his face and yelled, "Commandantico, how are you doing?"

"Very well," I replied. "How are you guys? Is everything in order?"

"Yes, yes," he replied. "Everything's in order. Che sent us to get you. He needs you immediately for something very, very important." He shook his head mockingly as he described the importance, implying that to Che, everything was of supreme importance.

I smiled slightly and did not elaborate on his supposed joke towards Che. I didn't know with what intention it was made. Knowing these people, if I smiled too much, he might tell Che a little later that I was the one who had made the joke in order to score some points.

I greeted the other two guards and asked, "How long ago did you arrive from the capital?"

"Only a few hours ago. We just stopped by the Regiment to see if we could find you there. Commander Escalona told us about the latest attempt on your life on the Havana Malecón. My God! What happened to you? Are you OK?"

"Yeah, I'm fine. A few bruises and scratches is all."

"After we saw the wreck the Mercedes had become, none of us could believe what Escalona said, that you were uninjured. I told my friends here that no doubt the Commandantico has more lives than a cat! Are you really OK? You're sure? You checked yourself with a doctor?"

I smiled as I replied, "To both of your questions I have to reply that yes, I've checked myself with a doctor and I'm fine. What Escalona told you is an exaggeration. I have a few scratches on my knee and a huge hematoma on my arm, but in regards to everything else I'm fine."

Fausto shook his head incredulously. "The way I saw that Mercedes, I thought I would find you in a wheelchair."

"You might say that as a joke, but in reality I had a great deal of good luck. My attackers were in two different cars, and I myself believed that I wasn't going to get out of that moment alive." I raised my right arm. "But that's a long story, and we're going to have a few hours during the trip to Havana. I'll regale you with all the details during the drive."

Both the guards and Fausto looked at me attentively. One of the guards pointed at my loaded pistol and said, "Commandantico, I think you forgot to completely holster your pistol."

I looked at him and pulled my pistol. "No, I didn't forget. I left it like that with a bullet in the chamber." I flipped it open so that he could see. "From now on, I will be prepared for the worst. Every moment could be my last, and I will shoot first and ask questions later. Nobody will ever get me by surprise again. I assure you guys, the next time you follow me, be very careful. When I got out of the car, I already had in mind I was going to shoot you, but I recognized Fausto. I'm getting a little paranoid. The next conflict I have with anybody, the first bullet in that fight will be mine."

Fausto looked at me askance and raised his eyebrows. "I don't blame you—if I were in your place, I would have weapons even in my teeth."

The Deadly Deals

I smiled and walked around the car. I reached in through the passenger window and pulled out the Thompson to show them. As I lowered it back down, I didn't realize that it was pointing at them. They blanched and took a couple of steps back.

Fausto yelled, "Watch out, Commandantico! Do you have the safety on that off, too?"

I smiled as I realized that the three of them had likely soiled themselves at that sight and said, "Oh, I'm sorry."

I carefully put the gun away to pacify them. I said to Fausto, "Go ahead and follow me to my house. I need to pack some clothes and things, since I have no idea how long Che is going to need me in Havana."

We returned to my house and I packed a couple of travel bags. We then left Pinar del Rio and headed towards the capital. During the trip, I had the leisure to describe in great detail my adventures of the previous evening along the Havana Malecón. They continually looked at me—even the driver. Fausto had to frequently remind him to keep his eyes on the road. When I finished, I realized that the three men were looking at me with even greater respect than before—even with admiration.

One of the men asked, "How the hell did you not lose consciousness when you hit your head on the wheel?"

"I think I might have, a little," I replied. "I didn't pass out, but I certainly was seeing double. I saw four tires in front of me, and I simply decided to shoot all four of them out instead of trying to figure out which two were the real ones!"

They burst out laughing at that. One of the soldiers said, "Commandantico, no doubt you have a supernatural power behind you, but also it's even more clear to me that you have huge balls—no doubt in my mind about that at all. I know grown men who, under the same circumstances, wouldn't even have the nerves to hit the accelerator, much less think to reach down and pull the pistol out from behind the goddamned pedal!"

"Guys," I said, "necessity is the mother of all improvisation, even when we don't have the luxury of making a choice."

A few hours later we entered Havana. This time, Fausto did not direct the driver towards Boca Siega but instead towards Cojimar, a small fishing village to the east of Havana. He pulled up outside a beautiful mansion right on the ocean. The house had probably belonged to some very elegant multimillionaire who had left Cuba. It had well-maintained gardens, trimmed fruit trees, and tall, wrought-iron black gates with golden tiger faces placed at regular intervals along the fence. Every door and window had multicolored Venetian glass and in stained glass style resembled famous paintings by Rembrandt, van Gogh, and other Impressionists.

Inside, the massive chandelier had Baccarat crystal in several colors, and I could not help but wonder how much it had cost. Perhaps enough, I fancied, to build a small town. I also wondered how much sacrifice and sweat on the owner's part it must represent and how much pain it must have brought to leave it all behind. Certainly they had extremely refined taste.

I was completely absorbed in my thoughts as we entered a formal dining room. It looked more like a luxury restaurant such as the Capri or the Hilton or like a banquet hall for European royalty. I thought to myself that they must have had everything imaginable available to them

The Deadly Deals

here. There were several dishes laid out in a vast banquet: multiple kinds of caviar, several kinds of fruit, gelatins, pate, yogurts, and other dishes I had never seen before. The centerpiece was a roasted suckling pig with an apple in its mouth. I was so completely overwhelmed by the sight of all that food that I could not for the life of me decide what dish to sample.

Che sat at the head of the table, reclining in a chair that had a tiger on its back. Before him was a large bowl of beluga caviar, and around him were various crackers and cheeses.

"Ah, Commandantico!" he said. "Come in, come in!" He held up a cracker with caviar on it. "You see this caviar? It's worth more than the car you destroyed."

Some of the soldiers, in an attempt to be refined, tucked napkins into their shirts at the neck. However, I was revolted by the way they started to eat with their fingers. The chair in which Che sat could easily have seated three, but he sat in the middle of it like a king surrounded by the commoners he was entertaining. He pointed out a new dish for the men to try, and they would scoop a handful into their mouths and rock back and forth as they exclaimed how wonderful it tasted to them. It seemed to me more like a three-ring circus, and Che was the ringmaster.

"Have you had lunch already?" Che asked me.

"No, these guys picked me up this morning," I replied. "I only had a light breakfast."

"Then you came to the right place!" he exclaimed. "Sit down, sit down! Enjoy this feast!" He picked up a cracker that had what appeared to be cream cheese on it. He scooped a spoon of caviar onto it and then a spoonful of capers. He then crammed the entire cracker into his mouth. With his mouth full, he said, "Sit down."

"I have to wash my hands," I protested.

"Of course," he said. "Go and wash, and come right back."

I went to a nearby bathroom to wash thoroughly. I carefully washed even under my fingernails, because I could tell I was going to be exploring some new dishes, and I wanted to make certain I was completely clean. It took me a little while, and I had to ask myself what Che had cooking in his head this time. I was a little worried, but I kept calm. By the time I returned to the table, Fausto had clearly given Che all the details regarding the crash, even though Che had already spoken with Commander Escalona by telephone.

He motioned over next to his chair. "Sit down over here."

I obediently sat next to him.

"Could you see the faces of your assailants?"

I shook my head. "Unfortunately not. Everything happened so quickly, and they took me by surprise." I added with strong conviction, "I'm ashamed of that, and it will never happen again."

He nodded. "A good learning experience for you, then."

"Well," I said, "to be fair to myself, the lights in my eyes from their cars almost completely blinded me. I fired my pistol whenever I could spot a target to shoot at, and at least I was accurate enough that one of them flew through the wall and crashed on the rocks in the ocean below." I paused for a moment. "You know, Che, what I still don't understand is how this happened in almost the same location where I saw the Belgian ambassador's car pulled out of the ocean. It could be just a coincidence, but even though I don't think they're the same people, they could be associates in some way."

He looked at me and stopped eating. "Why do you say that?"

I looked him straight in the eyes as I replied. "Because with so many locations and places in all the capital, why would they choose to do that to me right there?"

"No," he waved the thought off, "I can assure you this is pure coincidence. Go on, eat—you've been under a lot of stress, and it's making you a little paranoid. I can virtually assure you that the two things are completely unrelated." He began to eat once more. "How did you get out of that mess?"

"Well, due to the numerical superiority of my opponents, I decided it would be more prudent for me to retreat. As you said in your book about guerrilla warfare: retreat and regroup, and then return in greater strength."

He grinned broadly at my quoting him.

"I got out of there so fast that I think I left pieces of rubber from the tires on the sidewalk along the Malecón!" I said. "I decided not to give the ones alive and still in a condition to recuperate and take a window of opportunity to attack me again, much less the opportunity for them to regroup, themselves." I paused. "I have to apologize to you, most sincerely, because I really feel badly about the Mercedes. They damaged it pretty seriously."

He raised his right arm to fend my apology off. "Don't worry about it. The important thing is that you're alive. The Mercedes can be repaired, and even if it can't, who cares? We have thousands of cars, some even better than that one."

"Thank you again for understanding," I said.

He continued eating, and said, "Don't lose any sleep over that. Forget about it." I picked up a plate and selected foods that I might like from the table. "You see all this?" he asked. "It's a gift from our new administration to nationalize the restaurants in El Vedado."

I tried a variety of things, learning something about culinary dishes that night. Fausto made the occasional joke, one of them referring to how I had retrieved the Thompson out of my car. He laughingly said, "I could see that the safety was off, and I could smell the farts of one of the guys next to me. I nudged him and told him to stop, because the Commandantico would hear it and think we were shooting at him and would start firing at us!"

After we finished eating, Che told me to follow him, because he had something important to tell me in private. We got up, and some men who were stationed at the house started to clear the table. I followed Che into a room that looked like a small theater. We sat down in there, and he said, "I don't have to tell you, since you already know, the Belgian ambassador, Abdul Marcalt, is dead."

"Yes, I just told you—I was crossing by the Malecón that day, and I saw the crane pulling his car up off of the rocks."

He shook his head and smiled cynically. "That's why I said that the two events are unrelated. Our intelligence informed me that they had to put him down. He was becoming very dangerous to our future plans."

I felt a cold sweat break out in my armpits. Che reclined in his chair and crossed his legs. He looked me straight in the eyes as he stroked his beard. He looked at my pistol. "Why don't you close the bond on your pistol? It's open. I understand you're a little paranoid after all that's happened to you, but here in my house you don't have any worries. We're friends."

I reached around and snapped the bond over my pistol and nodded. I didn't let him see that I was unhappy about it—he continued to look at me in silence, which only added to my unease. It became a thorn in my neck, the way he was looking at me distrustfully. It was like he was trying to make me nervous to see how I would react.

I tried to control myself and imitated him by reclining and crossing my legs. My stomach was heaving, perhaps from the combination of stress and the food I had just eaten. I still had no idea what he had to tell me or why he had brought me here alone, much less why he had sent Fausto all the way to bring me in. I knew it wasn't just to talk about the death of the ambassador or to make a confession to me.

I kept my silence, and we continued to silently stare into each other's eyes. It was almost like the old competition about blinking. After a few seconds, he broke the silence to ask me once more, "You never said anything to Marcalt? You never contacted him, like I told you to do? Remember, I told you to get in touch with him, because he seemed to like you when he invited you to his party."

I removed my beret and put it on top of my knee. "Nope." I shook my head. "I've been too busy with so much stuff. The truth is that the Belgian ambassador didn't sit well with me, from the moment I met him at the French ambassador's house. Besides, I don't like that spy business, anyway. I cannot be a hypocrite."

Che looked at me and stroked his mustache. "Well, I don't think the feeling you had for him was mutual. Our intelligence deciphered a message to his contact that he sent in the diplomatic pouch. He told the CIA that he didn't know who you work for, but he was completely assured that you are a very well-trained spy. Even if you're not, you have unlimited potential to be one. He asked his contact to use every method at their disposal to try and recruit you as soon as possible because of your ties to all the elite members of this government."

When Che said that, my ears started to ring. Putting on an act of surprise and disgust at what I had heard, I spun towards him and said, "Where the hell did this man get that sack of bullshit when I only spoke to him once? And in front of Fausto and the French Ambassador. I don't believe it! Can you please retrieve that note from the diplomatic pouch? I want to see it!" I snatched up my beret and threw it to the ground. Making a display of angry disgust, I got up and walked away. As I did so, I covertly unsnapped the bond on my pistol. "You say your intelligence killed him? He should have been killed a long time before, if he put something like that about me on paper!"

Che looked at me very seriously. "This is not the best. The best is that Piñeiro has in his brain the suspicion that you are a spy from our enemies—he took all of this crap to Fidel at once."

"A-ha!" I exclaimed. I openly unsnapped my pistol. "That goddamned Piñeiro! I tell you, I'm going to put a bullet in his head. This is not the first time he's made this conniving accusation to Fidel. I'm positive now that this note doesn't even exist, and he's inventing it just to create problems for me and discredit me with Fidel! I'm going to put his red beard in alcohol and light a match to it!"

Che looked at me and leaned back as he put his hand on his own pistol in reaction to my display of anger. He said a little nervously, "Take it easy, take it easy! I've already talked to Fidel. Calm down! I already told Fidel that I sent you, which is true, to get information from Marcalt. I told him that I'd told you Marcalt worked with the CIA. I was the one who told you to talk to him. You didn't do it, but I assumed you had, and it made sense therefore that he would put that in his report. I didn't know if you'd followed my suggestions to get close to him or not. I know you don't like intrigues, espionage, and all this bullshit, but anyway it shut Piñeiro's mouth, and Fidel reprimanded him. He was very upset at this repeat behavior. He asked why he was doing this to you and why he was putting your loyalty in doubt constantly, without any concrete evidence."

I breathed easier at that. I'd been convinced I was going to have to shoot my way out of there.

"It's good to know somebody trusts me," I said. "Thank you."

He reached out to put a hand on my shoulder, but I instinctively snatched my hand towards my pistol. He realized I was still very jumpy and continued to try and calm me down. "You're welcome, Commandantico. Remember, I will never forget you saved my life. I know for a fact that you're not a traitor. Sit down. Calm down. I have to explain to you the plan we're going to follow from now on and the reason I sent for you."

I sat down by him. My forehead was a little sweaty, so I used my beret to discretely wipe the perspiration from my forehead. I pointed my finger at him and said, "Be careful with Piñeiro more than your worst enemies. He's a jealous, conniving, and insecure man. He's a resentful Machiavellian."

Che smiled. "Don't forget—he's also an ass-kisser for

Fidel."

I didn't smile. "Whatever he did to me today, he will do to you tomorrow. That is the inexorable law of the universe. That's why I will repeat to you—don't turn your back on him."

"You don't have to tell me that," he replied. "He's already tried to break my balls with Fidel, more than once." He shook his head in disgust. "Fortunately for us, we all know him very well, especially Fidel. No one has too much respect for his continual ass-kissing.

"Everything bad in life, however, has a good side. In the end, whatever all this crap turns up and whatever Marcalt communicated to the CIA about you will be of great benefit to us. Tremendous benefit—I gave them orders, with the green light from Fidel himself, to insert the note into the diplomatic pouch. If it didn't exist, then it was to be created. We took it that night to the courier at the airport before the news of the ambassador's 'accident' hit the local and international media, after we had removed everything important from it. One of our agents who works inside the embassy assured the courier that the ambassador had sent it but was too busy to bring it personally as they had agreed. Now his contact in the CIA will think that the information was delivered before Marcalt's death and think it valid."

He stood up and said, "Wait for me a minute. I want to turn on the projector. It will explain better what this is all about, and then I can go into details with you."

The Deadly Deals

Brigade 2506, the Cuban exiles trained for the attempted overthrow of the Castro regime at the Bay of Pigs

Dr. Julio Antonio del Marmol

Chapter 4: Blueprints to Corrupt the Bay of Pigs

Che turned on the projector and then turned off the lights. He came back over and sat down next to me. He put his hand on my shoulder and said, "The gringos are preparing an invasion of Cuba. But before I get to that, let me give you some of the details we found in the diplomatic pouch. We found Marcalt's codename as a spy: Albatross." He tapped his temple with a finger. "Remember this name, not just because it's very important, but for what I want you to do in the next few days."

The projector started to run. Images of a jungle started to display.

"This is in Guatemala. The pictures were taken by one of our agents who have infiltrated the Cuban Counterrevolutionaries in their training camp there."

Images of men training with cutting-edge equipment and modern weapons played. Their uniforms were green camouflage, but lacked any insignia or assignment tabs. The military advisers wore black camouflage.

After a few minutes, Che stopped the film, stood up, and walked over to the screen. He pointed at a man. "Look very carefully at his face. He is one of the highest level intelligence assessors, Mr. E. Howard Hunt.

He let the film run some more. Another man in black, bearded this time, wearing a military cap with a long visor appeared. Che stopped the film again. "Do you know who this man is?"

I stood up, walked over to the screen, and peered at the image. "His nose and face look familiar, but I cannot place where I've seen him before just yet. Give me some time."

Che smiled and stroked the beard over his chin. He let the film play once more. The man took his cap off and raked his fingers through his hair. He walked with the other adviser, under the large umbrella, rustically built of royal palm leaves. He pointed at some maps. Che stopped the film again. "Do you recognize him now?"

I looked at the image closely once more. I traced my finger along his image on the screen. I stopped at his nose and smiled. I put my finger over his eyebrow and smiled once more. "For sure, this is Yuri, the man you introduced to me the first time in the national bank."

Che looked at me in surprise. "How in the hell do you know that?"

"Because of his nose and the turn of his eyebrows," I answered.

He shook his head and smiled. "I know you don't like intrigue and espionage, but I think you were born for this. You have a photographic memory, no doubt about it. Even Mr. E. Howard Hunt doesn't know that we sent him as a double. Hunt's closest intelligence contacts don't know. As far as all of them are concerned, this is Lee Harvey Oswald, traveling under the code name of Alek James Hidell on his passport."

Che removed his beret. He pointed his index finger at me. "You are more than good to be able to recognize Yuri, even with that beard. You never mentioned any of the other three—you picked him specifically. Do you think you could determine who was who, if you had all four in front of you?"

I nodded. "I think so. After my initial confusion when you introduced the second one to me, I tried to examine them minutely, memorize a mark, and connect it with the name they used when we got acquainted. I looked at them as if I were learning the difference between twin brothers, looking for some tiny characteristic that allowed me to differentiate one from the other. You know—something so imperceptible as to ordinarily go unnoticed, like a tiny white hair on the eyebrow that the others don't have. For example, Yuri has something very different about his nose and the arch of his eyebrows. At a casual glance, you don't notice it, but when you pay careful attention to the details, you notice that the others don't have it."

Che grinned from ear to ear. "You have a special gift. I don't think I could determine that, and I don't consider myself a fool."

"Thank you," I said.

"You're welcome," he replied.

He crossed over to the film projector and turned it off. Then he switched on a slide projector. This time, he displayed a blown-up picture of the training camps. He went to the map and said, "You see? We have every single detail about the invasion except the most essential information: the exact point where they plan to come ashore and the day, month, and even the hour the invasion will take place. Our intelligence and counterintelligence have not been able to obtain those two pieces of information, even though they are like hungry dogs pursuing it.

"At the same time, the enemy's intelligence must be like

a hungry cat pursuing a sardine, trying to find where we have the fighter planes and bombers which could damage and destroy their forces while they're invading us. They also want to know what kind of artillery and internal support they could get from our armed forces—some of our discontented troops are ready to join them."

I scratched my head. "This, then, is the cat and mouse game that is also the cat and dog game."

He looked at me in surprise and then realized the comparison he himself had made. "Yes, you're right—it's between the cat and the dog. Let's hope we can continue to be the dogs, since the dogs always dominate the cats."

This time, I was the one who smiled.

Che turned off the slide projector and brought the lights up. He came back over to me and we sat down next to each other. He patted my shoulder. "Our enemies have been protecting that information very carefully, and we need to discover it as soon as possible. The invasion is imminent, according to our spies in the U.S. The man who knows this for sure is E. Howard Hunt, who is very close to the White House. This started as a joke, but it's grown larger. The information should also be in the hands of Lee Harvey Oswald—he and Hunt are like the nail and the cuticle."

I nodded and squeezed my chin in thought. I wondered what Che wanted from me and where all of this was leading. I was patient and asked no questions. I knew this was highly classified, and I didn't want to sound suspicious.

Che pulled out a large cigar and lit it. He wanted to give me some time to ask questions, but I reclined in my seat and crossed my legs. I looked at him. I could not forget that when we first entered this room and he started to interrogate me, he left me in the agony of intrigue for a while, possibly seeing how far my loyalty went and how he could break me. He was observing all of my moves and reactions, right up to the moment when I went into my act of righteous anger. I realized that it was only then that he came clean about resolving the situation—he had been testing me to see how loyal I was, or else he would have simply started the conversation with that and moved into this briefing. If he truly trusted me, I realized, he wouldn't have put me through that ordeal initially. Clearly, he thought he was so smart, but I knew what game he was playing. So I waited patiently until he decided to continue—I needed to show him I was disinterested and innocent.

Finally, he raised his eyebrows and nodded his head. "Tomorrow night, Lee Oswald will be here in Havana with us. He's supposed to come in with a group of investors and collectors for an art auction exhibition of very valuable pieces the Revolution confiscated. We will sell them to various collectors from Europe, American—anywhere in the world. Some of the people coming with him are probably either CIA or spies from other countries. The very last thing they want to do is buy art by Picasso, Rembrandt, or van Gogh. But we will play the game with them.

"That is where you enter into play. We will let you get close to Oswald and give you the opportunity to identify yourself with the Belgian ambassador's code name. Let him believe that you not only were working with him before he died, but that he did actually recruit you." He pulled a folded sheet of paper out of his jacket. "Let him have these plans, and get him to believe that this is where we are storing all of the aircraft. Of course, the planes we have there will be made of plywood and cardboard."

The Deadly Deals

He smiled cynically. "If you can convince him, you will offer to him the military unit number and geographic position where your brother-in-law, Canen, is in charge. We will tell him that Canen is in the position to give him full support with his troops, artillery, and most recently air-to-air missiles from the Soviet Union to the invasion." He squeezed my shoulder firmly. A strange light shone in his eyes. "If the cat bites this sardine, he will give to you the exact point of the invasion. It is vital, so that Canen can meet the invaders."

I looked at him dubiously. "Does Canen know about this?"

"No, no, no, no, no," he said emphatically as he raised both arms. He bit down on his cigar. "Under no circumstance can anyone know what we're doing. This is completely classified. Only you, Fidel, and I— and no one else—must have knowledge of what we're doing. We cannot, under any circumstance, trust anyone. No one—because, until now, Oswald hasn't given that information to anyone, not even our best agents. We have had him drilled by our best women. If we wanted to fish the cat with the sardine, it has to be in complete secrecy. We're depending on you to convince him of it so that he bites."

I stroked my cheek with my index finger. "I've got a question. If Lee Harvey Oswald is the cat, then what am I? The little sardine?" I looked at him seriously.

Che looked a little ashamed. He hadn't expected this question, and his comparisons were a little embarrassing. It took him a few seconds to search around for a graceful way out. "Well, yes—but you will be the golden sardine, because you will be the hero who saves our Revolution."

I nodded slowly, my face still grave. Che rushed on to

give me another rhetorical platitude. "Can you imagine the face of Piñeiro when Fidel gives to you the medal and recognition in the Plaza of the Revolution, in front of thousands of people? That you, and only you, without any help from anyone, are the hero that stopped and destroyed that invasion, with your courage and dedication? It's something Piñeiro has been unable to accomplish with all the counter-intelligence at his disposal."

I smiled and nodded. I needed to convince Che that I agreed and was enjoying all of the trite things he was saying. I didn't believe for a second that he believed a word of it himself. Even if this operation was successful, and I accomplished the impossible of sabotaging the invasion, I knew that Che and Fidel had been fighting like a cat and dog themselves to see who would get the glory and public acclaim. Both of them would fight and tell their respective groups that they were the ones who had accomplished and planned the entire thing. I had seen it multiple times before, and never had they mentioned any particular individual or given the credit to anyone else. Only the leaders had any credit—or someone who was already dead. But never did a living individual ever receive recognition; it was as if giving glory to anyone else would diminish their own glories. In Cuba, the only ones to receive any public recognition were the leaders or the martyrs.

"No, don't worry about me," I said. "All the credit is yours. If I accomplish this, I'm only going to execute the plan you tell me to do. It's all your idea, and I believe it's a great one."

Che smiled in satisfaction at my denial of any desire for

credit.

"I think it's a very high possibility that we can accomplish what you want," I continued, "because you've thought of all the details. It's just...." I stopped and looked at him dubiously.

His expression became one of concern. "What? What?"

"There's only one thing...." I trailed off again.

"What is that? Do you have any doubts?"

I shook my head and looked into his eyes. I leaned forward and rested my left elbow on my knee. I asked, "You told me Lee Harvey Oswald is not only a CIA agent but is somebody with some importance in that agency." I paused again.

Che moved forward and imitated me almost to the gesture.

"Yes—what is it?" he asked.

"If this is true, what is the motive for so many trips to Cuba? What is the excuse Oswald uses to his superiors to incur all of these expenses in traveling here? Under what circumstance—because I assume Uncle Sam is paying for all these trips—does he justify them with the Agency? You don't think he's playing you, as well? You are playing him, yes—but what if he's doing it to you, as well?"

Che leaned back with a huge smile of satisfaction. "The United States government has assigned billions of dollars for clandestine operations," he said. "The CIA and other counter-intelligence groups have unlimited illicit ways of creating funds for covert operations or what they call 'black ops.' Not even the Congress has the slightest idea that these exist. But in the case of Cuba, they consider it a top priority for geographic reasons to maintain possession of this island. We are the key to the Caribbean and in close proximity to their territories there. In the case of Oswald, we're making it very easy for them, and we make him an exception at our own convenience."

He took a long drag on his cigar. "If you confront a man physically, that man will fight you without hesitation, even when he doesn't feel comfortable to go to that point. But when you ask the same man with courtesy and diplomacy to come with you to have dinner, even when he knows you haven't the slightest sympathy with him and that you hate his guts, the simple fact that you are asking him politely and his fear of offending you make it likely that he will accept your invitation. He may have the fear that you could intend to poison him at that meal." He smiled sarcastically. "That is one of the things I love about espionage. Let the enemy think that he is in complete control of your mind and that you are at his mercy, and then, when he least expects it...." Che drew his finger across his throat. He smiled again and continued, "The man is completely decapitated."

I looked at him in concern. I didn't know for a moment if he was talking about me, or if this was purely rhetorical, as was his custom. I maintained my composure and showed him that I had no fear nor anything to worry about, even if the whole conversation was directed at me personally. He paused and said, "The best of all is when the enemy sees himself decapitated and doesn't have any idea about who or how somebody managed to remove his head. His friends are paralyzed in surprise by the sudden checkmate."

I smiled and stroked my chin. "Is that how you've managed to convince Oswald to be close to you and trust you? You showed friendship to him?"

The Deadly Deals

"Not only my friendship—beautiful women, exquisite meals in the Capri, Hilton, and other places, suites in the most luxurious hotels, cabarets, tickets all around the island—everything for free, courtesy of the Revolution. What else can you offer a man? How do you think we hold him and keep him so busy here in Havana, so occupied in his sexual pleasure for almost a week, while Yuri did his job in replacing him in Guatemala? Very simple—you will be meeting the Amazons in our Cuban counterintelligence. The three whites: Sonya, Tanya, and Yoska. They cut like a razor blade along the three points of the Y."

Che added proudly, "I've trained them myself. They are the best of the best, not only for their physical presence but for their dedication and loyalty to the Marxist proletarian cause. They are capable of doing and accomplishing everything we assign to them. They can remove your socks without taking off your shoes. Best of all, you wouldn't even know your socks were missing until you got home and remove your own shoes!" He leaned back and took a satisfied puff on his cigar.

I looked at him and the way he was bragging about himself in such arrogance. I thought that he needed to have his rear kicked very hard to bring him down out of that omnipotent cloud in which he thought he lived. It was no wonder that he and Fidel couldn't stay in the same room together for very long. If both of their egos continued to grow, one of them would have to leave Cuba, as the island would become too small to hold both of them. It was very difficult for me, and a knot grew in my stomach as I listened to all his self-aggrandizement. The superiority complex that these people displayed in their conversation was at odds with the socialist trope of being humble before the public. In private, however, they could not deny the Marxist totalitarian dictator's tendency towards gross stupidity.

Che looked at me with an assured smile. He asked, "Do you think you can handle this job for us and for the Revolution?"

I smiled. "For you, anything, Commander. For the Proletariats International Revolution, everything."

Che grinned from ear to ear. "Thank you very much, Commandantico. I want to give you a gift tonight. I want to take you to the Tropicana show and meet my Amazons. Their cover job is as dancers at the cabaret at midnight. We can have a midnight dinner, and I'll iron out the final details of what we're going to do tomorrow night."

"Very well," I said. "I'm here at your command."

"Have you ever been to the Tropicana?"

"No. I've seen it on TV, but I've never been."

"Well, put on your best clothes and tighten your boots, because you're going to have a night you're never going to forget. The most beautiful women in the whole world are there, and the elite of the elite of Cuba go there. And, of course, my girls are the best of the whole show."

"Very well," I replied. "Thank you very much."

He stood up and held out his hand to me. We shook hands, and he said, "Well, we're going to kick the gringos in the ass. Together, we will make history. We will see each other here at ten o'clock, OK? I have to go to a very important meeting all day at the Interior Ministry."

We stood up and walked to the door to the room.

"By the way," he continued, "don't even get close to the house at Boca Siega. We had a breach of security there. We're keeping it under observation, but we can't even find the guard we had on duty there. He's completely vanished, and until we find out what happened, we don't want anyone to risk going there."

I nodded.

"You thinking of going somewhere?"

"Yes," I replied. "I might go and visit my family. I want to check and see if my friend Chandee has returned from her trip."

Che pointed towards the garage. "You know where the keys are. Every place you go, they are in the same place. I want you to pick whatever car you like the most. They're all ready to go and all have full tanks of gas."

"Thank you," I replied.

He slapped my back in a friendly manner. "We're the ones who have to thank you. Don't be so polite. Whatever we have in the Revolution belongs to you, too."

He stopped in the dining room and yelled, "Fausto! Let's go!"

He picked up a portfolio from the table as Fausto entered the room with the rest of the escort, buttoning his shirt. He respectfully asked Che for the portfolio and took it. We said our farewells, and they left through the front door, two guards remaining on duty watching the outside.

After a few minutes, I entered the garage. I was in complete awe this time. If the garage before was large, this looked like the underground garage of a large office building. It was absolutely palatial compared with Boca Siega. There were cars inside of all makes and nationalities. I took my time to contemplate this beautiful collection of exotic cars. I got inside a few to try them out, but I kept my loyalty to my Lady Mercedes, selecting a 1960 convertible 300 XL, white with black stripes on both sides and with a red interior.

I took my travel bags so that no one would look inside them. I went into the kitchen, and as Che had said, keys were on a board in the same relative position as in the Boca Siega house.

I took the keys for the car I had chosen and headed into the city. As I drove, I thought how easy it was to become corrupted by the idea of simply enjoying the fruits of other people's work. Everything was free, since the previous owners had abandoned all their property—it was easy to adapt to this. No, I corrected myself, it was more like a drug habit. Using the excuse of helping the poor, they could behave this way to alleviate their consciences—those few who had consciences. I had counted in the mansion's garage no less than twenty-five exotic and very expensive cars. In terms of space, it was like the dancing hall of a hotel. The cars were stored there, of no use to anyone. It was one of the first things Fidel had criticized at the start of the Revolution. Not three, but twenty-five!

I hit the wheel with my hand and exclaimed, "Hypocrites!" I shook my head in disgust.

I could see a moon ranch along the side of the highway just ahead. They specialized in rotisserie chicken. In the parking lot outside stood a yellow and red telephone booth. I pulled over close to the booth and parked. I went inside and dialed Chandee's number. To my surprise, it was Chandee who picked up.

"Is it you? Oh, my God! Didn't you get my messages? I left you two messages at your house! I returned early this morning."

"No," I replied, "I didn't get your messages because I'm not at home. I'm here in Havana. I'm very close to your house."

"Oh, my God!" she exclaimed. "Really? You're here?" I could hear genuine happiness in her voice. "Very good—when can we see each other?"

"As soon as you're ready. I've got a lot to tell you, and I really would like to see you. I've been missing you."

"Me, too—and I have a lot tell you. I learned a lot, and you'll be very proud of me."

"I'm at your disposal all day long."

"Really? Come and pick me up at my house. I'll be waiting for you."

"Very well. I'll be there in fifteen minutes."

Chandee giggled. "You know, maybe you can invite me to go to the movies."

"No, I don't think so. The movie can wait until tomorrow. I don't think it would be an appropriate place for today, because I have a lot to tell you, and I don't think it would be polite to speak during the movie for as long as I need to speak to you. But you can bring with you a picnic basket, paper, and pen, so that you can take notes. We'll have a picnic. I know the perfect place: private, a little distance from the city. We might be able to have a snack or an early dinner. If you don't mind, we can leave the movie for tomorrow?"

"Of course not! It's been a long time for me since I've been on a picnic. I'll have a basket ready and will be waiting for you when you get here."

"Very well. There he goes—you hear the steps? That's me at the door!"

She laughed and we hung up. A little while later, as was her custom, she was waiting outside her house for me. At first, she didn't recognize me in the new car. As I slowed down next to her, however, she saw me in the driver's seat. She smiled. I got out and opened the door for her. We hugged and kissed each other on the cheek.

"Boy," she said, "new car! A Mercedes, and in my colors, black and white! These are my preferred colors in everything—and in a car, white with black accents to me is classy and elegant."

I smiled. "You see? Another thing we have in common."

We drove towards the Jose Marti International Airport and Rancho Boyeros.

Chandee smiled and asked, "Whose life did you save this time?"

I didn't get it at first because I was still distracted in my thoughts. "What? What do you mean?"

She smiled mischievously and gestured at the car. "Whose life did you save this time?"

I understood this time. "No, I didn't save anybody's life. Well, my own, but not anybody else's. My life nearly was ended."

Her demeanor changed immediately. "What happened? I see that bandage on your head."

I smiled. "A lot of things happened while you were away—mostly bad. We'll have time to talk about all that a little later." I touched the basket that she had on her lap and asked, "What did you bring for the picnic?"

She smiled. "Whatever I could find in our refrigerator. You didn't give me very much time to prepare." She opened it a little to show me. "Some soda crackers, some fruit, some croquettes, and four Jupiñas, because I know that's your preferred soda."

"Thank you for remembering me," I said.

"You're welcome. I like it, too." We passed by the El

The Deadly Deals

Parador coffee shop. "Oh, my God—this is the place with the greatest *media noches* in Havana, eh?"

"Yes," I replied. "Let me pull over, because your menu is a little poor. Let's add some *media noches*, and some coconut and guava pastries."

We went inside, bought our supplies, and returned to the car. I drove a few miles further into the Rio Cristal resort. I left the Mercedes in the parking lot, and we walked to the gardens, a beautiful tropical place that tourists frequented. Cascades of rivers mingled with the lush tropical vegetation to create one of the loveliest places in Havana. The caña brava bamboo trees grew in wild groves next to the river, and we headed in that direction to have some privacy. The riverbank was crossing by the back of the resort between the gardens.

We found the right spot; it had a small waterfall and a large truck of a fallen tree spanning the river. The basket between us, we walked towards the river until we found the tree bridge, acting like a young couple in love. We sat down on a smooth boulder. We put the basket down, and Chandee opened it. She pulled out a blanket, and I helped her put it down over a sand dune. She removed a spiral notebook and a pen.

We sat down on top of the blanket and spoke for several hours as we ate our *media noches* as well as the things she brought. I brought her up to date on all the things that had happened while she was away and the details of the plan I had concocted to push the G-2 back and punish the people responsible for Marlina's death.

When we spoke of Marlina, Chandee naturally shed some tears over her dear friend. I consoled her and told her the object of my plan was to create psychological panic in the minds of those responsible inside the government. I gave her the details as to how I was going to proceed with it in the next few weeks, and what I wanted her to do for me. I told her I would teach her how to do the black eggs for herself, and what the next step was going to be with the guerrillas in the mountains around the entire island. I wanted to create a more aggressive resistance to stop the oppression of the government's security forces and the G-2 by using their own medicine: intimidation for intimidation.

A few hours later, I said, "I will be in the Tropicana with Che, where he's going to give me the rest of the details for his plan and what he wants me to do for him."

She told me a little about her training and how proud she felt with all the stuff she had learned. She told me that all the counter-espionage tactics that they had been teaching her would come in very handy for our work.

A breeze started up and, combined with the tranquilizing noise of the waterfall against the trunk and all the food we had eaten, we fell asleep on top of the blanket. Time passed by quickly, and I felt something walking on my face. I started awake and touched my cheek. I was covered in ants. They had probably been attracted by the sweet crumbs of our sandwiches. I jumped to my feet and began to shake them off my body. I nudged Chandee with my foot, saying "Ants! Ants!"

She jumped up and shook her body and wiped her face, shaking her long hair. She turned around and said, "I think I have some on my back. Kill them, please!"

I checked her and noticed that they were a harmless variety of ant. We both laughed, and took the basket off of the blanket. We shook the blanket off.

"How did we fall asleep like that?" she said. "We're supposed to be spies, and yet here we were, sleeping like innocent children!"

I smiled and said, "Well, to some adults, we might still be children. But innocent—I think we have very little of that left."

Chandee frowned. "This Revolution steals the sweetest thing anybody can have: our innocence. Something so beautiful in life that our parents strive to preserve at least until our adolescence."

"I'm glad, to a point. I understand what you're saying, and I venerate the beauty of innocence, but unfortunately when you have that innocence you are abused, betrayed, and violated, as I've been, and my father, and many more by this Revolution and its leaders. Some even dare to call you stupid, simply because of your innocence!"

I shook my head in disgust. "I'm glad I'm not an innocent victim of these miserable liars, and I feel better with myself since they never will be able to lie to me again with their rhetoric and false promises. These depraved creatures stole from me my pure innocence before my puberty, but by the same token they gave to me the best weapon I could use against them to fight for my safety without even knowing they'd done it."

Chandee looked at me proudly. Impulsively, she stepped to me and kissed me on my cheek near my lips in love and appreciation for my supportive words. "You are always so eloquent. You take away the worst of my depressions with your great and beautiful words. That is very unusual, because you have the gift of being an optimist and seeing the best in the worst."

She stayed close to me, looking into my eyes in tender

admiration. She gave me a gentle kiss on my lips. I responded to it, but very softly and in moderation. I didn't want to cross the line like we had before, and I didn't want to be rejected once more. We stepped away from each other. With a smile, she squeezed my arm. "You don't want to kiss me?" she asked.

"Of course," I replied teasingly. "Do we have any G-2 watching us, and you want to pretend?"

She grinned in recollection of the show we had put on for the agents who had been tailing us before she went into training. She bit her bottom lip a little and playfully slapped my left shoulder. "No, this is true—if you want to as I want to, kiss me truly. Since the day we pretended, I've been thinking of your kisses and caresses night and day, every minute."

I held her neck with my right arm and kissed it tenderly. She returned the kiss passionately. After a few seconds, we lay down on the blanket in the sun, and slowly began to undress each other. Completely naked, we drew close to each other. I paused momentarily and tenderly held her face. I asked, "Are you sure you want to do this?"

She returned my gaze lovingly and passionately. "Yes, yes. I've been wanting to do this ever since I got to know you the first time. However, I didn't know what was going on between you and Yaneba, and so I stepped back, wishing one day that both of us would be free to make this decision. I was never more convinced that you were what I wanted until that night in the university parking lot when you poured out those kisses and caresses."

She pulled me close to her and kissed me passionately once more. She parted and said with a smile, "Please, be gentle and patient. This is my first time."

The Deadly Deals

I had never viewed her as anything but a friend until that night at the university; now, however, I looked at her with new eyes. I kissed her eyes, nose, cheeks, and chin tenderly before continuing on to the rest of her body. By the dying light of the sun, we made love to the music of the crystal water and the accompaniment of the breeze playing through the branches and leaves, bringing a romantic mysticism to that late afternoon. The sky was filled with many colors with the coming darkness, replacing the sun's radiance with the gentler wash of the resplendent moon. Gradually, the sky fully darkened, and thousands of stars shone brightly in the black velvet of the nighttime sky, displaying the full majesty of the universe.

In that beautiful tropical scenery, we looked at one another in satisfaction; it was then that I understood for the first time the fragile cycle of rebirth that is love. In that moment, I watched the birth of a new love in my heart, springing phoenix-like from the ashes of the old. It crept from the most intimate corners of the pain of our hearts, born from that trauma as the natural formula to heal the wounds we had previously suffered.

The happiness and sexual pleasure that moment brought to me was dampened by the memory of Yaneba and our first time. I could not help but think of her, and it made me feel doubly guilty. In the first place, my personality is such that loyalty is preeminent in my personal standards. I felt like I was betraying her memory, even though I knew that she was dead.

The second and worst guilt I had was that I had thought of Yaneba while I was making love to Chandee. It led me to keep silent as I looked at the starry sky.

Chandee rested her head against my naked chest, her

long hair smelling of recently-cut orchids splayed out over me. She asked, "Are you OK? You're so quiet."

I pulled her in with my right arm and kissed her head. "Never been better. Thank you for your beautiful gift."

She raised her head and picked my shirt to put on over her upper body. She took my face in one hand. "Look at me. I want to ask you something."

"Sure. What can I do for you, love?"

She smiled. "This is one of the things I like most about you: how gentle and pleasant you are."

"Thank you," I replied.

She pinched my lips together and kissed my mouth. She said, "I know whatever is established by our society's traditions makes you men feel guilty when you make love with a virgin." She waved her hand around vaguely, rolled her eyes, and shrugged. "And all these things," she added.

She put the fingers of her right hand against her forehead. "My honor is right her," she tapped her head, "and here," and she tapped her heart. She then pointed to her privates. "Not here. That is an old-fashioned notion that I don't believe in at all. I don't want you to ever feel obligated towards me simply because you were my first sexual experience. All I ask of you is that we continue to be the greatest friends, as we have been up to today, tomorrow, and for the rest of our lives. No one needs to know what happened here today. This is our own personal, intimate secret, and it will die with us. Are you OK with this?"

"Of course, absolutely," I said. "I'm not the kind of man who likes to talk about my personal life with anyone, much less something as intimate as this. You don't have to be so ugly and serious to ask me to do something like that. Any man who is even half a gentleman would never repeat it to anyone. Yes, and our society's customs require us to keep this even more confidential."

She smiled in great satisfaction. She asked, "Serious and ugly?"

I replied very gravely, "No, I didn't say that. I repeat: 'ugly and serious.'"

She bit her bottom lip and looked at me in recrimination. She picked up her blouse, wrapped it around her hand like a boxer, and began to hit me with it. I got up off of the blanket and ran towards the river in an attempt to escape from her beating. She ran after me, my shirt dropping off of her and threw her blouse at me. I entered the river, and she ran after me into the water. I stopped in the middle of the river by the trunk, where the water was chest deep on me. I held myself in place by the trunk.

Water splashed up and sprayed over her as she came through the water after me. Her wet body shone in the moonlight, and the droplets of water shone like stars. She moved more slowly as she hit the deeper water. I continued admiring her body as she drew close to me. She put her arms around my neck. Her kiss was tender at first, but quickly grew passionate. We started to make love once more, resting against the trunk of that fallen tree.

Exhausted, we left the water and returned to our spot on the sand dune. We dried off and dressed, picked up our stuff and walked towards the Mercedes. As I drove back to her house, she held my hand and looked at me lovingly as she said, "Thank you."

"Thank you for what?"

"You gave me so much, but I have to thank you because

you are so very gentle to the point I didn't feel any pain at all. It's my turn to say thank you, that's all."

I leaned in and kissed her lightly on the lips. "You're welcome, sweetie. It was a great experience I will never forget."

After we got to her house and arranged a time for me to pick her up the following day, she asked, "Could you leave some of the eggs *a la diabla* with me?"

"Of course," I replied. "Why do you call it that?" I asked with a smile.

"Because it must be the devil's work to remove this crap from any surface you drop it on."

I went to the trunk and pulled some out of my travel bag. I handed them to her. "Don't do anything crazy with these, OK? Remember what I told you—there's a purpose for them."

She smiled mischievously. "Don't worry—I will surprise you."

I left her at the house and drove towards Che's new place in Cojimar. I realized when I got there that Che was already back with his full entourage. Fausto told me that they had returned early and that Che was taking a shower to get ready. I told him that I was going to do the same.

As soon as we were all ready, we left the house in the three Oldsmobiles towards the Tropicana. All of the leaders and Commanders of the Revolution at this point used three black Oldsmobiles of either 1959 or 1960 make, simply because that was Fidel's preferred car. Later on, Fidel no longer felt unique and so took the privilege away from everyone else, reserving the Oldsmobiles only for himself.

On our way to the cabaret, Che asked me, "Did you have

The Deadly Deals

a good day? Did you visit your family?"

I didn't know if he had sent somebody to follow me, so I truthfully replied, "No, I didn't have any time to visit family. I spent the entire day with my friend, Chandee, who had just returned to town."

He smiled knowingly. "Well, women always have priority over our families. That is probably the reason you're so happy and in such good humor."

I smiled, thinking If you only knew. I asked, "Is it that obvious? I had a really good time."

He nodded and smiled. "Yes."

However, he said nothing further the rest of the way to the Tropicana. I could see he was not in the same frame of mind as I was. He looked worried and distant. I thought that he might have had some disappointment in one of his endeavors.

We pulled up outside the cabaret. I thought that, at worst, it might be another intrigue of Piñeiro's. I walked by his side silently and kept my calm. I kept my mouth shut and asked no questions.

As we walked inside the beautiful resort, I saw the most beautiful, voluptuous women I had ever seen in my life. They greeted us as if they had been waiting for us. It was likely that Che had told them we would be there. They put leis around our necks, welcoming us to the Tropicana. All three women were especially extravagant in their welcome to me, touching my hair and teasing Che by asking him if he were going to leave me with them. I felt this had to be part of the show, knowing that they had all been trained for this kind of stuff.

Tanya, the last to be introduced to me, caressed my long hair. She asked Che, "Can you leave him with me for at least a week? I will be on vacation in Varadero."

Che smiled and pointed at me. "It's up to him. By tomorrow, we will be finished with what he's doing with me, and it will be his choice. I cannot decide for him."

Tanya asked me directly, "If you decide to come with me on my weeks' vacation, and I would love for you to come to our home and meet my daughter."

I glanced at Che's face and saw his grimace of distaste. I could think of several reasons why he wouldn't want this to happen.

She held a card out to me. I ignored his expression and accepted the card.

"I would like very much for you to meet her," she said. "She's about your age and unfortunately doesn't have many friends. The work I do forces me to isolate her. Perhaps I'm overprotective, but I keep her away from most of society. Sometimes, though, I think she's very lonely, and she could use a good, trustworthy friend."

I nodded and said, "I understand. Every mom is like that. My mom goes crazy when I stay out of the house for too long." I bowed and gave her a reverence. I kissed the hands of all three ladies. "It would be my pleasure to go with you, ma'am."

"Don't call me 'ma'am,'" she protested. "Call me Tanya. You'll make me feel old."

"OK, Tanya. I'll spend your weeks' vacation with you. I need one myself."

Fausto, Che, and the others all grinned from ear to ear and chuckled, as they knew what I had recently gone through.

She turned and looked at Che. "This Commandantico is truly a gentleman."

Che smiled once more and replied, "Yes, he is. He's not only a gentleman but also very loyal with his friends." He proudly put a step forward and wrapped his right arm around my shoulders. "Not only that, he saved my life when the Counterrevolutionaries tried to kill me in Santa Clara. He's got steel testicles!"

Tanya, Sonya, and Yoska all looked at me with admiration and respect.

The premier maître d' of the cabaret came over to us and welcomed us. He greeted all of us with extreme pleasure, especially Che. It was clear Che was a regular there. He said to Che, "We have your table all prepared and waiting for you." He took us to a raised platform that was cordoned off with red velvet ropes and signs reading "Private; Entrance Prohibited" on them. Inside were four tables waiting for our party. As we walked towards the tables, Fausto leaned in and whispered something in Che's ear. Che nodded and whispered a response.

The Tropicana is a vast establishment built on an old estate. Though roofed, openings allowed the tall fruit trees to reach to the sky, providing the feeling of being outdoors. The theme was very tropical, with voodoo motifs, and it could easily seat 1,500 people. The large orchestra in front of the stage played music. At a distance, an open bar could be seen on the patio, decorated in tropical fashion with bamboo and palm leaves, while a large central bar provided immediate service for the tables. Most of the tables were level on the floor, while the reserved section rose above to command an unobstructed view of the stage. Overhead, among the tree branches were constructed catwalks along which performers strolled and danced.

We sat down and gave our orders to the three waiters assigned to us. Fausto excused himself and walked towards the front where the general public was sitting. We sat with the three beautiful ladies, but I noticed that none of the soldiers sat, even though there were several empty tables reserved for us. They formed a perimeter of protection around us. I also noticed that we were the center of attention to the general public. Every head was craned around to look at us and see who was in the VIP section. Fausto returned a few minutes later with three heavily built men. Even though they were dressed in very expensive, elegant suits, their gait lacked any refinement. It was clear that they were unaccustomed to wearing such sophisticated clothing; it was reminiscent of looking at young women wearing high heels for the first time: clumsy and inexperienced. One of them, the tallest of the three, said hello in perfect Spanish to Che as he waved to the others. "How are you doing, my friend Ernesto?" he asked.

Che replied, "Very well, *tovarich*[4] Vladimir. And you?"

Vladimir was nearly six-foot-seven with blonde hair and blue eyes. He replied, "I've been splendid." He gestured to the women. "Now, with this beautiful company, I'm even better. Who could feel bad with them around?"

Che smiled and held his hand out to the others, who appeared not to know him and apparently knew no Spanish beyond *hola*. Che spoke to them in Russian, which they clearly understood. They gave him their names, and said, "*Dobro pozhalovat Havana.*[5]"

The three men, the women, Che, Fausto, and I sat down

---

[4] Comrade
[5] Welcome to Havana.

around one of the tables. A little while later, the ladies had to excuse themselves to get ready for their midnight show, promising to return afterward. Tanya winked at me and gave me a kiss on my cheek before she left. Vladimir said jokingly said, "What, no *besos*[6] for us?"

With a twinkle in her eye, she pulled out a peso from her purse. "One *beso* costs a lot of pesos," she said teasingly.

We all burst out in laughter except for the two Russians who didn't understand what was said. Vladimir translated for them, by which time their laughter sounded oddly delayed, as the rest of us had stopped laughing by that time.

I sat on Che's left with Vladimir between Che and Fausto. After the women left, Vladimir said to Che, "Our people are very, very worried. Your friend Fidel says one thing and then does another. That is not a good thing to do in our position. It does not sit well with the Kremlin; you know that better than anybody. Today I spoke with our ambassador. He will return tomorrow to Moscow, and he told me that Fidel is not at all reliable. We have to be careful; we're putting too much money in the form of weapons in the hands of this maniac. I need you to give me a reassurance that we won't have a fiasco here."

The waitress served drinks. Che picked up his glass and took a long drink. He was clearly uncomfortable. Vladimir was speaking to him as a superior speaking to his subordinate. "We need to know what you've been doing to protect our interests."

Che put his hand on Vladimir's shoulder. "You guys

---

[6] Kisses

worry too much, and for no reason at all. Remember, I know Fidel like the palm of my hand."

He tapped his index finger of one hand into the palm of the other. "I also know that Fidel sometimes behaves like a prostitute. Anyone who shakes their ass to him and offers something, he'll go with him. If the Chinese offer him something, he'll go with them. If the French offer him something, he'll go with them. He doesn't stay with anyone; he takes what will be of advantage to him, regardless of who is offering. That is his game. In the end, however, he always will be with us, even though it occasionally looks like he's about to abandon us. He knows for a fact that, with us, he will only get security. No one else can offer that to him: not the Chinese, not the Europeans, no one else will pull his ass out of the fire when the gringos fabricate an invasion of Cuba. He is very clear about that."

Che took another drink. "Don't worry; tell the ambassador to relay this message exactly as I said before, and make Moscow certain that everything will continue as we planned it. Don't create waves by going to Moscow and putting such fear in the Kremlin. I have everything under control, and no one will kick us off of this island—not even Fidel, even if it becomes necessary to put him down to prevent it. I've already planted the necessary roots to establish an intercontinental Marxist base here in the heart of the Americas. It will last for a hundred years or longer, if no one makes the mistake of destroying my work. We will set the gringos' tails on fire."

Vladimir grinned broadly. He picked up his drink and said, "I trust you, Ernesto. I repose all of my confidence in you, and I will relay your message to the ambassador." He raised his glass to Che, and the two of them clinked glasses. "You haven't failed me so far. Now, more than ever, we can take your word to the bank, since you're the president of the bank."

They both burst out laughing at that. I pretended not to listen to their conversation by keeping my attention to the stage, where the orchestra was playing beautiful music. The show started, and women wearing flamboyant costumes came out on white horses. Some of them swallowed fire, and others performed magic tricks. It was like the Cirque du Soleil under the stars, which appeared to become the roof covering the spectacle which unfurled before us. The magnificent choreography was what made this place internationally famous. All the time I had been around Che, I had never seen him so submissive and almost timid—not even in front of Fidel.

Vladimir stood up to say goodbye, downing the rest of his vodka. Che virtually jumped up as a gesture of extreme respect. He put one of his hands on Vladimir's shoulder and said, "Boss, you can return to Moscow and sleep well. I know how I can manage Fidel." He smiled. "He's egotistical, egocentric, and paranoid, but," he continued as he held up his left hand, "we have him right here. He knows very well that without us, he's a dead fish in the water without any future. If he turns against us, he will disappear quickly from the book of history—assuming he even makes it to the first page. Just like Sandino in Nicaragua was completely wiped out of everyone's memory."

Vladimir replied, "Very well—Fidel is all yours. Keep me posted if anything gets out of your control. We've invested a fortune here, and we should keep the Central Committee in Moscow updated of every single thing going on here."

After Vladimir finished, Che nodded his agreement. Vladimir opened his arms, and they exchanged a bear hug. The three men said their goodbyes, and they disappeared into the crowd of people.

Chapter 5: The Chinese Infiltration

Che wiped his brow and took another long drink. He sighed in relief as Vladimir departed.

Fausto moved his chair closer and asked, "Is everything OK, Commandante?"

"Yes, yes," Che replied vaguely. "The same old shit. Go and get the Chinese. Tell him I'm ready for them."

Fausto nodded his head and took a sip from his glass. He got up and walked towards the patio bar.

Che turned and put his arm around my shoulder. "How do you like the atmosphere?"

"Very beautiful and elegant," I replied. "I've heard about this place and seen coverage on television, but nothing I've heard or seen compares to what I've seen tonight here."

Che smiled. "You haven't seen anything yet. At midnight, you'll see the real show! Then you'll have something to tell your kids about. It's an unforgettable experience, and the women are the most beautiful in the entire world." He raised his glass with a smile. "Prepare yourself to watch the best show you'll ever see in your life." He checked his watch. "Only half an hour more."

Fausto returned with four Chinese, three of whom were tall and slim, though muscular. All were dressed impeccably in cashmere suits of light colors. The shortest one was plump and dressed in white cashmere with a red silk shirt and a white tie with red stripes.

Fausto introduced everyone, but the short man ignored them as he walked over to Che and embraced him warmly. He was introduced to us as Mr. Wong and appeared to be the leader of the group. Che indicated that Mr. Wong should sit next to him where Vladimir had been sitting. The waitress came over, and Mr. Wong ordered a drink. His entourage were already holding drinks with little paper umbrellas in the glasses. A few minutes later, the waitress brought him a tall glass with pieces of pineapple and other tropical fruit on a stick. She also put a large platter of assorted tropical fruits before him on the table.

Mr. Wong and Che spoke for a while about the necessity to strengthen Cuban and Chinese relations. He promised Che that there should be no worry and that China would be able to supply Cuba with all the rice and other grains that would be needed for a long time to come. He also asked Che if their help was needed in creating conflicts in the Americas, Algeria, Palestine, Lebanon, Ethiopia, and anywhere else in order to distract U.S. military forces while victory was achieved in Vietnam. The Chinese goal was to unite both North and South Vietnam into one country under the red banner of the communist flag.

As I listened to this, my mind flashed back to the American movie Casablanca, in which an Italian spy in an American cabaret plotted with Nazis to unite the world during World War II. It was strange to me how life imitated art, as the same thing essentially was happening here in the Tropicana. The setting was larger: instead of a small cabaret, the Tropicana was huge, and instead of just Hitler, the conspirators were from different countries. The purposes were similar, but these people were unscrupulous compared even to the Nazi leader.

Evidently, these were more sophisticated spies, as they were plotting these schemes surrounded by gorgeous women, eating exquisite meals, and drinking the most delicious liquors as they planned the deaths of innocent people in this sinister game, just to satisfy their political ambitions. I smiled grimly at the irony and shook my head, even as I pretended that I was hearing nothing and was fully transfixed by the scenery on stage. I thought about the people who had left Cuba in the hopes of finding another country in which they could live in peaceful happiness, not even considering that the country they selected might, in the future, be living under the same shadow of Marxism as the next victim on this black list that was even now being drawn up.

The meeting finally concluded, and the Chinese stood up to say their farewells. The master of ceremonies came out to the microphone at that moment to announce the start of the midnight show. A fanfare followed his announcement. Che asked the Chinese man, "Why don't you stay for the show?"

Mr. Wong said, "Unfortunately, I have something else to attend to tonight, and we have to get up very early in the morning to get to our embassy. But thank you very much; it's been a pleasure to see you again, my friend. Together, we will make history." They embraced once more.

The house lights dimmed, and lights were brought up on stage. The orchestra's music swelled in volume, and dancers emerged from the wings. The show was phenomenal; Che certainly hadn't exaggerated. The show surpassed the best dancing I had seen in films. My eyes took in every aspect of the show. About fifteen minutes later, during the best moments of the show, we heard explosions mixed in with the music. It was like someone was firing off firecrackers in the midst of the music. However, we soon heard screams of people in distress. The guards immediately surrounded us to protect Che, loading their weapons in combat positions. They communicated to Fausto that something was not right, and we needed to leave immediately. Many people stood at their tables in confusion. Some fled the place, others stood around in an attempt to see what was going on.

Fausto said, "Come on, let's go, let's go!" He cocked his pistol.

The music stopped momentarily, and we heard the emcee attempting to keep people calm as we walked away. "Ladies and gentlemen, please keep your seats. Do not try to leave, as it will cause more confusion and damage, and you could get hurt. There will be a momentary intermission until we discover what is going on. We have reports of gunshots being fired in the parking lot. Please keep calm until we know more details."

However, as soon as he mentioned gunshots, more people began to leave. The orchestra continued to play, but other performers rushed to vacate the stage by its rear entrance. We followed Fausto and the escort to the back and into the gardens. Some of the escort formed a screen in front of us, while the rest followed at the rear. We came to a corridor formed by planters on both sides of the passageway. The first thing we saw was the body of one of the tall Chinese men who had been sitting with us, lying on top of the bushes in one of the planters between the dance floor and the main show room. A member of the escort

The Deadly Deals

gestured for us to stop and duck down. He trained his weapon forward and moved the body of the man. As he turned the body, we could see a bullet hole in the corpse's head. He leaned down to take the pulse and indicated that the man was dead by drawing a finger across his throat. He continued on, and we walked out towards the parking lot.

The soldiers almost shot a woman as she darted out unexpectedly, shrieking, "Oh, my God! They're dead! They're all dead!" In spite of the high nerves, they managed not to shoot the woman. She was just an innocent bystander who was running across the corridor.

No one knew what was going on, which only made matters worse. We walked another ten steps before finding the moaning form of another of the Chinese man. He was nearly dead, sitting on the sidewalk with a pistol still in his hand. One of the guards walked over and kicked the pistol away with his boot. He kicked it once more to give it well out of reach. Suddenly, another shot rang out, and everyone stopped and ducked. The moaning stopped as the soldier knelt down to try and talk to him. He took the man's pulse and looked up at us, shaking his head.

The guard and Fausto gestured for us to wait. A few seconds passed, and no further shots were heard. We continued onward. With all the screaming and people running around, it was clear that a full panic was setting in. The only thought in the crowd's head was to put distance between themselves and whatever was going on. From our angle, we could see the entire scene: people piling into their cars, vehicles colliding with one another as people attempted to drive away rapidly, even lone people nearly getting shot by our soldiers, as they had gotten lost and suddenly popped up near us. We walked another fifty feet.

We were nearly clear of the structure, out of the bush-lined corridor that emptied out into the parking lot. Before we went into the open, Fausto signaled for a halt. A form sat against the gate, both fists under the chin. It was the third Chinese man who had accompanied Mr. Wong. This time, Fausto went forward to the form. He nudged it in the chest with the barrel of his pistol. There were no signs of life. He removed the man's hands, and we could see a bullet hole that had been covered right at the base of the man's throat. Fausto checked his pulse and shook his head.

We continued into the concrete of the parking lot. Only a few steps from the gates under a palm tree, we heard the voice of a man screaming, "They are the ones! Damn traitors!" We moved close to them, and saw it was Mr. Wong. He was bleeding profusely from a chest wound. One bullet had cleanly taken the skull from the right side of his head, exposing his brain. In spite of his hand clasped over the chest wound, with each breath he took more blood pumped out from between his fingers. In agony, he tried to speak again.

Che went to his knees and held Wong's face close to his. "Who did this to you?"

Mr. Wong gasped, "Rus...rus...."

"Who?" Che shook him slightly. "Who did this aggression against you?"

As if with the last of his strength, Wong's eyes opened wide in apparent recognition. "My friend—the Russians!" He began to relax into death and haltingly gasped out, "Vladimir's . . . men. Vladimir . . ."

We were in shock for a moment. He had said "Russians" very clearly in Spanish, and "Vladimir" was likewise very clear, with the final R being drawn out. Che remained by his side, taking his pulse. He was shocked and very disturbed by this unpleasant surprise. It certainly didn't look like something he had expected to happen tonight. He remained there longer than one would take to register a pulse. He was lost in thought, possibly wondering what to say to us, perhaps in shock from what he had just heard from his friend's lips.

Finally, he took a deep breath and stood up. He turned to Fausto and me and bit his bottom lip. "We cannot give any credibility to what Mr. Wong just said. He was wounded in the head and the emotional state of mind he must have been in, so close to death, it could be that the whole thing really was a mirage. It's an unrealistic accusation of the people that he didn't like very much." He rubbed his forehead as if he were himself unconvinced. I had never seen him so demoralized. He closed his eyes and stroked his chin. Still looking down, he said, "I would appreciate it if none of you guys repeat a single word of whatever you heard here to anyone.

We stood in stunned silence.

"Do you guys understand what I'm saying?" he demanded.

Wordlessly, we all nodded. He rubbed his forehead once more as we stood there for several more seconds.

He might have felt betrayed by his own superiors, or perhaps, to a point, humiliated by them, as it was obvious that no one had consulted with him about this plan. On top of everything else, it was done, effectively, on his patio. His face was contorted and red, his ears like baby tomatoes. He looked once more at the dead man and said in resignation, "Oh well."

He shook his head in an attempt to justify in his mind

what had just happened to his friend and co-conspirator. "We all have to die sometime. Might as well do it in a place like this. Let's get out of here before I completely lose my patience. Whoever did this tonight not only ruined my night but your night as well." Without another word, he started to walk towards the cars.

The ambulances and police cars had started to arrive. Che walked so fast that he moved ahead of us. We started to run to keep up and the advance guard to stay ahead of him and protect him. The space where we had left our car was the special part of the lot reserved for dignitaries and high government officials. There was consequently greater security there, especially when such a prominent figure as Che was there. The guards immediately recognized us, and the young valets tried to wave to us and greet Che in a friendly manner. Che, however, did not respond, and he brushed by them without a glance, as did the guards with him. I felt uncomfortable, and so I was the only member of the group to salute them in recognition of their greetings.

We were about twenty feet from the cars. Fausto and the soldiers, still running ahead of Che, got there first. Fausto screamed in rage, "Son of a bitch! Who the hell dared to do this to our cars?" He turned around and bellowed, "Guards! Attendants!"

Several guards and valets ran over. The two black young men who valeted there in Tropicana uniforms approached us. We could see that all three of the Oldsmobiles had been bombarded from the front with black paint. I realized that this wasn't the work of one or two eggs—it looked more like three or four eggs had been used on each car. The windshields were completely covered in black paint. One of the young men nervously took a bottle of window cleaner in an attempt to clean the windshield with a small towel. However, the paint was partly dried, and instead of helping, his attempts made matters worse. The moist portions of the paint simply moved around. He looked over himself, and saw that black paint covered his white shirt, coat, and pants. He tried to remove his jacket, but gave up when he realized it would not help matters.

The other valet had completely frozen. He did nothing but observe. He tried to shift any guilt from himself by saying, "I just came in for the midnight shift. I only work here part-time, a few hours, to help my family!" He spoke with a quivering lip and eyes bulging out of their sockets. The young man was in total panic about what might happen next.

The security guard headed towards the entrance. "I'll just go and tell my boss," he said as he hurriedly left.

Che checked his watch and asked loudly, "What time did you come in to work?"

The attendant replied in even greater nervousness, "At eleven forty-five, *compañero*."

Che looked at his watch again. He shoved his watch in the man's face. "What time is it right now?"

The young man replied, "Twelve thirty." He looked at Che with an expression of discontent on his face, knowing full well what was being implied. We remained silent, except for Fausto.

"Every one of you guys, without exception," Fausto bellowed, "is responsible. If none of you did this, then at best you are all negligent and incompetent. You would have to be blind to not see that this had been done, since the paint is almost dry! *Que carajo* have you guys been doing? What were you thinking when this happens in front of your eyes, and you don't even notice?"

I felt sorry for those poor kids who looked like they were still teenagers, being so verbally abused by Che and Fausto. I knew they'd had nothing to do with it, and I had a pretty good idea who was responsible. Unlike Che, I wasn't taking it personally that she would do something like this without consulting me first. I swallowed and silently asked the Lord that this would stop here and not escalate any further. Che looked like he was about to completely lose control, and for a moment I thought that the accumulation of everything that had been happening lately that I knew about, combined with things I had no knowledge of, was taking him to the border of total emotional collapse.

When he screamed at the two youths, the other attendants drew towards us, curious about the commotion. He gestured at all of them and bellowed, "You will all wind up for a long time in the Guanacabibes Rehabilitation Camp if we don't find out really soon who is responsible for this criminal act!"

The attendant who had already spoken yelled back indignantly, "That is not fair nor logical, and it is not Revolutionary, *compañero*!" He said it in a rush, without any pause and possibly summoning up all the courage he possessed to say such a thing to Che Guevara. He lowered the finger he had pointed at Che. He continued, "Especially with me! I only started to work, not even half an hour ago!"

This time, Che put his hand on his pistol menacingly. He walked towards the boy and nearly put his face in the youth's in an intimidating way. In a low, threatening voice, he asked, "What is your name, kid?"

With trembling lips, he held his ground. "My name is Aurelio Almeida Rodriguez, *compañero*. What can I do for you?"

Che grew even angrier at the lad's attitude. Not once had he been addressed by name or military rank, as he was accustomed to being addressed. He leaned in even closer and thrust the watch once more in his face. This time he bellowed, "Do you know how to count, or don't you? Are you pretending to be stupid? It's not half an hour—it's forty-five minutes that you were already here in your work place! That means you are equally responsible as anyone else, even those in the previous shift, for what happened here tonight! What is wrong with you?"

"*Compañero*," he said, "we don't have any good paint in Cuba that dries in forty-five minutes. I can see that this paint had already been drying for at least two or three hours. That means I have nothing to do with it or what has been done."

At that argument, Che could only say as he shook his finger in the boy's face, "If you say another word more, I will send you to La Cabaña under charges of being a counterrevolutionary, where you will rot for being a party of the crime of destroying the interest of the people."

The attendant looked at Che with moist eyes filled with indignation and frustration. He swallowed his rage down at that and decided not to antagonize Che any further. The rest of the attendants, hearing what was going on, tried to clean the windshields, some with squeegees, others with razor blades, but the paint would not be removed. The oil of the paint smeared across the glass and continued to obscure the driver's vision. Without the proper types of paint thinner, nothing was going to remove these black stains.

Che's patience reached its limit. He snatched a rifle

from one of the escort soldiers, and beat on the windows, front and rear, of all three cars until the windows were broken in. He said to the attendants, "Clean this up. Bring some trash cans, and scoop up all that glass and toss it away. Be thorough about it." The attendants obeyed and brought trash cans forward. A short while later, all of the pieces in the car and still hanging from the frames were cleaned up. After all that work, Che said, "You will all receive a visit from the G-2. You had better cooperate and tell them what you know, because in the best case you'll wind up in jail. The worst case is that you'll be executed for treason."

Entrance to the Tropicana Club in Havana

Some of Che's "Amazons"--dancers at the Tropicana

The Deadly Deals

Our Freedom Is Priceless

Freedom, it is beyond price. All the blood and tears we give, it is worth it all.

Lady Freedom smiles with such beauty, to see her face is beyond value.

We must do and dare the most impossible deeds to keep her by our side.

Dr. Julio Antonio del Marmol

Dr. Julio Antonio del Marmol

Chapter 6: Chandee's Graduation

We finally left the Tropicana without any glass in any of our cars save for the side windows. On the trip back to Cojimar, Che told Fausto to take the Oldmobiles to the Transportation Ministry with some of the escort, to drop them off there, and to bring three more, as he had a very important meeting at 10:30 with the French ambassador. After we arrived at the house, Che sat down with me to give me the final details for the plan we were to follow the next day, including the place and time that I was to meet with my contact. He told me that he was not going to be in the city, wished me luck in my assignment, and said that he would be in touch with me. I did not feel very good about hearing this. He also recommended that I take my friend Chandee with me to the meeting with Lee Harvey Oswald as a distraction.

I said, "I don't know if she'll be available, but I will ask her."

It was strange to me how abruptly he had given all of his instructions to me. It also seemed suspicious that Che would want her to go with me to such a meeting, but I thought that it might be a good idea for me after all, since she could watch my back. Nevertheless, I went to bed very worried.

It made no sense to me that he would send me by

myself, without even Fausto to back me up, when I'm supposed to meet with a sophisticated CIA agent and give him the plans of the locations of the concealed planes. By his own words, destroying the planned invasion from Guatemala was of such importance that I could not believe that neither he nor anyone else would be supervising. I knew he wanted to make me believe that he had complete confidence in me, but I also knew that was untrue. Che was incapable of trusting anyone, even his own shadow. The whole thing started to sound like a rat trap. As Cisneros had told me many times, one had to be careful, because when you least expected it you could find a very disgusting hair in your soup.

I decided to meet with Chandee even earlier that we had planned so that we would have plenty of time to discuss the new details regarding my meeting with Oswald the following night.

I was completely absorbed in my thoughts and concerned about the following night. I fell asleep and slept soundly until after 10:00 that morning. Between one event and another, I didn't get to bed until 3:00 a.m. After a shower and a light breakfast of fruit and yogurt, I headed towards the center of the city.

One of the soldiers had told me that Che had left that morning in a very disappointed and bad mood. Instead of new Oldsmobiles, the Minister of Transportation had sent Buick La Sabres. By order of Fidel Castro, the Oldsmobiles were now to be reserved solely for the Commander-in-Chief. The Minister was also less than happy with Che's decision to break the windows of new cars when the paint could later have been removed.

I smiled as I drove, thinking that this might be the worst

week Che had had in a very long time. I stopped at a gas station near the entrance to the city. While the attendant checked and serviced the Mercedes, I called Chandee. I explained that I had called a little early because something had come up and I needed to talk to her as soon as possible.

"Remember, you promised to take me to the movies today," she said.

"Yes, yes," I replied. "Nothing has changed. But I wanted to let you know ahead of time that I want you to dress elegantly, because if it's no inconvenience for you, after the movie I want you to come with me to the art auction, where they're selling all those paintings by van Gogh and those other crazy guys. I need your help in what I have in mind to do. It's at eight o'clock tonight."

"Where?" she asked.

"In the Palace of Beautiful Art," I replied.

"OK," she said. "Just come and pick me up in an hour. I want to take a shower and have plenty of time to get dressed."

"An hour?" I asked in surprise.

"You forgot so quickly that I am a woman?" she asked with a laugh. "Well, well, OK. Don't get too agitated because you can't have surgery on your heart. Just make it half an hour, OK?"

"OK, in half an hour I'll be there with you."

"Very well," she replied. "Ciao."

I hung up and paid the attendant for the few gallons of gas he'd put in it. He praised the car and complimented me, and as was my habit, I let him know that it wasn't actually mine. "It belongs to Che," I told him.

"Oh, my God!" he exclaimed. "You'd better take care of

that machine, man! If you scratch it, that crazy guy will cut your balls off."

"You must be kidding," I told him. I turned and showed him my pistol, unsnapping it. "Why do you think I've got this?"

"Oooh," he said as he backed away in jest.

As I walked back to the phone, I said to him, "Believe it or not, this is the third one. I've wrecked two already. Let's hope I don't wreck this one!" I entered the booth again and called Chopin.

Chopin answered. "Hola."

"Chopin?"

"Yes, who is this?"

"The Commandantico."

"Oh, my God!" he exclaimed joyfully. "How are you, *compañerito*?"

"Very well," I replied. "Thank you for asking. Is everything OK with you?"

"Yes, yes. Everything is fine, thanks to God. By the way, Ricardo called me and told me that he's very, very grateful because he received your letter. He told me to let you know that you are a full gentleman. He thanks you for keeping your word and everything about it."

"Very well, I'm glad he received it. It gives me a great deal of tranquility to know he's happy. Thank you for letting me know. Do you think you can meet me in the bakery on La Gran Via?"

"When?"

"In the next ten or fifteen minutes, if that's convenient."

"I will be there."

"Thank you. I'll see you there."

I hung up the phone, and entered the bakery parking lot

a few minutes later. I walked inside, took a cart, and picked up a box and a pair of tongs. I filled the box with napoleons, éclairs, and other pastries. A few minutes later, I noticed Chopin beside me with a small cart and his own box of pastries. We greeted each other nonchalantly, as if we didn't know each other. When we were able to speak more, I asked, "You didn't have any problems, did you? When I left, I saw the G-2 cars descending on you, but I haven't contacted you in case you were being watched and it would give you problems. I've been worried sick all this time."

"Nothing major," he replied. "They paid me a visit and asked me a few questions. The guards at the embassy told them I had been there that day selling oysters when the two G-2 agents were found dead in the bushes. They wanted to know if I had seen anything unusual that day. I said that when I'm working, the only thing I can see are my oysters and whatever ingredients my customers ask for me to add. The rest of the world doesn't exist. If I distract myself from any client, it could cause dissatisfaction, as I could wind up adding hot sauce instead of cashews, which would be a great tragedy for some people. It happened to me once, and a very angry customer threw the cocktail in my face, as he was allergic to the hot picante sauce I had accidentally put in." He paused and said, "That really happened."

I nodded. "I believe you," I said.

"But the G-2 men probably thought I'm just a stupid black man, and they got the hell out of my house, like dogs you kick in the ass, with their tails between their legs. After that, they've never come back to my house. I've continually gone to the embassy since that day to sell my oysters so I don't create suspicion." He smiled cynically. "I have to give to you the most sincere thanks, because you found for me the best location to sell them. Every single day I sell my entire stock."

"I know just by looking at you that as a black, you have strong genes." I shook my head and said, "But I have strong doubts that you have any single gene in your body to be stupid. By the way, I will need you at the Palace of Beautiful Art tonight at eight." I breathed deeply and picked up the tongs and a tray to get some pastries. I put some guava pastries into the box.

Chopin asked, "What do you want me to do in there?"

"All I need is for you to be on standby in case we have a situation and need to leave in a hurry. You know, like we always prevent problems, you will be my emergency exit. You can park on a parallel street, and you'll see us as soon as we are at the front door."

Chopin raised an eyebrow. "Us?"

"Yes," I replied. "I will be accompanied by a young Chinese girl. Her name is Chandee."

Chopin smiled a little slyly. "Business or pleasure with this new Chinese connection?"

I smiled. "Both. She is the daughter of one of the good friends of my uncle. On top of that, for me it is a great pleasure, and I'll enjoy very much having her work by our side."

Chopin grinned. "Oh, man!" he exclaimed mischievously. "You are more slippery than butter. You never give me a straight answer." He waggled his eyebrows and poked his forefinger through the circle he made with his other hand suggestively. "You know what I mean." He looked at me expectantly.

I looked at him nonchalantly and nodded. "Yes, yes. Chandee and I are great friends, and we work together."

He threw his hands up in surrender. "Ah! There you go with the same answer!" He bent over slightly and used his tongs to fill up his own box. He realized that I was not about to give any information about my personal relationship with Chandee. He turned to me and asked, "Do you think I should bring a weapon?"

"No, no, no—I don't think it will be necessary," I replied. "This shouldn't be anything dangerous or anything like that." I tapped my forehead. "At most, it's going to be a head game. But it's your personal decision, whether you wnt to bring a weapon or not."

He pursed his lips in serious contemplation. "Who are we having that meeting with?"

"Well, he's supposed to be a North American double spy," I said.

He nearly broke his neck as he turned to me. "What? Holy shit! A double spy who's a North American, and you tell me there's no danger!?"

"Calm down, man," I said reassuringly. "It's going to be an exchange of information, that's all."

"Are you sure? You don't want to bring any reinforcements?"

"I'm sure," I said with conviction. "There won't be any need for violence there. The whole thing probably won't take more than fifteen or twenty minutes—at most half an hour."

"That's enough time to kill an army," he replied.

I shook my head. "I repeat to you: this guy is coming from out of the country. He'll know better than to bring a weapon to this meeting."

Chopin looked a little more relaxed, but unconvinced. "Very well—I'll be there at seven thirty, so that I have time to carefully scout out the whole area. That way, I can be fully prepared—just in case some fly falls into the soup."

I smiled. "Thank you, brother. We'll see each other tonight."

We said our goodbyes. He paid for his pastries and left before me, heading towards the right of the store. I waited for a few minutes, paid, and left by the opposite side.

I drove out of the parking lot and headed towards Chandee's house. It had been more than forty-five minutes, as it had taken me longer than I had expected with Chopin. She was waiting impatiently outside her house, flashing her wristwatch at me as I pulled up alongside the curb. I stopped and walked around to open her door.

She smiled as she said, "You told me to hurry up, and then you pull up at the same time I told you before that I needed to get ready."

I kissed her on the cheek and said, "How are you doing today, sweetheart? We didn't sleep together last night as far as I know."

She realized my meaning and said, "I'm sorry, but you know how we women are."

I smiled and walked around the rear of the Mercedes. After I got in, I said, "Love, the only reason I got here a little late was to give you more time. I went to a short meeting with someone who will be a great support for us tonight in our mission at the Palace. Just a precaution in case something goes wrong—we should have a back door open in case something unexpected occurs. I thought about arranging it after picking you up, but I decided to do it before so that you would have more time to get ready with more comfort. It also gives me more time to spend with you and give you the full details of what I have in mind."

She apologized once more as she held my right arm and squeezed it in sincere repentance.

"It's OK," I said. "You only have to apologize for something else—the shit you caused last night with Che's Oldsmobiles at the Tropicana, without letting me know in advance what you were going to do. You caught me completely by surprise."

She grinned broadly and slapped me playfully on my shoulder. "Well, what about it? Did you like it, how I got in and out like a ghost, the way you taught me?" She added proudly, "No one will ever have any idea how I got in and out of that high security area: on the very roof of the same van that brought the security guard detail's relief! They then brought me out without realizing it after I had finished my job, hanging from the back of the van, dressed as one of the van's custodians."

I smiled and looked at her in surprise and pride. I shook my head as my smile grew to a grin. "Congratulations, because you also gave Che a tremendous kick in the butt—something he's long overdue for. You deflated his ego completely. I've never seen him so disturbed and confused. But just for both your security and mine, don't give me any more surprises. When you're going to do something like this in the future, give me a little advance notice so that I can be prepared, OK?"

Chandee looked at me in worry. "What happened? Something negative because of me?"

"No, no—you've been great." I stroked her hair with my right hand. "It's just Che threw a tantrum bigger than the

Tropicana show that night. He threatened to send the valets to La Cabaña prison, or to the Guanacabibes camp, or even to the firing squad under accusation of being Counterrevolutionaries and damaging the interest of the people." I added sarcastically, "Of course, we all know those cars belong to the people." I grew serious again. "One of the kids had the courage to confront him, and for a moment I thought Che was going to summarily shoot him on the spot right in front of us. That's how outraged he was."

Chandee clapped her right hand to her mouth. "Did he lose his mind, this unscrupulous assassin?"

I nodded. "Sure enough, he is an assassin. Just never forget that. All of this caught me completely by surprise, and I had no idea what I would say at that moment if he had confronted me. One of the men we met in there looked like one of Che's bosses in the KGB. They are even bigger criminals than Che is, and since they don't like competition, they killed three Chinese intelligence agents right there. It looked like they were making some kind of economic and political negotiation with Che. The hit took place in the gardens of the Tropicana, right in the middle of the show! They didn't care about the scandal or commotion it created, or anything else."

I steered with my right hand as with my left I massaged my forehead. "It completely caught Che by surprise. I saw him utterly confused and frustrated, more than I've ever seen him before. For the first time, probably because I was guilty in my knowledge of where the eggs had come from, I feared for my life. Those vehicles looked more like large chocolate balls than cars anymore. I was completely petrified, and I didn't know how Che was going to react." I paused for a few seconds, and then turned and asked her. "By the way—how many eggs did you use? That wasn't the work of one or two eggs! It looked like you had diarrhea and covered the cars from one end to the other."

She smiled and scratched her head. "I really don't remember, but I think at least four or five for each car."

I shook my head and exclaimed, "Ugh!" I smiled ironically. "No wonder! It looked more like tar than paint."

Chandee pouted. "I only wanted you to be proud of me."

I turned my head slightly and replied, "Of course I'm very proud of you, honey." I put my right hand on her left knee and squeezed it affectionately. "But remember the purpose of those black eggs: to mark our enemies so that the guerrillas can identify them and bring them to justice, meting out appropriate punishment for their wrongdoing. We don't need to completely paint their houses and cars; if we do that, we'll need a large paint factory to accomplish the purpose."

Chandee burst out laughing and covered her mouth with her hand. "I'm sorry I didn't warn you about what I was going to do. But I have to tell you something. The truth is that I didn't just want to give you a surprise; I wanted to get back at that bastard."

"Yes, yes—you made your point very clearly and accomplished your purpose. I guarantee you I wasn't the only one taken totally by surprise."

Chandee bit her bottom lip and smiled. "I felt so good after I dropped the first two eggs, and I had in my heart and soul so much satisfaction, because they're so silent, that I decided to keep dropping more. It was like painting great art, and I didn't want to stop that feeling of gratification."

"Yes, yes, yes. I understand you very well, and you have become an Asian Black Picasso, crapping all over Che's Oldsmobile." I could not help but smile.

She smiled back. "You might be saying that in jest." She put both hands over her stomach. "And forgive me for the vulgarity, but that is exactly the same feeling I had while I was doing that and the same kind of pleasure."

I glanced at her. "You're a nasty girl, Chandee."

She nodded her head and squeezed her lips with a hand. "Yes, I know. That is why I have to ask your forgiveness."

We arrived at the Hotel Riviera. It was built right across from the Malecón. I tossed the keys to the Mercedes to the young valet, and we walked into the hotel. After a nice lunch at this beautiful, elegant place, we went out by the pool. A sign read, The water in our pool slept last night in the ocean. Near the bottom, in very small letters, a further caution read, Salty water—be aware. The water was pumped from across the street by submerged pumps a very short distance to the hotel's pool. They would fill it at night and then empty it the following afternoon.

The Hotel Riviera

We sat down in the bungalow reserved for guests. It was a very ultramodern, exotic tent with mosquito netting and expensive armchairs and sofas. Beautiful silk curtains covered in white mosquito netting bordered in gold protected the entire space from pests—a problem due to the close proximity of the coast. I ordered an orange juice while Chandee ordered a *materba*, a very popular soda at that time in Cuba.

Once the waitress left us, I explained to her the plan that Che had given to me. I told her, "This is supposedly the schematics from the military where they have the fighters and bombers, and Che wants me to give them to Oswald, this supposed spy from the CIA, and try to convince him that this is the real thing. That way, when they drop their bombs in this particular location, they will believe they've destroyed all the air defense that could frustrate their invasion they are currently preparing. In reality, these planes are made of plywood and cardboard. The real planes are in a different secret location, which they are holding in reserve to give an unpleasant surprise to the invaders."

Chandee asked, "How the hell are you going to figure out a way to tell this spy Oswald that this map is a decoy, and not the real one?" Before I could answer, she asked, "Do you know if this spy speaks Spanish?"

"I believe a little. I only spoke to him once. I don't know for sure how much, but my belief is that his Spanish is very limited. I don't want to take any unnecessary risk communicating to him verbally. There will be people all around us, and I bet my life Che, Fidel, and the others will have a thousand eyes and ears in that place. That is why I came up with the idea to write him a note behind the map I'm supposed to give to him. If, as is very possible, they're watching me when I give him that map, everything should look perfectly normal. The only thing I'm doing is what I'm supposed to do—give him a piece of paper."

"It sounds like a good idea, but..." She squeezed her lip and chin in thought. "What if you get caught with the map and it ends up in the wrong hands?"

I smiled cynically. "That can't happen by any means. If it does, I'm a dead man walking. I don't want to wind up on one of those stainless steel beds with those vampires sucking the blood out of my arms before they put me in front of a firing squad for treason."

"You don't think this smells funny and could be a sophisticated trap to test your loyalty, after all the doubt

Piñeiro has instilled lately?" She bit her lip and grimace sourly. "I don't know, but it really smells fishy to me. Why you, precisely? They have hundreds if not thousands in their intelligence groups to do this job to perfection. Why does it have to be you? Have you asked yourself this?"

"Of course," I replied. "I even asked Che that, and the reason he gave me was that they had tried in different ways with Oswald, and nothing worked. Since I had associated with the Belgian ambassador, as I explained to you before, they think it could work, especially if it's my brother-in-law's unit that supposedly joins with them in the invasion. They would need that location, of course."

Chandee shook her head. "I don't think I would swallow that pill, not even with Jupiña."

"Me, either," I answered, "but I'm in the middle of a difficult dilemma. I have to at least play the role that I'm actually trying to do it. I have to play my cards right so that Che and whoever is behind all this crap will be convinced that I did what they asked me to do."

Chandee looked at me gravely and nodded. She clucked her tongue. "I understand perfectly. This son of a bitch Che has put you in one of the worst dilemmas and has backed you against the wall with a sword to your chest. If you don't give the map to Lee, you're not loyal anymore and they can't trust you. If you do it and at least don't try to persuade Lee that this is a decoy, it would be a fiasco for our friends that are attempting to free our country with this invasion. Boy, boy, boy, boy." She opened both arms. "They're putting you into a straitjacket, which leaves a huge problem."

I smiled and raised my eyebrows. "Really? That is brand-new knowledge you're bringing to me now. Why do you think I told you I need to find an exit for this?"

She shook her head with a smile. She touched my shoulder. "What if they change the plan at the last minute and ask you to give them back the map? Can you imagine what Che's people would do if they saw the message you wrote on the back?"

I hadn't thought of that.

She shook her head and clucked her tongue once more. "I think this is extremely dangerous. The note to Lee should be separate, and you should write it and insert it into the fold of the map as you're carrying it. That way, if anything unexpected or dangerous shows up, you can quickly remove the note from inside, destroy it, and still retain the map in your possession."

"Honey," I said, "I think you just earned another *media noche*!" I stroked my chin. "Yes—I like that idea of yours. We will cut a piece of paper the same size as the map, and write a simple note, and insert it so that when the map is folded it looks simply like the back of the map. I'll tell him not to open the map under any circumstance until he is in a secure location. How is your English? Mine doesn't go past 'Tom is a boy and Mary is a girl.'"

She smiled. "My God! That's the first line of the elementary primer for English!"

I shook my head. "Yes, you are completely right. Unfortunately, that is the only thing I have been able to learn. The first teacher the government kicked out of my school was my English professor the first year I was to learn the language. My English is limited to what we learned in one single hour before the prohibition to learn it in any school or university came down from the government."

She grimaced. "Mine is a little better, since I got past the first lesson in the book, but I don't think it will be much better than yours."

"Uh, oh!" I said. "I think we're in trouble then." I pulled out the small English-Spanish dictionary my uncle had given me. "With this little book, I think you and I can prepare a brief message—just what I want to communicate to Oswald."

We started to work on it, and a little while later, we finished. With the help of the dictionary, we wrote: This is a trap. I'm not the contact for Albatross. I'm not associated in any way with him. This map is only a decoy, discard it. Get the hell out of Cuba immediately, because your cover is blown and your life is in immediate danger. We went back and forth, reviewing it once more with the dictionary.

"Well," Chandee said, "if I haven't qualified for a *media noche*, I've at least earned my ticket to the movie theater today."

"You have a *media noche*, the box of pastries I have in the car, and the movie ticket, all before you helped me with this note! You deserve that and a whole lot more, sweetheart."

She stroked my cheek affectionately. "Thank you, and thank you for being so gentle."

"You're welcome," I said. "We're done with our work, unless you want to ask for something else here."

"No, no, I'm fine. That stuff and the *materba* has filled me to my throat."

"What movie are we going to see?"

She held up her finger. "Ah, ah—surprise, surprise."

"OK, Mrs. Surprise, so long as you don't select a Russian film where you don't know any of the stars or how it ends. Otherwise, any film from any country is fine with me."

The Deadly Deals

Chandee smiled as we walked through the hotel lobby. "Well, if what you just told me is true, let's hope you don't repent of it. The movie we're going to see is a little different, from what I've been told."

I smiled and squeezed her arm affectionately. "You've got me in total suspense with the theme of the film. Boy! You would be a great advertisement for the company to watch their movie. I don't even know the title, and my curiosity is piqued."

She smiled. We walked out to the valet station, and when my car was brought by, I tipped the valet. He stepped on the accelerator and said, "Man, this is a beautiful car! How much did it cost you?"

"Nothing," I replied. "It belongs to Commandante Ernesto el Che Guevara."

His eyes grew wide and he exclaimed, "Ooooh!" He jumped out of the car like the seat was suddenly too hot for him. "I'm even afraid to smear the seat with my butt!" He began to carefully clean the mirrors and dashboard.

"Don't worry," I replied casually. "I've already wrecked two of his cars. He has plenty others, so it's no big deal. If I smeared the car, it was a blessing."

We pulled out of the valet structure, and I asked Chandee, "Which theater are we going to?"

"To our theater," she replied.

"Be careful—we can't own anything in Cuba, much less a theater."

"Of course, to the Astral! You know what I mean—the theater where we always like to go. It's my favorite here in my patio, close to Chinatown."

"You don't like the Radio Centro?" I asked her. "You know, across from the Hilton. Everyone prefers that theater."

Chandee grimaced. "No, no, no. Too many people there, and the parking is terrible. I have to admit, it's very modern and beautiful, but it lacks character. Besides, the location is extremely central, and too many tourists hang around."

I nodded in approval. "Yeah, you may be right. There are a lot of foreigners always hanging around that place in La Rampa. But when I go to that theater, I park across the street in the Hilton valet. That way, I avoid the issue with the parking."

Chandee glanced at me and replied with an expression of approval, "That is not a bad idea."

"Of course not," I teased. "When do I ever have a bad idea?"

She slapped my shoulder. "Stop it!"

We arrived at the Astral and cruised around, looking for parking. "You see?" I said. "Sometimes we can't talk, because it comes back to bite us in the butt." I glanced up and saw a space a distance away in a side street.

As we walked up the street, I saw the marquee read in large letters, Clark Gable and Vivian Leigh in *Gone with the Wind*. Smaller letters continued, A love interest and intrigue set in the conflict of the Civil War in the United States. I turned to her and smiled. "Honey, this is a love story. I don't mind love stories, so long as it's not a Russian love story that becomes a trial to endure. This is a surprise?"

"No, no, no," she said. "That is my movie. Yours is *The Young Lions* with Marlon Brando and Montgomery Clift. It's a war movie about loyalty, bravery, and deception."

"Oh!" I said in surprise. "A love movie for you and a war movie for me. A very well-balanced program. I have to give you ten points for that!"

Chandee grinned from ear to ear. "Really? Really, honey?"

These movies were well-received by the public. Not only was there no parking nearby, but I had never seen so many people in that theater. We enjoyed the films as well as the popcorn, M&Ms, and other snacks.

Chandee shed a few tears over the trauma of Scarlett's ordeals, and I felt frustration at the unexpected death of my favorite character, played by Marlon Brando. He was so filled with deception that it was impossible for him to be loyal to both friends and enemies, and he ended up being shot after he had broken his weapon against the trunk of a tree. It was extremely different in those days; I had never seen before in my brief life a principal character die in a film. Both films had spectacular cinematography. Both were stories of great courage and sweeping human emotions which really spoke to me. However, because of our real life situation in dealing with intrigues, deception, and stress, they didn't sit well with either of us, and so neither one met our expectations.

As we were walking towards the Mercedes, we crossed the road, and Chandee asked, "Did you like the movies?"

"Yes," I said a little unconvincingly. "They are great productions."

She smiled. "You're a very bad liar." She shook her head. "No, that I already know. What I'm referring to is the stories—the whole plot and structure of the films. To me, it was too much sadness in both of them. Don't you think so?"

"Yes," I said as I held her hand. We continued to walk. "You're completely right. Too much of the same kind of drama that we live in every day. But they had great messages that we need to digest, especially everyone like us who is losing each day the most precious thing a human being can have in life: freedom. You cannot give it up, and you have to keep on fighting for it."

She pouted and said, "I'm sorry. It's my fault; I didn't read anything about the movies before picking them. I only went by the word of mouth of other people."

"You don't have anything to apologize for. Even though they're sad, they are really great films. They will eventually become classics of the North American cinema. Both have very different flavors and themes, historically, but they're very identifiable in the everyday life of those like us who are enduring similar situations."

Chandee nodded and smiled. "Well, after all, my selection wasn't all that bad."

"No, no, sweetie, under no circumstance! Your decision was magnificent."

She smiled again and took my arm. She squeezed my arm against her body. "Really? Truly?"

I smiled and nodded, showing my approval on my face. "Yes, really."

We walked a little further. When we almost reached the Mercedes, I noticed through the rear window the head of someone that appeared to be hiding on the other side of the car. My first reaction was to reach for my holster and unsnap the safety. I snatched my arm from Chandee abruptly as I did so. I leaned to my left as I reached toward my pistol.

Another individual came up behind us out of the darkness. Something cold and metallic touched my neck. A voice said in my ear, "Don't even think of pulling that gun out, unless you want to die here tonight."

I didn't turn around but leaned forward. As I did so, I kicked my right leg up, striking him solidly in the groin with all my strength with the heel. The man screamed in pain. Chandee kicked his arm with her left leg, and the pistol flew up into the air. It landed on the concrete of the sidewalk and skittered away. As the man started to collect himself, I stabbed down on his neck with my ring.

The man who had been hiding behind the car rose up, a pistol in his hand. He yelled, "Don't move, or you both die! Hands up, hands up!"

The stricken man started to limp around the sidewalk in the darkness, seeking his gun, one hand still clapped over his privates, the other clapped to his neck. As he walked, he moaned in pain. A black car with a white roof on the opposite side of the street turned its lights on. It circled in the middle of the street and pulled up right next to us. The driver leaned over to open the passenger door, shoving it fully open.

He yelled over the running motor of the car, "What are you waiting for? Take that gun away from him and bring him to the car!" He seemed very nervous and agitated. Chandee and I looked at each other, standing there with our hands raised. The man covering us didn't dare to approach us, obviously not wanting to run the risk of suffering the same fate as his associate. When I heard that, I thought that I might lose my life in that place that night, but I was not about to get into that car under any circumstance save for unconsciousness or death.

The man with the pistol pointed to the man searching for the gun and yelled back at the driver, "Toño is the one to disarm them. How am I to do that while protecting myself at the same time? You don't even have a gun!"

Toño found his gun and started to walk towards us. Before he could get close, however, the convulsions started. He looked like he was doing some kind of voodoo ritual, the convulsions growing more violent. Before long, he dropped his pistol, and clapped both hands to his neck. He was having difficulty breathing. The man covering us saw it clearly and yelled to his friend, "What happened to you, Toño?"

Toño tried to answer, but could only croak unintelligibly. He started to foam at the mouth, and fell to the ground as the convulsions grew more violent. He yelled at the driver, "What are you waiting for, carajo? Get out of the car and see what's wrong with Toño!"

The man got out of the car, leaving both doors open. He was a small, skinny man. He walked towards Toño, who by now had his eyes rolled up into his head, the whites fully showing. He rolled him over and did his best effort to pick the stricken man up. Toño, however, was a large and heavy man, and the little driver could only pick him up waist high. In exasperation, he yelled, "I need your help, for God's sake! I cannot raise him up!"

The man with the gun grew angry. "Carajo! You're not even good for letting the dogs out to pee!"

The driver dropped Toño, who fell heavily onto the ground, striking his head with a thud on the concrete, the gun skittering once more into the shadows. He waved his arms angrily and said, "I've told you, don't disrespect me, especially in front of strangers! I've said this many times! The next time you do, I'm getting the hell out of here and leaving you to handle it yourself, since you're so macho and can do all these things!"

"OK, OK, OK, I understand. Pick up his gun and bring it to me."

The driver searched in the darkness for a few seconds. "I can't find it."

"OK, come over here."

The driver timidly moved by us. The look he gave us was that of someone who was there not of his own volition, but was either under threat or because he was being paid. When he reached the side of the man with the gun, the larger man forced the pistol into the driver's hand. He was showing him how to hold it, like the man had never held a gun in his life. "Keep this on them, OK? You fire it by pulling this trigger, and you'll kill both of them. If they make the slightest movement, you shoot! You got it?"

"Yes," the little man replied in an unconvincing tone. He flipped a hand towards the larger man in an attempt to be bold. "Go on, you do what you have to do!"

The large man walked towards Chandee first. He frisked her. As soon as he realized she wasn't armed, he came over to me. With his left hand, he opened the holster while he tried to remove the pistol with his right. As he balanced forward to do this, I stepped away suddenly. As he fell forward, I jabbed him in the neck with the ring on my left hand. At the same time, I tried to snatch my pistol free, but he grappled me as soon as he felt the sting on his neck.

I yelled to Chandee, "Get on the ground!" I rolled on the ground with the large man, trying to get my gun free. However, the man was both larger and stronger, and he was also trying to get my pistol.

As I struggled on the ground with the man, I heard a shot ring out and felt a piece of the sidewalk concrete strike my cheek. Out of the corner of my eye, I also saw the spark from where the bullet struck the ground, far too close to me. Since neither of us was hit, I continued to wrestle with the man, my fingers locked over the pistol. I could see the small man drop his gun, run to the car and enter it by the passenger door. The tires of the car squealed and the smell of burnt rubber wafted through the air as he sped away out of there. The large man grabbed my gun, and I clapped both hands over it to prevent him. He would let go his hold with one hand to punch me in the face. I would take advantage of those moments to jab him once more with my ring.

Chandee ran towards the dropped pistol left by the little man in his hasty departure. I knew that it wasn't going to be long before the poison would affect the large man, and so I locked my hands like iron. His life was now measured in seconds, but those seconds seemed to slow and seem like an infinity. The man continued to punch my face, and one blow hit my forehead wound. I felt the warmth of my blood flowing out of the reopened injury towards my eye.

Chandee ran back with the gun. She put it right to the back of his head and yelled, "Stop it right now, or I'll blow your brains out!"

He felt the barrel against his head and heard the click of the hammer being pulled back. He stopped at once and moved off of me. It was at that point his convulsions started. I wiped the blood from my face and moved close to him. "Who sent you? You better tell me in the next few seconds, or you're dead!" I showed him my ring. "You have a poison in your system that will kill a parade of elephants in a few seconds. Imagine what it's doing to your internal organs right now." I looked at my watch. "I have the antidote, and you don't have much time. Tell me now, while you can still talk." I pointed at the now-weakly convulsing Toño. "Once you reach that stage, our negotiations will be concluded, because you won't be able to speak anymore. Or do you want to wind up like your friend?"

I could say no more, because the violent convulsions began. Foam spurted from his mouth, and he fell to the ground as he lapsed into the unconscious stage. I took Chandee by the shoulder and said, "Let's get out of here." I took out one of my handkerchiefs. "Even if I apply the antidote to him now, it's too late."

Chandee looked at my bloodied face. Not only had he reopened my forehead wound, but he had also given me a fresh cut over my eyebrow that was bleeding profusely. "Let him die," she said. "That's what they deserve. It's probably what they wanted to do to us. Look at what he did to your face without mercy while you were down on the ground."

She dabbed the handkerchief in her mouth and began to clean my wounds.

Chapter 7: Piñeiro's Trap and Humiliation

We walked to the Mercedes and I said, "You'd better drive. My right eye is starting to swell up."

As I sat in the passenger seat, I pulled the visor down. While Chandee drove, I moistened the handkerchief with my saliva and attempted to clean my face.

"I think we'd better go to my house and clean those wounds," she observed. "You're not in any condition to meet anyone with that face."

"No, under no circumstance can we do that." I looked at my watch. "Maybe the purpose of this whole thing is to delay me so I won't show up. They could then blame me. It's only six o'clock," I said in reassurance. "We have two hours. Let's go to a pharmacy to get disinfectant and change my bandages. I hope the stitches my doctor in Pinar del Rio gave me haven't been pulled. After I wash and put some ice on this eye, you could put some makeup to cover the bruising, and I should be presentable by eight this evening. If these people were sent to keep me from showing up there, those not expecting me now will be completely surprised when they see us arrive."

Chandee shook her head. "No doubt now that your head is a lot harder than mine. With all these scratches and cuts on my face, I would only be going home."

"OK, don't worry. Drive to the nearest pharmacy. We'll

fix this."

We left that place, leaving the still convulsing bodies there on the sidewalk. When we reached the pharmacy, Chandee got an ice bag, some ice, and a first aid kit. As I iced my eye, she cleaned the wounds and used peroxide to disinfect the small abrasions and cuts. Luckily, the stitches on my forehead had not pulled; they were held in place by the strong bandages my doctor had put on.

Chandee made me lean back in my seat for nearly an hour and a half with the ice bag over my eye. It worked, and the inflammation was reduced by about 75 percent. She dried my face and put clear makeup over the worst discolorations. I looked fairly normal, save for the bandages over my right eyebrow and over my left forehead. I looked like a boxer who had just come out of a difficult fight but still had the dignity of emerging victorious from it.

I got behind the wheel and said, "Well—there he goes. I'm ready; are you ready?"

Chandee grimaced at my appearance. "Well, after what's happened tonight, I think I've completely graduated and am ready for anything. By the way, I would like very much, whenever you think it's convenient, if you would be so kind as to let me have a ring like you have. I saw how effective it is."

I raised my left hand. "This was a gift, but I'll see what I can do to please you, sweetie."

Chandee smiled and nodded.

We left the pharmacy and drove towards the Palace of Beautiful Art. When we arrived, I immediately noticed Chopin's car. It looked like he was bringing Chia with him. I nodded very discretely as we drove by.

"Do you see that car?"

"Yes, what about it?"

"Those are my backup friends. I don't expect any trouble or acts of violence here. But, in case anything unexpected happens, your exit from this place will be with them. Understand?"

"Very well," she reassured me. "Let's hope we can get out of here together like we're coming in. I have in mind to end this complicated night with a golden brush by celebrating with a romantic moment with, like we had in Rio Cristal. That way, we'll better cultivate our experience."

My eyes widened. "Really? Thank you, sweetie, for giving me that motivation, so that I'll want to get the hell out of here as soon as possible and in one piece."

Chandee smiled and asked, "A very pretty stimulant, no?"

"A beautiful and extraordinary stimulus."

She leaned over in her seat to kiss me on the cheek. We smiled, and I returned her kiss.

We parked the Mercedes and walked towards the building. People were coming in and out. It was a crowded place, with everyone dressed to the nines—the men in black tie and the women in full evening dress with elaborate hairstyles.

As we entered, the wait staff were all dressed in frock coats with long tails. They held shining silver trays with crystal glasses filled with champagne, fruit drinks, and other beverages. A circular table in the middle of one of the rooms was filled with cold cuts, pastries, croquettes, and other delicacies.

It was a high-class event, with the walls filled with artwork—each with a golden tag bearing the title of the painting and the name of the painter. Next to the work was a larger plate with a brief history of the details surrounding the picture and how the artist had been inspired to create the magnificent piece.

Near one end, close to the wall, a small glass table held fliers of high-quality paper with lists of the other paintings of each artist and the years of their creation. The place looked like it no longer belonged in Cuba but would be more at home in Europe. In the past, the Revolution had so criticized the bourgeoisie and their opulent lifestyle. Only two years later, we could see it still displayed in the food on the table, the jewelry worn by the women, and the magnificent and exquisitely aromatic floral arrangements all around. The ministers and commanders of the nationalized corporations of the Revolution enjoyed it in plenitude.

I realized that there were plenty of undercover G-2 agents in civilian clothes in addition to the uniformed armed guards. Their tell-tale posture and radios indicated that the G-2 men were not merely attendees.

I leaned in to Chandee and whispered, "When I identify Oswald, and you see me approach him, go immediately to the bathroom. We will meet at the main exit door."

"Very well," she replied.

We went over to the buffet table, took a couple of plates, and filled them with the delicacies we both liked. As we did so, I looked around, trying to locate Oswald. He was nowhere to be seen yet. I saw a very tall, good-looking man with dark hair with a similarly tall, blonde woman. She was also good-looking, and her hair was permed. They came over and smiled at us. I didn't recognize either of them, but when the man spoke in a friendly voice, I realized he was Commander Franco.

"What a pleasure to see you here, Commandantico," he said. He put his right hand on my shoulder and pointed with his left to his companion. "My wife, Vivian."

I extended my hand to her and discreetly moved to my opposite side in an attempt to get Franco's hand off my shoulder as I kissed her hand. "Mrs. Vivian, it is a pleasure to meet you. My name is Julio Antonio del Marmol, and this is my friend, Chandee."

Chandee extended her hand and said, "Nice to meet you."

After the introductions were made, Franco and Vivian started to serve themselves from the buffet table. As we walked around the table, Franco asked, "What happened to your face?"

"Not much, really," I answered. "You don't want to see what happened to the other guys."

Franco smiled. "Che told me, before he left the city and gave me the invitation to come here tonight, that I should be here with you, because you would appreciate very much to see a friendly face, especially one from Pinar del Rio."

Chandee looked at me when she heard that. I glanced at her in confusion and dissatisfaction. I wasn't happy that Che had sent someone over to me. I was discreet, however, and replied to Franco, "Of course—it's always pleasant to find great people and friendly faces, especially if they are good friends."

Franco and Vivian smiled and expressed their thanks. Franco said, "Commandantico, you have to remember that I always consider you a great friend of mine. Just remember that in the future, even if we have different ways of seeing that friendship. But I always respect you, because though you're young, you are completely a man."

I smiled and looked him directly in the eyes. "Thank you, Franco. I really appreciate your understanding and the difference in between all of us in life."

After we filled our plates, we said goodbye to them very politely, saying we would see each other later.

We left the room.

Chandee said, "I sense you were a little uncomfortable around those people."

I smiled. "You women—you're always a step ahead of us, because intuition makes you guys see what many men don't ever perceive. I don't want to talk about that now. I don't feel uncomfortable with his wife—I feel uncomfortable with him. Just a little. But you are very good to notice."

We walked into another room. Soft music played there that we hadn't heard outside. The room was well-designed acoustically, and the doors had remained closed. The elegance was undiminished from the previous room as couples danced to the orchestral music on the dance floor. The orchestra consisted entirely of string instruments plus a piano and saxophone. The musicians were all dressed in white tuxedos. As I started to close the door, a foot halted the process. I looked and saw Chopin and Chia behind us. Both were dressed elegantly. He had been observing us and followed us inside to exchange a few words with me.

Our hands were full of plates of food, and we hesitated by the door, uncertain about the appropriateness of entering such a room with them. After I introduced Chandee to my friends, we found an empty table at the extreme right of the door. It was nearly imperceptible from the door, but it afforded us a full view of anyone coming or going from the room. We sat down and shared our plates with Chopin and Chia, who had not even seen the buffet table in their distraction of searching for me.

After a little while, I explained to Chopin what the plan was, and how we would all walk out of there without trouble if all went as planned.

"If, however, anything goes wrong," I said, "please get the hell out of here and take Chandee home."

After I explained things to Chopin, he nodded and excused himself. He and Chia left to take up their positions. I said to Chandee, "I wonder with how many people Che has shared the details of my mission here tonight. I like this less and less. How many people know that I'm here and so would be an easy target? What else is he telling all of his spies?"

I rubbed my forehead with the fingers of my right hand. I continued, "This man Che is either irresponsible or has multiple faces—which I already know he has. But I was hoping he would be a little different with me. The only thing we need now is to see the face of Barbarojas, Commander Piñeiro, in this place."

Chandee said with an expression of awed surprise and displeasure in her voice, "Oh, my God! Speak of the Devil and he will show his horns." She pointed her left index finger at the door.

When she said that, I thought she was joking. Then I turned slightly towards the door, I saw that she was right.

Piñeiro stood there with two men, peering in through the half-opened door. It looked like they were looking for something or somebody. They looked all over the salon at the people dancing—and at the tables. I leaned back

The Deadly Deals

further to be out of his line of sight, and Chandee followed my example. They remained there for a short time.

After they closed the door, I said, "I don't believe that Oswald will be here tonight. Maybe I'm wrong, but I think all of this is an elaborate trap to catch me with my hands in the cookie jar. Go back with Chopin and Chia to your house if I don't return in ten minutes. Do you understand?"

"Yes, I do."

"Very well." I squeezed her arm with mine and smiled. "Tell Chopin and Chia that I have to go, because it's an emergency. Tell Chopin that the Red Nose is here—he will understand."

I got up from the table and left towards the door. After I left the room, I walked towards the bathroom. I saw Franco and Vivian. They tried to say something to me, but an interposing group allowed me to pretend I didn't see them.

I walked into the corridor and rapidly entered the bathroom. I went to one of the stalls and secured the lock. I pulled my pants down and sat down, pretending to answer the call of nature.

I took the map that Che gave to me from my pocket, unfolded it, and put it against the wall of the stool. I took the note that Chandee and I had written to Oswald. I rolled it into a very tight cylinder. I took the roll and made it even smaller. I then took a roll of toilet paper off of the wooden dowel. I removed the spring from the middle of the dowel, separating the two wooden sections. In the hollow middle, I concealed the note, and then reassembled the entire structure and returned it to its place. I rolled a bunch of toilet paper around my hand, dropped it in the bowel, and flushed the toilet. I pulled up my pants, and went to the sink to wash my hands. I heard, over the intercom, a female voice announcing the imminent start of the art auction. I checked my watch and saw that it was 8:30 p.m. We had been there for half an hour.

I walked outside and looked up to meet the eyes of Lee Harvey Oswald. He asked me the time, and I showed him my watch.

For a moment, the man had me fooled completely, and I thought to take him inside the bathroom and remove the note from its place of concealment. I figured for a moment that I was being completely paranoid and was overreacting, and I recriminated myself for that. I had Oswald right in front of me.

But then I looked at him once more. He had a pencil thin mustache and a thin, anchor beard. It was then that I also noticed that he was faking a North American accent, but his Spanish was Castilian and perfect, right down to the slight lisp. I looked at him more closely and saw that he seemed a little nervous. I suddenly realized that this man was more perfect than any of the other Oswald doubles I had yet met. The only difference was that his chin was squarer, while Oswald's more pointed—the difference was virtually imperceptible to any normal person, and it explained the beard he had grown.

He held out his hand and said, "I'm Lee Harvey Oswald."

"I'm Julio Antonio del Marmol," I replied. I looked him straight in the eyes and asked, "North American?"

He answered, "Do we know each other from before?"

I said, "No, I don't remember ever seeing you before in my life."

He looked at me in confusion. He let it pass, and smiled. "Yes, yes—you can tell by my accent, hey?"

The Deadly Deals

"Yes, a little."

He laughed, and even that sounded like Oswald's. "I've just recently come back from Belgium. I'm a very good friend of the ambassador here in Cuba, but he unfortunately died not too long ago in a car accident here in Havana."

"A-ha," I said.

He looked me in the eyes and asked, "Did you know him?"

"I only met him once," I said casually, returning his stare. "At the home of a mutual friend— the French ambassador."

Every single detail I saw in his nose, ear lobes, eyebrows—I wanted to ingrain everything in my memory so that I would be able to tell this one apart from Oswald and the other three. He turned his head to look around the room. As he did so, I saw just below the hairline on the back of his neck a tiny black, blue, and red tattoo of a Chinese dragon.

"It's really a pity that I cannot stay for the auction tomorrow. I believe that is when they will be bringing the most valuable paintings up. But I have very important business to attend to in Miami, and have to leave very early tomorrow morning."

I held my hand out to him. "Well, I wish you a good trip. I hate to leave now, but I have someone waiting for me. Perhaps we'll meet again in the future."

He held my hand without letting go. Looking straight into my eyes, he asked me, "Do you know the Albatross?"

I looked at him in surprise. "What?" I gently but firmly disengaged my hand. "I don't know what you're talking about, sir."

He smiled and nodded. "Yes, yes—it's OK. I believe I made a mistake."

He turned and left towards the exit to the hallway. As he walked, he raised his hand as if signaling to someone. Two men in black suits appeared at the end the man had disappeared from, and two other men, identically dressed, appeared behind me.

I wondered what to do. Violence would only make me guilty. The tallest, who looked like the leader, pulled out a badge, revealing himself to be from the Special Unit of the Prime Minister's Office.

"Could you please come with us? The Commander-in-Chief needs to speak with you in private, and he asked us to come pick you up."

"Very well," I answered.

The man was tall, dark-haired, and heavy-set. He hesitated. "I'm sorry, but you have to give me your weapon."

"Why?" I put my hand over my pistol. "It is not customary to disarm me before speaking with the Commander-in-Chief"

He moved away cautiously, not certain about my reaction. "I don't know—those are the orders they gave me."

"Who gave you those orders?" I demanded in an unfriendly tone. I showed them no fear.

The man shrugged his shoulders. "My boss, Captain Ricardo, who is in charge of Fidel's escort."

I put the fingers of my left hand to my forehead in displeasure and discontent. I considered how I should react and what I should do in this predicament. There was something greatly wrong with this new request that I disarm myself. Nothing good could come from it. I realized, however, that I had no alternative; in fact, any further resistance would give them the excuse to shoot me right there for resistance or endangering their lives by being difficult or aggressive.

I raised my hands and said, "No problem. I'm going to unsnap my holster, and I'll pull my pistol out and hand it to you."

As I proceeded to do that, I knew something was terribly wrong and that my situation was serious. Every man, without exception, when I reached for my pistol, reached for their guns. Two of them even pulled their weapons and covered me. Very slowly, keeping my fingers clearly displayed and my other hand held high, I pulled my pistol out with two fingers and held it by the grip so that the muzzle pointed directly at the floor.

I held it out to the man, who rushed quickly to snatch it out of my hands. I noticed him sigh deeply in relief as he did so. He was clearly concerned that there would be an incident with me. All of the men surrounding me funneled me so that I could only go where they wanted me to go. They did it with practiced efficiency, demonstrating that they had done this many times before.

On the way out, we passed by Franco and Vivian, who looked at us in surprise. I walked slowly in the middle of this group along the corridor to the main entrance. As we approached the front door, I saw Chopin and Chia walking slowly with Chandee next to them. They looked at me, understanding that something strange was happening. I did not smile at them, but I caught Chandee's eyes and nodded with imperceptible grimness.

We left the building and walked towards one of the cars

parked along the curb. They put me in the back seat, one guard sitting to one side of me and the team leader on the other. The remainder of the escort piled into the car behind, which started and followed behind our car very closely. Knowing my surroundings as well as I did, I could immediately tell that we were not headed towards the Prime Minister's office but were instead heading in the opposite direction.

I asked the leader, "Where are you guys taking me? We're not going to Fidel's office. This isn't the way there."

He looked at me, uncertain how to reply to me. He looked at the other guard hesitantly. Finally, he replied, "We received a last-minute order over the radio that we should take you to Villa Marista."

That was the headquarters for the G-2.

My stomach churned as a knot formed in it. My ears started to burn. I knew what that signified: Piñeiro was involved in all that was going on, beyond any doubt at all. The only thing I thought of at that moment was that unless he had something concrete against me, he would never cross this line. The only people taken to Villa Marista were obvious Counterrevolutionaries.

I swallowed my nervousness and kept silent, trying to remain calm. It could simply be a bluff or an intimidation ploy by the red-bearded chief of security. He could have gotten so desperate he was playing games to break me, trip me up, and force me to admit what he could not prove.

The guard leader looked at me hesitantly. He wanted to say something but clearly was trying to figure out a way to say it. He pulled out his handcuffs. "You don't have to do it now, but when we get to the building, would you please put these on? It's a regulation at Villa Marista."

The Deadly Deals

I took the handcuffs from him, my face grave. I held them up and stared at them as if in contemplation and played with them for a few seconds. I held them up and asked, "To talk to the Commander-in-Chief? Since when was this regulation implemented, that they would have to do it unarmed and in handcuffs?" I tapped my empty holster with the handcuffs and then shook the restraints at him. I smiled in obvious sarcasm.

"No, no, no, no," the guard said quickly. "The regulation is applied when entering the building with a prisoner...." He paused for a few seconds as he realized what he had just said. "Well, we cannot make any exceptions to anyone we bring in for questioning, even if that person isn't under suspicion of doing anything and is just going to be there for a few minutes." He was rambling, clearly rattled at his slip.

I smiled once more as I continued to play with the handcuffs. "Prisoner—or suspect? In which category am I being classified here? Or maybe both?"

The guard's eyes bulged in panic, and the car was deathly quiet. "Do you guys know if the Commander-in-Chief has any knowledge of what is going on here? Or is this only an order from your boss, Piñeiro?"

The leader shrugged and raised his right hand. He said seriously and nervously, "I don't know anything about that. I'm only following orders and doing my duty. Nothing else."

I asked once more, "Orders from Piñeiro?"

The guard shook his head without admitting anything. His tone was pleading as he said, "Please, Commandantico, don't complicate my life or position. I know that this is all a very bad mistake and that very soon everything will be cleared up. My comrades and I have no idea what's going on. We're just soldiers following orders."

I said once more, "From Piñeiro?"

He didn't dare reply.

"Of course, who else would dare disarm me, put me in this car, and on top of it all accuse me of being a suspect to bring me to Villa Marista?"

The leader shook his head in disgust but did not reply.

I mumbled to myself, "I can't wait to see what Fidel will say when I tell him they put me in handcuffs—in handcuffs, for God's sake, like an enemy!"

The silence grew palpable. I continued to play with the handcuffs, debating whether or not to put them on. I wanted to push to find out to what extend these guards were going to obey orders—whether they would be rough with me or gentle. This was the only way to find out. I decided to attempt to intimidate him, asking, "What is your name, *compañero*?"

He asked defensively, "Why do you want to know my name?" He looked at me in concern.

I smiled. "Well, it's good to remember those men we find along the road in life that follow orders, do their duty, never convert themselves into accomplices, and maintain their honor and decency in the process of fulfilling their duty. Honestly, I have to say to you that you haven't crossed that line—yet. As you said a little while ago, when everything gets cleared up, as I know will happen, the men in charge or behind these insidious orders always clean their hands like Pontius Pilate to blame the ones like you who are only executing orders. Those like you are the ones who wind up for many years in a labor camp or executed for cowardly conduct. They will say that they never told you to do this and that you decided to do this yourself. I have never seen any of the big leaders ever admit that they are wrong. They'll say that you were told to bring me to the Prime Minister's office or even to Villa Marista but that they never told you to put me in handcuffs."

The looks of concern by the escort grew even deeper. The leader gulped nervously and nodded.

He sat in silence for a few seconds. He held his hand out to me and said, "Lieutenant Jose Manuel Castellano."

I took his hand and shook it. "I'm Julio Antonio del Marmol, at your service."

He smiled in reply. "Like the great patriot, Donato del Marmol Tamayo, during the Great War of Independence from Spain."

"The very same. He is my great-grandfather."

"We all know you as the Commandantico, but it is a pleasure to know your name and that you are from a family of patriots who are in the history books of our country. You have a great role model to follow."

"Yes," I replied, "and some very big shoes to fill—so big that sometimes I think I could use them like a lifeboat. But I try to do my best and live with the same honor my ancestor gave as my example to live for. That way, I will leave behind me the best example for the generation that follows me and for my country."

Jose Manuel stayed silent after I spoke. He looked out through the window next to him, lost in thought and contemplating my words.

I looked at him and saw through the window a car coming up next to us. It signaled by honking the horn to the driver to stop and pull over. Another car followed that one as well. As soon as they could, one of the cars pulled over to block further progress as we pulled over, while the other pulled in and blocked the way out behind.

In the back seat of one of the cars sat Piñeiro. The other car held Commander Franco.

All the soldiers save for the drivers of all the cars got out, keeping a distance from Piñeiro and Franco, who were evidently having an argument. I could not hear what was said from inside the car, but I could see Franco point to the car in which I sat and saying something to Piñeiro. I could tell from Piñeiro's innocent reaction and gesturing that he was not happy with what Franco was saying.

It was clear to me that Piñeiro was trying to minimize the seriousness of the situation, and make it sound like I was being taken in just for some routine questions. To make it appear worse, I slipped on the handcuffs. Before the driver could do anything, I opened the door and jumped out.

I screamed at Piñeiro with all the strength of my voice, raising my handcuffed hands up, "Can you explain what the hell I'm suspected of doing? According to your guards, I'm also a prisoner!"

Franco completely lost his temper at that. "Why are you putting this kid in handcuffs? Have you guys lost your minds or what? I'm not telling you again—these are the orders I have directly from Fidel!"

Piñeiro threw his hands up in the air. "You do what you want, and I'll tell Fidel what you said. It's in your hands now!"

Franco called his escorts and walked towards his car where his wife was sitting in the back. I looked at his departure and wished fervently that, for once, he would take me with him.

Piñeiro's nerve broke, and he called out, "OK, OK—take him with you. I'll take care of this with Fidel myself." With both hands in the air, he gestured to Jose Manuel to release me from my restraints and let me leave with Franco.

Jose Manuel pulled the keys to the handcuffs out of his pocket. He walked immediately over to me and released me. He returned my pistol to my holster. "I'm sorry, Commandantico," he murmured in a low voice, "for all of the problems. You see? I told you everything would be cleared up."

I nodded and looked him in the eyes. "You want some advice? Look for any other officer to work with. All Piñeiro will do is bring trouble to you. Mark my words, and never tell me if I see you in the Cabaña or somewhere else that I never warned you."

He said nothing but nodded. Piñeiro had the audacity to wave to me with a smile on his face as he got into his car as I walked towards Franco's car in response to his signals.

I looked at Piñeiro and returned his cynical smile with one of even greater cynicism. I didn't wave at him, but turned and said, "Jose Manuel! Thanks for the ride!"

The entire group smiled at that, appreciating the grim humor. They responded in kind by waving and saying their farewells to me. The smile was wiped off of Piñeiro's face, and he turned forward and tapped the driver on the shoulder to get moving.

As I drew near, Franco said, "Come with us. I have to drop my wife off at my home in Miramar. This son of a bitch Piñeiro spoiled our evening. We will talk later, but I'll take you to Fidel, OK?"

I replied, "OK, thank you."

I got silently into the car without questions, and we drove off.

After we went a few blocks toward Miramar, Franco shook his head in frustration. "This goddamned Piñeiro is a pain in the ass! To him, everyone is a traitor or a spy or in a conspiracy to take away Fidel's power. At worst, you could be an agent of the CIA, or the Israelis, or the English! He always has something to accuse people of!"

He took his hat off and put it on his knee. "I think, whenever he has nothing to do, he creates conspiracy stories so that he can justify to Fidel that he's working hard, twenty-four hours a day. Looks like he's afraid that Fidel might take this sweet candy out of his mouth at any time, and he'll lose his privileges."

I smiled and thought that his observation applied to all of his comrades. Like dogs around the master's table, they only concerned themselves with the bones he might throw to them. I shook my head and said, "One of these days, Piñeiro will find some quicksand in his path, and he's going to wind up ending his bullying and abuses, because no one will be around to give him a hand to pull him out. That quicksand will show him exactly the same mercy he's shown to anyone else that's come under his power."

Franco and his wife smiled, and Franco said, "Exactly! Let's all hope that he finds that quicksand hole soon!"

We arrived at their house, and Franco took his wife inside. He returned, and we drove to the Prime Minister's office.

A few minutes later, we entered past the checkpoint. It once more reminded me of the Nazis and how a previously peaceful neighborhood was turned into a military headquarters with large national banners hanging from the windows. We parked and walked into the largest house which housed Fidel's offices, a place I had been to several times. Franco took me to the conference room, which looked like a luxurious room in a five-star hotel.

I remained there, alone, for six hours, waiting patiently. I fell asleep, but was awoken by a noise at the door. I looked at my watch, and saw it was 3:30 in the morning. Fidel, Che, Franco, and Piñeiro entered the room. I looked at them, still half asleep. "Hello," I mumbled.

Fidel smiled. "Sleeping, eh? That means you must have a completely clean conscience, if you can sleep under all this pressure!"

I smiled vaguely as I wiped my eyes clear. After a few seconds, I asked myself what Che was doing there. He wasn't even supposed to be in the city—he must have lied to me once more. I kept my mouth shut, limiting myself to straightening my hair and adjusting my beret as they all came in and sat down around the vast table. They looked at me in silence.

Fidel broke it. "What happened to your face? It looks like you came out of an ambush."

"You're right about that," I replied. "Evidently someone doesn't like me too much and ambushed me with several people. They almost killed me as well as my friend Chandee. When I got ready to go to the Palace tonight, three men attacked us."

Che looked at me in surprise. "Again?" he asked.

I nodded and showed him my new cut. "In a little while, I'm not going to have any place to get new scars or wounds."

Che, Franco, and Fidel slowly turned and looked at Piñeiro. No words were spoken, and Piñeiro silently and slowly shook his head in denial. I knew at that moment that Che, Fidel, and Piñeiro were in agreement on something. The looks from Fidel and Che were silent demands of Piñeiro as to why he had gone way beyond whatever they had agreed to.

Che asked me, "Why didn't you take one of the men from my escort with you?"

He and I both knew that he had only suggested I take Chandee with me. "You never suggested it," I told him. "That's beside the point, though—I would never have taken one with me because I wouldn't have considered it to be necessary, especially going to the Palace of Beautiful Art. It's a very secure and public place, full of people—what better refuge could I have had than to be in front of that crowd of people?"

I took my beret off, put it on the table, and raked my fingers through my hair in agitation. "It never even crossed my mind that this incident would happen. That threw me off completely. Besides, I can defend myself. I know how, and that's why I have a weapon with me." I gestured with my index finger. "I assure you guys, though, that the next time this happens, I will shoot before anyone even says a word to me. I guarantee you that."

Fidel asked me, "What happened with the map that Che gave to you?" I opened my shirt and removed the map. I handed it to him. Fidel took the map and unfolded it. He looked at both sides of it, and handed it to Che. Che also looked at both sides, and then handed it to Piñeiro, who looked at it, and then passed it to Franco. Fidel asked, "Why didn't you give it to the spy Oswald, like Che told you to do?"

I looked Fidel in the eyes as I said, "I don't know who the hell that man I met tonight was, but I assure you, Commandante, that he was not Lee Harvey Oswald."

The Deadly Deals

"Are you sure?" he demanded, looking at me intensely. I returned his gaze calmly.

"Why do you say that to me?" he demanded in an authoritative tone.

"That was not the same man I met with Che and who was introduced to me as Oswald. Che told me he was a double spy who works for the CIA, and so I carefully studied his face. The man I met tonight is another double—physically very, very close and much better than the others I've previously met, but still a double. I never saw him before in my life, and I don't know what his name is, but I guarantee all of you that I will let you guys pick the most horrible name you can imagine and then re-register me under that ugly name if you can prove to me that I'm wrong."

Che smiled to suppress his laughter, while the others maintained their silence. I ignored Piñeiro completely, and focused my attention entirely on addressing Che, Fidel, and Franco. I quietly thanked God for keeping me ego-free and following Chandee's suggestion to not write anything on the back of the map. Chandee had feared the map would fall into enemy hands; she was a little short, since the map was in the hands of the Devil himself on that island.

The silence at last was broken by Piñeiro, who said distrustfully, "Even if that is true, your duty was to give the map to the individual who fit the description of Lee Harvey Oswald. He was in front of you, practically begging and screaming for you to give it to him. You didn't give the map to that spy, knowing yourself the supreme importance this implied in destroying that invasion! It was imperative for you to make this happen, or they will easily disembark on our beaches and destroy our Revolution. They will kill all of us. Maybe that is what you want, and I'm pretty sure you're not going to shed a single tear over the death of any one of us or the Revolution." He stopped and looked at me expectantly.

I looked at him with contempt in my eyes, and I bored into his. I leaned back in my chair and slowly inhaled. I prepared myself for battle and pulled from the reserves of my spirit all the courage I could muster to reply to this miscreant everything I had in my heart. I picked up my beret and dropped it on top of the table. "If reality is like you say, Commander Piñeiro," I pointed to the cut over my right brow and then circled around my face, "I believe this is only a good excuse to simply not attend that meeting at all. Of course, it only offers to you another proof of disloyalty, something you will celebrate with pleasure. Let me show you something, a little higher than this."

I picked up a jug of water on the table. Making a mess on the floor and table, I poured some into my hands. I rubbed my face vigorously to wipe off the makeup Chandee had put on to cover my bruising. I dried my face with my handkerchief and tossed the now bloodied cloth at Piñeiro. I raised my head up so that they could see that both my eyes were swollen and blackened. Che, Fidel, and Franco all looked at me in surprised awe. All three heads swiveled back to look at Piñeiro, this time with recrimination in their eyes.

I continued speaking. "In reference to the point that I might enjoy our being destroyed by our enemies as well as our beautiful Revolution, I would remind you that the Revolution has already cost the life of one of the members of my family during the attack on the Presidential Palace in our attempt to bring down the Dictator. It also nearly cost the life of my own father to one of the most sadistic assassins Batista had, along with thousands of young Cubans who died for this Revolution. To me, what you just said is not only an insult, it is unfounded and a malicious accusation, only proper from someone filled with hatred and resentment."

I raised my right hand and pointed to each man in turn. "For Fidel, for Che, together with all the leaders of the Revolution, I don't know how many tears I would shed." I pointed at Piñeiro. "But for men like you, who only know how to cultivate hatred and division, I don't think I would shed a single tear, unless it be a tear of joy to see you taken to your rightful place of origin in Hell!"

While I spoke, I undid the bond on my holster and cleared the leather.

He looked at me, his eyes shining with indignation. He remained silent for several seconds, growing angry when neither Che, Fidel, nor Franco said a word in his defense. He stood up violently and put his hand on his pistol. He pointed at me with his left hand. He screamed, "You have to respect me, you snot-nosed kid!"

At almost the same moment, I sprang up. My snap was off, and my hand actually was grabbing my pistol. "The only ones who can demand respect," I said, "are those who give respect to others. You haven't shown me any in your previous accusations or in any conversation. You have the same respect from me that you've given me—no more, no less." Not letting go of my pistol, I pointed with my left hand at my chest. "No one—not you, not anyone—can intimidate me! Go ahead and pull that gun out, if you dare!"

At that, Che, Fidel, and Franco jumped up and got clear of any impending gunfight.

Che was nearer to me, and put his hand on my shoulder and squeezed it reassuringly in an attempt to calm me down.

Fidel screamed, "*Cojones*, what the hell is wrong with you, Piñeiro? Why do you think you could say all these horrible things to the Commandantico and he would sit there and do nothing?"

Piñeiro was still angry and pointed at me. "This is why I wanted to disarm him and restrain him! I knew this little shit would do something like this!"

Franco yelled, "You already had him disarmed and handcuffed in the car!"

Che said, "What!?"

"Yeah," Franco said, "when I picked him up he was already in handcuffs and disarmed."

Fidel whirled on Piñeiro. "After all I told you, and you found nothing, you still did that to him?" All three had rounded on the red-bearded man by now.

Che said, "You had no reason or motive. You are completely out of line, Piñeiro."

Fidel raised his right hand and tapped the palm of his left with his index finger. "There is no doubt in my mind that the Commandantico passed the test you put him through with flying colors. I told you before that this kid is truly a loyal Revolutionary, but you insist and insist, and it makes no difference what I or Che tell you! For God's sake, he saved Che's life!

"But you convinced us and got away with your shit, and we let you do it, because you said you would prove that the Commandantico is the famous spy, the Lightning, you

The Deadly Deals

have been unable to catch all this time."

Fidel threw his arms wide as he screamed, "Where is the proof that you assured me you had?"

Piñeiro was completely demoralized at being singled out and the center of this humiliation. His aggressive attitude seemed to leak out of him, and his hand slipped off his pistol, and he placed both hands on the back of the chair, his shoulders slumped in resignation.

Fidel raised his hand once more. "Can you imagine it, Piñeiro, having your own men in that goddamned sewer under the Palace, pumping the toilet, looking for your evidence supposedly flushed down? You could have had them doing things of importance, but you had them instead in the middle of human bowel and all that crap, pumping and sorting through the tanks with strainers to see if they can find even fragments of a note? You were so certain that this sophisticated spy would feel trapped and drop some kind of evidence there that you assured us you would find it! According to you, if he didn't do that, the evidence would be written on the back of the map."

He held up the map and flipped it over on the back. "Where is it, Piñeiro? You assured me two things—first that the Commandantico would never give this map to the spy, Oswald." He smiled wanly. "I'll grant you that, but it's not because of what you're assuming. It's because he is a lot smarter than you gave him credit for, because he realized that it was a double you sent, and he decided not to do it. The second assurance I had was that I would never see this map again. According to you, he would write something in code on the back to communicate to our enemies that it's a decoy meant to misinform them of where our planes are!"

Fidel looked disgusted as he shook the map around. He threw it to Piñeiro. "Do you see any message or code here? Why don't you take it to Villa Marista and have your people study it carefully? Maybe it's written in invisible ink!"

Piñeiro looked ready to explode from this stream of abuse. He turned slightly as he shook his head. He pointed with his right hand and said, "My Commander, I can guarantee you that I haven't been wrong. Maybe I was a little crazy, but in my heart I feel that this spy that's done so much damage to us, the only reason he could get away with it is because he has to be this little son of a—"

Fidel interrupted him. "Be careful, Piñeiro. Be careful! In order to respect yourself you have to first respect other people, remember? Don't blow up at other people just because he got in your face."

Piñeiro continued obstinately, "Only a person like him who moves around all of our ministers and around our compounds, including this office, has the power to locate the information to be used against us." He shook his head again.

Fidel threw his arms out and then waved at us. "Everyone, sit down, sit down—please."

I sat down, my hand still on my pistol.

"Let's sit down in peace," Fidel continued, "and you, Piñeiro, please tell me which of his hands or his legs you would like to have him cut off himself to put up as a trophy in your office to finally convince you that you're wrong and that he's a loyal Revolutionary and not a spy like you think. There are hundreds of people around us with the same kind of access he has—why does it have to be *him*? Do you like him or something? Are you turning to the other side? What is wrong with you?"

The Deadly Deals

Franco looked askance at Fidel at that.

"You think he is good-looking or something?" Fidel continued taunting. He pointed at me. "It's true—that young kid is handsome, eh?"

Even Piñeiro smiled at that. He shook his head and replied, "No, no. It is not that at all, and I don't want to do any damage or hurt the Commandantico. In reality, if he is loyal to the Revolution and I'm wrong, I have a great idea how he could finally convince me."

Fidel threw his hands up in exasperation. "How can he finally convince you, Piñeiro?"

Piñeiro said, "Very simple. We can sit him down with a polygraph. If he passes, I promise you guys I'll never bother him again."

I looked him straight in the eyes and thought how the serpent could be nearly dead on the floor and yet still try to bite you again with its last breath. Che shook his head and said, "I think this is enough. More than enough, and I think an apology is in order from you, Piñeiro, in front of all of us, to him."

Piñeiro stayed silent.

Fidel said, "Well, what about it?"

Piñeiro said, "Oh, I apologize, no problem." He turned to me. "I'm sorry, Commandantico, really."

Fidel said to me, "What do you think about this, Commandantico, this lie detector test? I think, like Che, that you don't have to prove anything to anyone anymore. We know who you really are. Even though he apologized, I know he'll keep trying things with you. If you want to—you don't have to, mind—you can convince this old mule of your loyalty. Not for any of us, not for the Revolution, but for this hard-headed mule, you can do it." He laid stress on his next words. "Only if you want to. I don't think it's necessary, and Che agrees with me."

I thought about that for a few seconds. If I said no, it would probably get worse. I would need to get somebody to train me to pass it, but with time I could then get clear by convincing them in this way I had nothing to hide.

I turned to Piñeiro and said, "If I do what you're asking me to do, and I prove to you by passing that test that I'm loyal, and not only that, doing this when I don't have to do it, that means I don't hold any grudges towards you, even with all the conniving things you did without any basis or foundation, even putting my family in Pinar del Rio as victims of your paranoid crap by sending your dogs to search my house...."

"No, no," he interrupted, "I had nothing to do with that."

"You had everything in the world to do with that, and all of us here knows that," I said. "I want you to give me your word of honor, in front of everyone here, that you would clean your head and your heart of every single suspicion you have against me, and never, never bother me, my friends, or any member of my family ever again."

Piñeiro nodded happily. He looked a little confused at my voluntary acceptance of taking a test which he thought would only reveal my guilt.

I asked once more, "Are you sure of this?"

He nodded once more, smiling.

I put the index finger of my right hand to my ear. "I don't hear you. Can you articulate the words, 'Yes, *compañero*'?"

He said, "Yes, *compañero*." He obviously couldn't believe that he might have gotten me to voluntarily put myself into a trap he hadn't even planned for me. "Yes,

The Deadly Deals

Commandantico, if you pass the test, I will not only be convinced and completely satisfied, but I will also give you an apology in writing for you to put on your wall."

"No problem," I said, "just one condition."

"What do you want?" Piñeiro asked me.

"The test has to be done here, in this very office, in front of the same people we have here: Che, Fidel, and Franco. I'm going to return to you your own pill—I don't trust you at all with a hundred-mile pole. You make me feel extremely uncomfortable when I'm around you. Since we're being honest here, and you're telling me what you have in your guts, I'm telling you what I have in mine. And you really stink like crap. You should go home and take a shower or bath, because I think you stuck your hands in that sewer."

"Yes," he admitted, "I did." Che, Fidel, and Franco burst out laughing.

I took my only clean handkerchief out, wrapped my hand thoroughly in it, and held it out to Piñeiro. "OK, then I think we have a deal. I extend to you my hand in friendship and my last intent to maintain cordiality, because all of us here are Revolutionaries, and we should fight our enemies, not each other. When you have your technicians and the machine and have coordinated with all three Commanders, you let me know, and I'll be here."

Piñeiro stood up and shook my hand. Fidel, Che, and Franco all stood up and burst out laughing. He said, "My guys will take you back to where you left your car at the Palace."

I held up my hand and said, "No, no, thank you. First of all, that's not my car, it belongs to Che."

Fidel said, "It doesn't belong to Che, either. It belongs

to the people, to all of us."

I said, "Whatever. I'll leave with Che. I have some things I want to share with him in private about the meeting I had tonight." I looked at my watch and saw it was 6:30 a.m. "Well, let me correct myself—the meeting I had last night."

Fidel walked a few steps to me and put his hand on my shoulder. "Come on, let's go. I want to talk to you a little bit."

We walked out of the room together, and he said, "You did very well to not give the map to that individual when you didn't know who he was. Che will explain to you everything later, but I have to tell you now before I leave that this Piñeiro is a goddamned crab on your balls. Deep inside, he's not a bad person. You did well to say you don't want to have grudges against him."

I said, "Commandante, I've been diving for almost two years, and I cannot find the bottom of good in him yet."

"Well, he's a little paranoid to such an extreme that one day he'll accuse me of being a Counterrevolutionary." He smiled. "That will be the day I dye his beard green and send him to Mazorra with the rest of the crazy maniacs like Nogueira." He squeezed my shoulder reassuringly. "If by any circumstance he comes around and bothers you again, you come here directly and tell me. I'll take care of him. You understand?"

"Yes, Commandante, I understand. I will. Thank you."

He said, "You're welcome. Go to Che, he's waiting for you in the hall now. Who knows what conspiracy Piñeiro's been telling him now."

Piñeiro and Che were standing at the end of the corridor. Franco waved goodbye to me and walked away.

Fidel said, "Go and get some sleep. You need to

The Deadly Deals

recuperate your energy from this bad night we've all had."

He said goodbye and walked off with his escort in the other direction.

I stayed there for a few seconds in thought. It was logical that Fidel and Che hadn't accepted the plan from Piñeiro simply to please him. They had dropped the hook in front of me to see if I bit. In the end, they wouldn't lose anything, and the blame could all come on top of the paranoid Piñeiro. I realized once more that I had to walk very carefully with these two. With Piñeiro, I could see it coming. With them, however, I wouldn't see it coming, and when I least expected it, they would be jumping down my back.

I walked down the hall. Seeing my approach, Piñeiro turned and left, avoiding my presence. Pretending for Che's sake to be friendly with me, he raised his arm to me in farewell. When I reached Che, the first thing he said was, "I have to apologize with you very sincerely because I had no alternative than to follow Fidel's lead with Piñeiro. When Fidel told me about this and said that this was what Piñeiro was proposing for that meeting in the Palace, even though I didn't agree, Fidel insisted. He also insisted this would be the last time, as Piñeiro had assured him of having completely convincing evidence but no proof, and this night was to provide that proof. As you see, like always, he couldn't produce anything. Fidel assured me that we should do this one last time so that we can finally get the stupid idea Piñeiro has that you are the infamous spy he's been looking for. It's like accusing me of being that spy: completely delusional."

I stayed silent while we walked to the new black La Sabres in the parking garage. Fausto and the escort were half-asleep when we walked up and Che commanded we get out of there.

We drove towards the Palace of Beautiful Art, and on the way, Che said, "We have to use another contact to bring that map to the invaders. Apparently someone made too much noise, and the gull has flown away to another patio. Oswald's plane never made it to Havana, and he was supposed to land yesterday after leaving Guatemala. Our U.S. contacts told us early yesterday morning that Oswald landed in New Orleans. Some of the Cuban Counterrevolutionaries received him at the airport. Today he was supposed to go with some of the CIA agents in that city to a very important meeting."

Che stroked his beard as he crossed his legs. "What happened last night not only was a test from Piñeiro. I decided to test not your loyalty but your excellent observational skills with physiognomy. Since I knew Oswald wasn't coming and the fifth wheel was here in Havana as part of his training for our plans to eliminate the mother serpent in the USA, I decided to use him to approach you as Oswald. When I spoke to him half an hour after you left the Palace, I could verify that you're not only good—you are excellent! Our Arzate—that is the fifth wheel's name—told me that it took you only at most two or three minutes to realize that he was not the real package. That is truly extraordinary!"

Che paused and then continued, "This man, Arzate, is our best asset. He looks almost identical to Oswald. How the hell did you realize when you had never seen him before that he was not your man?"

I looked at him gravely. I could not forget that the deceiving Che had been in cahoots in all the schemes of

Piñeiro. I tried to be civilized and not show him my discontent at this deception. In the end, after all, I could expect nothing less from an unscrupulous assassin without loyalty to anyone but himself. I leaned back in my seat and said, "Little details. But the biggest one of all was his strong Spanish accent. Tell him from me that the next time he approaches anyone to impersonate Oswald not to open his mouth and speak Spanish to anyone. That will be a serious mistake, unless he removes that stupid accent from his tongue." I paused and asked, "Arzate—with an 's' or a 'z'?"

"With a 'z'," he said.

I smiled and replied, "Very strange name in a Spanish language. But nothing surprises me from the Spaniards when they call their kids *Casimiro*[7] and the women *Torquata*." I shook my head. "These names are so horrible that if we were in North America they would only be used in horror movies."

Che smiled at my jest. He asked, "What other detail did you notice in the fifth wheel?"

"Well," I replied, "I don't know if he thought because of my age that I was just a stupid kid, but I almost burst out laughing in his face when he tried to create a North American accent. He sounded like Tonto in the Lone Ranger." I tapped my chest. "What you want me do, Kemosabe?" I laughed.

"Really?" Che asked. "He did that? It was so obvious?"

"Not only obvious," I said. "It was stupid. I repeat to you—I had to make a great effort not to burst out laughing in his face. Thanks be to God I could control myself, especially when I asked him if his origin was North

---

[7] "Almost seen"

America. He replied to me with a really stupid laugh that he was and asked if I could tell from his accent! I almost could not hold a straight face. I said that's true, but I wanted to say 'Yes, with that Andalusian accent, not an American one!'"

Che looked serious, not pleased at what I was saying. "The only thing that sounded like Oswald was that idiotic laugh. But physically, it was an extraordinary resemblance. For the first few minutes of that meeting, I thought it was actually Oswald, and I nearly gave him the map. But as soon as he started to speak, I realized he was a fake and withdrew myself from the situation."

Che nodded his head. "It's no doubt absolutely that you should be trained to work with our intelligence groups. Even though I know you don't like this kind of work, it would be a criminal waste of those talents you possess."

I shook my head. "Thank you, really, for your compliment. But every time you or somebody talks about intelligence and I look around and see Piñeiro, I get sick to my stomach and my digestive juices get acidic. If there's anyone on this Earth that I don't want to even remotely resemble, it's that idiot Piñeiro."

Che smiled and asked, "What about me? Would you mind looking like me?"

I smiled and looked at him knowingly. I said, "Like you? That would be something entirely different. But you don't work with intelligence."

Che looked me in the eyes like he had a secret. He raised an eyebrow and said, "How do you know for sure?"

I stroked my chin with my left hand while I scratched my ear with my right hand in a show of innocence. "Well, you have the capacity and education. You could possibly be a great master spy."

Che smiled. "If it were like that, would you like to learn from me that kind of work?"

I looked him in the eyes and smiled. "No, no, no. I don't think I would be good at that, believe me. I like very much to express what I feel. You saw me telling what I feel tonight to Piñeiro, and a spy cannot do that. He has to hold himself in, tell people whatever he needs to please them to keep himself alive and show completely different feelings from what he really has. This, for me, would be very difficult if not impossible to do."

Che looked at me seriously this time. "Is that not exactly what you did tonight with Piñeiro in front of all of us? When you held out your hand to him? I know for a fact what you wanted to do was pull your pistol and blow his brains out."

He held his fingers an inch apart. "I know you a little, and I know the last thing you wanted to do on this Earth was give your hand to that ass-kisser, but in doing that you completely destroyed him." He pointed at me. "And that is what a professional spy does!"

He paused as he shifted around to look at me in detail. He was observing my expression, hands, posture—everything said he was carefully scrutinizing. I wondered what kind of cat and mouse game Che was playing with me now. It was possible that Che was now concluding that I was the one they were looking for, and my heart started to beat a little harder. I knew the first thing I had to do was calm my nerves and then quickly give him a straightforward, proper answer to eliminate from his brain the last idea Piñeiro might have planted there before leaving.

After a few seconds of silence, I replied, "Maybe, like you've said on several occasions, I'm a natural spy, even though I don't know it or want it. Something like those kids who play instruments without anyone ever teaching them who start playing like professionals because they were born with a natural gift. Talking about music as an example, I've never received a single piano class, and the past few weeks I was at home in Pinar del Rio, watching my mother and sister play, I've been learning to play by ear in just a few hours. I can even create melodies now that can support my singing the songs I hear on the radio. It completely surprised both of them. That is why I came to the decision I want to learn music."

I waved that thought away. "Leaving that behind and coming back to what we were talking about, as you told me, that in extending my hand to Piñeiro to try and keep the peace, even though you know I don't like him and feel I'm wasting my time with that moron, I learned something from my old man. Before you completely execute your worst enemy, you should give him one last opportunity to repent. That is why I gave him my hand today: it was his last opportunity from me. Let's see if he makes good use of that opportunity or wastes it. But I offered it to him sincerely with my best intention."

Che looked at me, smiled, and shook his head. "I will give you a small advice: when somebody attacks you repeatedly, they've identified themselves as your enemy. When you have your first opportunity, don't hesitate— eliminate him. If you don't, he will eliminate you. Don't give him the chance."

He drew his finger across his throat. "What your father taught you is very noble and gentlemanly, but it's not practical, especially in this age. In the world we live in today," he once more drew his finger across his throat, "if you are merciful, you're dead. Only the strong survive in the jungle. We live in the jungle of asphalt and cement. Do you understand what I'm saying?"

"Yes," I replied. "Thank you for your advice."

"You're welcome." I realized from his demeanor at that moment that I had accomplished my objective to distract him and remove from his mind the possibility that anyone had been training me from any organization, that my skills were natural and untaught, and so explain how I had managed the situation with Piñeiro so well.

We reached where I had left the Mercedes. I said, "If you don't mind and you don't need me the next few days, I've been thinking of accepting the invitation from Tanya to spend that week at Varadero Beach. I don't want to get back to my house in Pinar del Rio and hear my mother screaming when she sees the condition of my face. Besides, after everything that's happened lately, I think I not only deserve but need at least a week of rest."

He looked at me and smiled. "Yes, yes, of course—go to Varadero Beach with Tanya. She and her daughter will take good care of you," he added with a knowing wink.

I smiled back and said, "Thank you."

"You're welcome, no problem. When you come back, whether in a week or two, if you don't find us at the house in Cojimar, take the Mercedes and use it however you want in Pinar del Rio. Don't worry, we're not leaving the country anytime soon. If I do, however, I will send somebody to let you know. I would like you to eventually come with me on one of my trips to Africa. There's a lot to learn on that continent."

We said our farewells.

As I got out of the car, he said, "Don't worry too much. The gull of Lee Oswald flew and you couldn't complete your mission. Even though he's flown far away from us, we've already put the ring of our intelligence on his leg. It doesn't matter how hard he tries to shake it off, it will remain with him until he's dead. If he doesn't want to come back here, we don't need him here anymore. We have his body; as far as I'm concerned, I hope he doesn't drop dead yet. We still need his image around for the plan. By the way, I have to apologize to you once more. I hope you understand I felt obligated by Fidel's orders to not communicate anything with you of what the plan was all about at our meeting until our mission with Arzate concludes."

I had my hand on the edge of the window. He put his hand on my arm and squeezed it in a display of repentance and affection. "I want you to know that I'm very happy that you passed the test. From the bottom of my heart I tell you this."

I nodded and smiled. "I know. Thank you."

We said goodbye once more, and I walked the short distance to the Mercedes. As I walked, I realized that none of the three Buicks had moved until I opened the door and got in. It made me think that, perhaps, deep down, Che had a small spark of remorse on his conscience. It was also possible that he really had no feelings at all and was just putting on a show for my benefit so that he could continue to use me each time he needed me.

Even though I always prefer to view things optimistically, the more I looked, the more I could not find in any of the leaders of the Revolution even the smallest

The Deadly Deals

feeling of grace, altruism, or generosity—something they preached to the world as their sole motivation for their socialist ideas but never practiced to anyone's observation. They used this to continually criticize capitalism, free enterprise, and democracy, even though they never showed it.

Azarte, in his cover passing out pamphlets in New Orleans

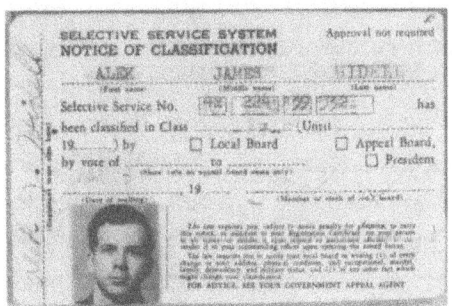

Marcelino's false ID card

Dr. Julio Antonio del Marmol

Chapter 8: Chandee's Loyal Devotion

After I entered the Mercedes and the men in Buicks departed, I was surprised to find someone lying fast asleep in the passenger's seat, her long, black hair covering her face. It was Chandee, her seat fully reclined. She had clearly spent the night in the car, hoping for my return. I touched her shoulder, and she awoke. She straightened her seat, looked at me, and asked, "What happened to your face? My God!"

I smiled and replied, "You forgot what happened last night so quickly?"

"No, no," she said. "How could I forget, even if it gives me nightmares of those sadistic men? We were fortunate that the effeminate man panicked and dropped his pistol to run away, or I don't think we would have survived that ordeal. What I'm referring to is the makeup I put on to make you look better. It's gone. What happened?"

"Oh," I apologized, "I'm sorry. I used my bruises to demonstrate to Che and Fidel that it was likely Piñeiro who was behind that criminal assault last night before we reached the Palace. By the way, the whole thing, I discovered, was a huge trap—large enough that I think they were intending to catch elephants. I believe that Piñeiro, Fidel, and Che all were in cahoots to put me through a test. In the end, they instead wound up with a big fiasco. I'll give you the details later. I couldn't sleep all night and have been under constant stress for six hours, waiting for the worst. What I want to do right now, before anything else, is give you a big hug and kiss." I leaned over and held her tightly in a hug and then planted a long, loud kiss on her cheek. "Thank you, thank you."

She shook her head sleepily. She looked at me in surprise and wonder. "Why are you giving me thanks? I haven't had much opportunity to do anything except stay here all night, dying of worry. I've been driving myself crazy thinking about the worst that could be happening to you."

I looked at her in tender gratitude. She returned my gaze with a smile. "What? Why are you looking at me that way?"

I replied, "What do you think was the first thing Fidel asked me when they took me to his office and left me alone for almost six hours in an attempt to break me? Think. Guess. What was the first thing?"

She looked up in thought. Her face lit up. She asked joyfully, "The map?" She clapped both hands to her mouth. Before I could reply, she continued, "I told you!"

I nodded and said, "You were right, all the way, it was exactly as you told me."

She sighed deeply in relief, her chest heaving. She asked anxiously, "Of course, you already took the guts out of the map, right?"

I nodded. "Thank God."

Chandee crossed herself. "Oh, God—thank you." She looked at me. "Where did you leave the note for Lee?" I pointed towards the building across the street. She raised her eyebrows in astonishment. "Is it in a secure place?"

I smiled and said, "As secure as I could find under the

circumstances."

She nervously fixed her hair. "We have to go in as soon as they open and retrieve it. If it winds up in the wrong hands—oh, my God! I think you'll last less time than a candy bar at the front entrance of a school. It will be a tremendous calamity if our enemies get a hold of it."

I said at once, "Take it easy and don't worry. Where I put it, it will take a very long time to locate, and it would be a huge coincidence if someone finds it. It would be a major mistake to go there at once, since we have no idea if Piñeiro has people watching us right now to see what our next move will be. If we walk straight into there today, we could wind up taking them directly to where I left the note. We might as well leave it alone for a little while. I'll retrieve and destroy it later, once everything's cooled off and I feel that we're no longer being watched."

"Yes," she said, "you're right. We don't have a reason to rush, if you're certain that its location is well concealed. They didn't find it last night, and I'm pretty sure they even searched inside the toilets." I smiled at that. She looked at me and asked, "What? What did I say now?"

"You don't even know what Piñeiro did," I said. "He actually disconnected the sewer from the toilets in there, and used a strainer himself in the midst of all that crap to see if they could retrieve the note I wrote to Oswald. I found out all of this in Fidel's office, but I'll give you details later. It's a very long story."

"Oh, no!" She exclaimed. "That's not fair! You're going to go to sleep, and Heaven knows when I'll see you next. All that time, I'll be wondering what happened last night and how the Devil you were able to slip through their fingers again." She shook her head discontentedly. She clasped her hands together in supplication and pouted at little. "Please," she implored, "please. Curiosity is in my genes. It's my Chinese descent, because we're the oldest civilization in the world, and have always been experimenting. I'm also a woman, so I have an innate curiosity. If you add to all that that I was involved with you last night in all this ordeal—please! You're going to kill me if I have to wait hours before finding out what happened. Please—why don't you come with me to our home, where we love you so much and always treat you with courtesy, instead of going to Che's house where you know they don't like you so much and doubt you all the time?"

She touched my face with her hand. "I will tell my mother to make her best breakfast for you, and we'll clean your wounds and ice your swollen, rainbow eyes, and you'll see in a few hours how you'll be a brand-new man. In the process, you can tell your *chinita* all the details. That way, nobody can take you by surprise."

She looked at me expectantly and then smiled slyly, shaking her hands and head in an exaggerated dramatic display. "This won't take more than a couple of hours, and then you can sleep all day. I will personally see to it that nobody bothers you. I will be your guardian angel while you sleep. My father is out of the city; maybe, with a little luck, I can convince my mom that, since you're wounded, that you can stay in my bed. Then, late this afternoon while my mother and sister leave to go to the temple for daily prayers...." She waggled her eyebrows suggestively and smiled mischievously. "We might have a few hours of romantic privacy."

I grinned broadly. "*Chinita, chinita*, you are *una*

verdadera diablita[8]. You have convinced me to go along with your program. I don't have any desire at all to go to Che's place in Cojimar after what he did to me, if I can be honest with you—not to sleep, not for anything— until I have some time to forget for a little bit what a deceiving traitor he is after what happened last night. Let's go to your house, and I thank you for the invitation."

Chandee smiled and said, "You like the program, eh?"

"Of course, my love, even though it's not for the good things you want to do for me but to satisfy your curiosity."

She slapped me on the shoulder.

"Ouch!" I said. "You hit me on one of my bruises!"

She leaned in towards me and kissed my shoulder. "I'm sorry, I'm sorry." We both smiled. She kissed both of my wounds on my forehead and eye. "Is there any other place where you have a boo-boo?"

"Well," I mumbled as if in pain, pointing to my mouth, "I have a little boo-boo here."

She leaned in and kissed it tenderly. The kisses continued until they became passionate. Just then, there was a tapping of a key on the window of the car that broke the passion completely. I turned and we both looked at the source. Standing there with a white, toothy grin was Chopin. He held the keys to his car in his hand, and he was nodding slyly in a knowing manner. I put the window down.

"Good morning, Commandantico. Good morning, Chandee," he said. He looked at my face and winced. "Ouch! What happened last night? Your face didn't look like that when I saw you last."

---

[8] Truly a little devil

The Deadly Deals

I opened the door with a smile. "Yes, yes. My face last night was exactly like it is now, but it was camouflaged by the makeup Chandee put on my face. I'll give you the details later. I had to remove it to prove to Fidel and Che that I had been victimized by people who were perhaps contracted by Piñeiro to assault us."

Chopin shook his head violently. "That son of a bitch Redbeard! Everybody in Cuba without exception hates and despises him! One of these days, he will end up with a hole in his face, and I assure you it will not be made by him to hang an earring."

I smiled and asked, "But what are you doing here? Where is Chia?"

He put his right hand on my shoulder. "Take it easy, my friend. Chia is fine, sleeping and relaxing at home. Unfortunately, I had to spend all night here because your girlfr—I mean, your friend Chandee didn't want to leave the Mercedes here unprotected. That meant that I couldn't leave her here by herself all night. So I drove Chia back home and returned here, parking close by so that I could keep an eye on your car and protect Chandee. She assured me that you have something extremely compromising in your travel bags in the trunk of the Mercedes. If by chance the G-2, Piñeiro, or anybody else found it, your cover would not only be blown out of the water, but that bomb would explode with Che and Fidel. She told me it was up to you to let me know what it was, but whatever you have in there has to do with why Che no longer rides in the three Oldsmobiles. It sounds like Fidel got pissed off with him because the Argentinian was trying to imitate him. So that Che didn't ruin any more Oldsmobiles, Fidel downgraded him to Buicks. I saw the evidence of that myself a little while ago when they brought you back here."

He paused and looked at me closely. "Really, though—what the hell do you have in those travel bags? Chandee makes it sound more destructive than the bombs we used in the fight against Batista."

I smiled and shook my head. "Ah!" I said as I clapped his shoulder. "When will you learn not to listen to women? All she was doing was putting wood on the fire of your curiosity. I will explain everything to you in detail very early tomorrow morning. I have to see you before I leave for Varadero Beach."

He looked at me pleadingly, uncannily similar to the expression Chandee had just used on me. "Tomorrow morning?" he asked plaintively.

"Oh, no," I said. "You, too? I'm very tired, I ache all over from the bruises and cuts I have all over me, I didn't sleep all night. I have to meet with you anyway. Tomorrow morning, we'll get together, and I'll update you on everything. You'll find out about the bags' content, because I need you and your people to help me in the execution of this plan."

"OK," he said unenthusiastically.

I smiled. "My God, you guys are so alike it's unbelievable."

"What do you mean?" he protested.

I gave him a hug. "Thank you very much for your support last night and staying here all night long. That means a lot to me."

He patted my back appreciatively and waved off my thanks politely. "For me, it's a sincere pleasure as well as a duty to do what all of us are doing." He smiled impishly. "I left you a present in the trunk of the Mercedes." He raised his right hand. "I swear to God that, even though I'm dying of curiosity, I did not open the travel bags to find out what Chandee was talking about."

I smiled and replied, "Even if you did, I assure you that, unless I explain to you what they're for, you wouldn't understand it."

He threw up both of his hands in mock exasperation. He smiled. "Now you are dropping more wood on the fire! You keep clanging the gong of mystery."

"No, man," I said. "I'll tell you everything tomorrow." We smiled and hugged once more, and he waved his farewell to Chandee before leaving. I got back into the Mercedes and said to Chandee, "Well, I'm all yours for the rest of the day and maybe all night tonight."

Chandee wiggled her eyebrows mischievously and squeezed my arm with both hands. She rested her head on my shoulder. "I like it like that."

We drove off and went to her house. I drove around to the alley and parked the Mercedes inside the commercial parking lot where Mr. Xiang had once directed me to go when we didn't want to attract the attention of the neighbors. I walked through the main door of the store. Chandee, her sister, and her mother showered attention on me. Chandee told them that my wounds were the result of an automobile accident—not entirely true, but for the most part accurate. After I took a long, hot shower, Chandee cleaned my wounds and changed my bandages with the assistance of her sister. After a wonderful breakfast, we retired to Chandee's room, as Mrs. Xiang believed I was going to spend only the afternoon with them.

Once we were alone, I satisfied Chandee's curiosity, filling her in on what had happened in Fidel's office in the early morning hours. After our long conversation was finished, I shared with her my idea of visiting the leader of the guerrillas in the mountains as soon as I returned to Pinar del Rio. I informed her what the purpose of my visit was going to be. She was completely against that idea and tried to convince me that it was a bad and imprudent idea, as my uncle had, asserting that personally conducting such a meeting was an unnecessary risk to my security.

She took my arm and looked me in the eyes. "I can go and meet with Mr. Correa, and I can arrange for him to take me to the leader of the guerrillas. That way, these men won't know who you are. Just think about it—if any one of these men gets caught by the forces of our enemies and is tortured, he might break and mention your name." She clapped both hands to her head. "Can you imagine it? This is exactly what Piñeiro has been looking for all this time—he wants to take not just your hand but your head to the firing squad. Poof! And all the young people you've inspired to fight against this government will lose all the hope you've been giving them. Do you think that is worth it?"

"OK," I replied, "I understand perfectly what you're saying. My uncle already told me the same, and he made the exact same comparison you just did. I realize that my mere presence in the guerrillas' camp might be difficult to justify if I got caught in there. For you, it could be different. You might be able to dress like a peasant and pass as one of those country farmer's daughters. I think it will be a lot easier for you to communicate with these leaders."

She smiled in satisfaction. "I will give your instructions

to the guerrilla leaders and make sure they follow those instructions to the teeth. I will tell them to spread to the other provinces' guerrilla leaders the same plan."

"Very well, sweetie," I said, "you win. You will do this as soon as possible."

"OK," she said, "now that all of our business has been taken care of and we're in complete harmony and agreement, I think it's time for you to go and rest."

I yawned deeply.

"Yeah, I think you need it very much."

"Yes," I replied, "I told you I'm exhausted. I need to sleep for a while." Chandee walked me to the bed and helped me lie down. She covered me up and kissed my cheek tenderly. She closed the curtains over the windows and left me in the darkened room, closing the door quietly behind her.

Between the exquisite food Mrs. Xiang had prepared for me and the tilo tea I had drunk, I slept like a baby in the womb for several hours.

When Chandee finally woke me up with a kiss on my face, it was already dark. She had opened the curtains, and I could see from my position on the bed the bright, white light of the moon shining through the window. Chandee sat on the bed next to me, caressing my hair. Her lips formed a beautiful smile, and she said, "I believe you will lose the opportunity. It's been more than half an hour since my mother and sister left for the temple. I'm sorry to wake you up, but I started to think that if I didn't, you would confuse one day for the other."

I looked at my wristwatch. "My God! Eight thirty! Why didn't you wake me earlier? I've been asleep for over ten hours."

She smiled and said, "Not ten—try twelve. And you

snored like a train, you slept so soundly." She looked at me lovingly, caressing the bandage over my right eye with her hand. "The inflammation has almost disappeared."

"Really?" I said.

Chandee picked up a hand mirror and held it before me so that I could see. I realized that, while there was still a little bruising, most of the swelling over my right eye had gone away. I felt better about that. She leaned over me and said, "You see? My kisses over your wounds have healed you."

"Uh, oh," I said. "You want to start the whole thing again?"

"No," she answered. "No games." She leaned in and kissed me tenderly on the mouth. The kisses started to grow passionate, and she lifted the sheet to slide under with me. We continued kissing and caressing as our clothes flew onto the floor. Very soon, we made love in her own bed for quite a while. All unnoticed by us, the time rapidly passed.

Suddenly, we were surprised to hear the voices of Chandee's mother and sister walking through the antique store and into the house as they returned from the temple. We both jumped out of bed and scurried around to quickly gather up our clothes. We tried to get dressed quickly to avoid being caught in a very embarrassing situation. It would have been worse for me, as I was the guest in that house.

No matter how fast we rushed, however, we heard the door to Chandee's room start to open. I was only in my underwear. I sat down on the cloth-covered table where Chandee kept a Parcheesi board set up. I used the tablecloth to conceal my lack of dress. Chandee ran and sat down on the other side. I put my pants over my lap and let the legs dangle down over my bare legs. Chandee had managed to get only her blouse and underwear on, and so concealed her state of undress similarly.

The door opened, and Yein entered with a big smile on her face. "Oh, my God! Julio Antonio, you look a lot better! All you needed was some rest, eh?"

I smiled and nodded. "Yes, yes, but also both your angelic hands healing me."

Chandee nudged me with her foot under the table. Her face was cautionary in expression, clearly warning me not to overindulge in conversation with her sister. We pretended as if we were in the middle of playing the game. Yein walked over to the bed and asked her sister, "Would you like me to fix your bed?"

"No," Chandee protested, "let me do it. I want to change the sheets and pillow cases. If you want to help, please go and tell Mama that Julio Antonio hasn't eaten all day. If she would prepare some soup and stuff, I will join you, since I scarcely ate when you did. I wasn't hungry yet, and now I'm famished!"

Yein smiled and got up from the bed where she had been sitting. "OK, I'll go and tell Mom and ask her if she needs any help." She clearly was trying to appear older and responsible beyond her thirteen years in an attempt to impress me. Chandee rolled her eyes in exasperation.

"That is very good, little sister. Go quickly, because our guest is very hungry."

"OK," Yein replied, and quickly left the room, closing the door behind her.

Chandee immediately got out from behind the table and ran towards the bed. She searched and finally found her skirt and the rest of the clothes. She retrieved them from under the sheets while I finished putting on my pants. I had just finished tying my belt with the door opened once more.

Yein popped in with a smiling face. "Mama asked if you want to eat in here or in the dining room. I can bring the food in here to you guys, if you want." Her tone was complacent.

Chandee was nearly done fixing the bed, and replied, "Tell Mama that we'll both come to the dining room. We'll be there in a little while, OK?"

"OK," Yein replied. She left, closing the door once more.

Chandee walked over to me and kissed me tenderly on the lips. "Let's go. I'm really hungry."

"Me, too," I said. I followed her to the dining room where Mrs. Xiang, as was her custom, had prepared a variety of Chinese food. We both fell to it and ate with great appetite. Even though Yein and Mrs. Xiang hadn't been eating, they sat with us at the table, sipping tea and snacking.

I said to them, "Stay here at the table. Don't go away, OK?"

I picked up the keys to the Mercedes and walked out of the house. I went to the trunk of the car and got the box of pastries I had forgotten in all the commotion. I noticed in there something that looked like tubes of canvas secured by rubber bands. I unrolled one of them, and it looked like a painting. I was taken by surprise, and I remembered what Chopin had mentioned before about leaving a present for me there. I was so tired and in so much pain that I had completely forgotten about it. I rolled the painting back up and wrapped the rubber band around

The Deadly Deals

it once more. My curiosity burned, as I had no idea how Chopin had obtained them. I counted five rolls of canvas. As I walked back with the box in my hand, an idea flashed through my mind, but I discarded as utterly crazy.

Back in the house, we shared the pastries, and I let them know I had bought them because I wanted to see if they would like them as much as I did. I knew that they had different customs, and I had no idea how the pastries would taste to them. They seemed to enjoy them very much, as all three ladies each ate two pastries. When they finished them, they all bore pleased smiles of satisfaction on their faces. Yein even asked if she could have another.

I smiled and said, "They're all for you guys. It's not up to me."

Mrs. Xiang said, "No, she has eaten too much already. She's going to get sick."

I spread my arms helplessly. "There's the captain who says yes or no to you."

Mrs. Xiang smiled at my words. "OK, I'll get one and cut it in half." She took one of the pastries, cut it, and held one piece to Yein. "Only half—you get the other tomorrow."

Yein smiled in satisfaction as she snatched the pastry and began to eat it.

Chandee and I excused ourselves after I thanked Mrs. Xiang for all her attention and cooking. Mrs. Xiang replied, "Thank you for all the pastries—and very exquisite pastries they are! We have enough for the entire week."

We went to Chandee's room and sat down on pillows on the floor. We listened to her Paul Anka records and those of other modern musicians who were no longer heard on the radio. Slowly, month by month, the government had nationalized all the radio stations, now even taking over the smaller stations. It was becoming rare for radio stations to play this kind of music, and even the ones that were yet to be nationalized knew the rules. There was not yet an open censor, but the few stations left untouched didn't dare to play any of the music the government considered inappropriate.

After a few hours of listening to music, all thoughts of spending the night together were dispelled by the sound of the front bells ringing in the store. Chandee went to see who was coming in. A little later, she returned with a long face. She let me know that Mr. Xiang had returned from his trip early, and as soon as she had let him know that I was there, he said that he had something extremely important to communicate to me immediately. I fixed my hair, adjusted my beret, and went to his office to see what he wanted.

He was seated behind his desk waiting for me. We greeted each other, and he gestured for me to sit down. He said in a very serious tone, "You should tread very carefully. The invasion of Cuba is imminent. Our people in here are prepared to join the invaders. The G-2 has intensified their circles and started to pick people up who have nothing to do with politics or anything we're doing, and they're arresting people simply for applying for passports to leave the country. They've opened facilities in the country for doctors, attorneys, or anyone they think would be a potential enemy. They're picking them up on any excuse to bring them to these camps, no matter how ridiculous the excuse. They have very sophisticated intelligence about this invasion from the double agents they have infiltrated within our forces. They don't have any idea of the magnitude of this invasion, or of the direct

The Deadly Deals

support the United States government will be giving to it or how prepared the Yankees are or what they are willing to risk in front of global public opinion to ensure the success of it. Not even we know that. It all depends on the size of the balls of this new Democrat President, John F. Kennedy. Only history will tell us.

"This is absolutely confidential and classified, to be known by only the highest people in our group. Don't tell a soul. The point of disembarkation will be Villa de la Santísima Trinidad. If this is not changed at the last minute, do you have any adverse opinion about this location? Could something throw it off that we have to pass along to our intelligence?"

I shook my head. I removed my beret and put it on top of his desk. "The only thing I know about Trinidad is that Che has one of his largest training bases for the International Guerrillas there. He told me that himself. Personally, I've never been there. I don't know anything about this base or where it is located. The one I know of, according to Che's description, is smaller but similar. It's the one I visited in Caibarien." I raised my right hand high. "I sent you pictures from my camera pen with Chandee not too long ago."

Mr. Xiang held his hand up to slow me down. "Yes, I remember. That is from the trip you took to Santa Clara with Che."

"Yes. Do you have a pencil and paper, please?"

He opened a drawer and pulled out a composition book and a pencil. As we continued to talk, I placed the book on one of my legs and began to trace. Mr. Xiang observed me with curiosity but asked no questions.

Instead, he said, "We have recent information that the

Cuban government is planning a change of currency in order to pick up all the foreign currency in the country. This will let them limit the amount of money anyone can have in a personal or business account. Do you know what they're trying to do?"

"I have an idea," I said.

He pointed at his ear. "Well, keep your ears open. We need to know when it will take effect. This will damage us tremendously in our activities and put an economic restriction on our movements. We will not be able to use the dollars we'll be smuggling in."

I continued to write on the paper.

He looked at me and paused before asking, "Do you think that your brother-in-law, Canen, will want to join his troops with our people and the invasion force?"

I raised my head and shook it. "I doubt it. I believe strongly that, even though he's anti-communist, has no sympathy with what is going on right now, and is really upset with the Castros because of his religious principles, he'll consider the invaders as coming from the same people who supported Batista. Like most people, his information is based on this government's propaganda which associates such people with worms and boot-lickers of the Yankee Imperialists. To my mind, this will hold him back from uniting with them. He would consider himself a traitor to his own brothers in the fight for this Revolution. Even though hundreds or thousands of officers like him are willing to do something else to do something to bring down this regime, I don't think they'll follow this invasion."

I handed my sheet of paper to him now that it was finished. "I believe all these rebel officers, like Canen, want to take the power out of the hands of the Castro brothers and bring back the Revolution and freedom in a democratic way, as had been promised to the Cuban people from the outset. But they won't unite with those whom they consider their enemies. Not yet.

"Eventually, they will realize that this idealistic way of thinking of overthrowing the Castros without superior forces will be smashed by the forces of Soviet intelligence here. They don't yet know this game is not a Cuban revolution; it is a master game of a Soviet conspiracy to swallow the world. This is part of the international Marxist conspiracy developed by the most sophisticated of their agents, KGB agent Number 066614, who we now know is Commander Ernesto Guevara de la Serna. This man knows the appetite for power and the grandiose ego Fidel Castro has. Very cleverly, he's prepared a great table with one unique plate. Castro's covetousness for power forces him to eat only from the dish of Soviet communism, making the clandestine operations nickname for him, Alexander the Great, very appropriate. What Che never told Castro is that he is himself a KGB agent. He's also never told him that he has himself been played all along by the master rulers in the Soviet Union. In the end, they are both zeros to the left of the decimal point, and mean just as much: nothing."

Mr. Xiang looked at me gravely. He shook the paper and asked, "What is this?"

I returned his gaze. "That is the disinformation map showing the location that Che and Fidel want the invaders to drop their bombs. They want them to believe that with this they will destroy our FAR aircraft. In reality, that location only contains cardboard and plywood dummies. The decoy was placed in a rural farm with school dormitories for children that have been brought from the city for voluntary labor and to learn agriculture. On the roofs of these dormitories they have placed Chinese quad mount anti-aircraft guns to make it look more like a military establishment. This operation will kill hundreds of thousands of kids.

"Please let it be known to our allies, through any channel, that if they received this information, they should dismiss it at once and put the question mark on the person or entity that produced it. I can guarantee you ninety-nine percent that the one who provided it is a double spy, and one percent could be that the man has been very cleverly conned by Castro's forces."

I pointed at the map that Mr. Xiang was still studying. "Be very sure that the map I just made out of the recollection of my memory never lands into our enemies' hands. I will die if it does. If I'm right, I'm one of the few who had possession of this information for a very few hours. This past early morning, Fidel himself asked me very worriedly for the return of that map. They wanted me to give it to a double spy named Oswald; unfortunately for them, it was frustrated. It looks like Oswald smelled something rotten and never arrived in Havana like they had expected. I assure you that they will look for and find another way or connection to get this map into the hands of whoever is in charge of this invasion."

Mr. Xiang looked worried. "You haven't had any problems, have you? When something in an operation of this magnitude goes wrong, the blame never winds up on the floor but on the shoulders of someone involved. In this case, you are the weakest link in the chain, so you would be the logical victim."

I smiled. "You're right. Piñeiro, mostly, tried to place all

The Deadly Deals

the blame for the entire matter on my shoulders. Not just that, but a lot more. He tried to involve me in one of his insidious schemes, but I believe I was able frustrate his designs once more. I managed to come out of it smelling like a rose, unlike Piñeiro, whose nails smelled of the crap he had been digging around in as he tried to discover my caca. To be completely open with you, I owe a tremendous debt of gratitude to Chandee for her great help. Thanks to her savvy advice, which I followed to the letter, I was able to avoid falling into a huge trap set for me not only by Piñeiro, but I also believe in my heart, Fidel and Che. I don't want to go into this too much. Chandee can give you the details later on.

"Right now, I think the most important thing is for you not to waste any time. If possible, even tonight, use whatever sources you can find to send this plan of misinformation to the people planning the invasion. I don't want to give the major bureaucrats any time to develop the idea that this is real and so force things to end in a big fiasco."

He shook his head. "No, it's not possible to move until tomorrow morning, but I will give this information the top priority."

I said, "The most unbelievable thing is that they placed those anti-aircraft guns on the roofs of the school in this camp that is the supposed 'secret military airbase' in order to create a perception of reality. They even have a small army unit with real trucks and jeeps to further validate the appearance. This way, when our allies drop the bombs there, the first thing Cuban television will broadcast around the world through their solid contacts in the international media will be the bodies of the dead and mutilated children, probably with a graphic that there were no military installations here—only a school for the children of poor families and orphans protected by the Revolution."

Mr. Xiang shook his head in disgust. "This is unbelievable. How deeply does evil run in these men? How could they dare to prepare ahead of time their unscrupulous propaganda without regard to the lives of those children?"

"You're right, my friend," I replied. "This is not a common, everyday enemy. This is a special enemy, trained by the master of hypocrisy and deception, and they've prepared to do whatever is necessary to obtain their objective."

Mr. Xiang stood up. "You know what? I have to go to bed early, since I need to get up early enough to send this information ASAP to our contacts at the naval base. Are you going to stay with us tonight?"

"Yes, if you don't mind. I don't want to be a bother, but I would rather stay here than Che's house in Cojimar. It's my only option, since my family are probably in bed, and I don't want to embarrass myself by knocking on the door at this hour, especially since I've been so busy that I haven't even had the time to stop by to say hello."

"Of course," he said. "For God's sake, you're a part of our family, as well."

"Thank you. I will leave very early in the morning, probably even before you, so that I can meet one of my contacts before leaving the city."

"Very well. I will talk to Chandee to bring whatever you need to make your stay comfortable—blankets, sheets, whatever."

"Thank you once more," I said respectfully. "I really appreciate your hospitality."

Mr. Xiang held up his right hand. "You don't have to thank me. Like I said: you're a part of this family." He smiled broadly and said goodnight before leaving the office.

I removed my gun belt, beret, and other things, and gathered them on the chair. There was a knock at the door, and Chandee came in with blankets, a pillow, and other bedclothes. She gave me a tender kiss on the cheek and then began to make up the sofa bed that was to be my accommodation for the night. When she finished, she was about to kiss me once more, but there was another knock at the door. It was Yein with an extra pillow and a silver tray with a pitcher of water and a couple of glasses. After we said goodnight, they both left the office while I turned the lights off and lay down in preparation to sleep.

I lay there in the dark for a while, deep in thought. I wondered what would happen if the invasion were successful. It would be a great accomplishment, as it would restore Cuba to the rule of law and democratic freedom. I knew it wouldn't be easy. These people were hungry and thirsty for power, and were not going to easily let it go. The potential for a great deal of bloodshed and loss of life was more than a mere possibility.

I fell asleep. Several hours later, I heard the door quietly close. I saw a silhouette in the dark, and I turned slightly, my hand reaching under my pillow for my pistol. Instead of my weapon, however, I found a soft, long-fingered hand that squeezed mine.

Close to my ear I heard Chandee's voice whisper, "Take it easy, love. It's me, your *chinita*, who loves you very much and has come to caress your skin, not bruise or wound it."

I smiled when I heard that, even as I was aroused by the feel of her naked body and the aroma of the light jasmine smell of her hair. I turned towards her, our faces very close together.

She smiled and said, "Hi. Surprised?" She stroked my cheek with the back of her left hand while her right slid down my chest towards my underwear. Her eyebrows wiggled suggestively. "Uh-oh," she said with a smile.

She kissed me tenderly on my lips. "Thank you very much for your recognition of me you gave my father. You made him very proud of me, because it's been a long, long time since he spoke to me in the kind, loving way he did a few hours ago. My father is a great man, and I love him very much, but he can be very cold and inexpressive. Maybe that's our Asian culture, an excess of respect that's only heightened by our ancient traditions and education in our homeland of China. His father had been beaten with bamboo sticks as a child for discipline. My grandfather did to him something that's not even appropriate to do to animals in Western culture."

I shook my head in distress at that, my expression sad. "I'm really, really glad that my conversation with your father changed his mood and put him in that loving disposition of character. When he left the office, he wasn't in a very good mood because of what we discussed. I love very much that the word I had with him softened him so much towards you. It's an important relationship between a father and daughter, or between father and son, for that matter. I'm truly happy about that."

I wrinkled my brow in puzzlement. "I didn't say that much—only the truth, which we should always do in life whenever we recognize the qualities and merits in others.

I only said to your father how much you helped me in last evening's situation, especially regarding the map—even though you offered me a little resistance to my idea of not writing something on the back of the map. But in the end, you agreed to that."

She frowned mockingly at me. She didn't let me finish as she started to tickle me. "Liar! Liar! That is not what you told my dad. He told me the whole conversation."

I tried to defend myself, but she continued tickling me. My laughter grew uncontrollable, since she had caught me by surprise, and she began tickling me everywhere. I finally leaped out of the bed in an attempt to get away from her and put a safe distance between us.

As I stood naked in front of the door, it opened. The light of the neon sign at the front of the store flashed on and off, and when it was on flooded the room with light. It completely illuminated my body. I froze, and saw the form of Chandee's sister, Yein. She stood there, her eyes fixed entirely on my erection. She stood there mutely, transfixed as if hypnotized. Save for the strobe effect of the flashing sign, we were all frozen in a kind of tableau.

Chandee was the first one to recover. She covered herself with the sheet as she sat up in bed and whispered in a strong, exasperated voice, "Yein! What the hell are you doing here?"

Yein didn't reply at once. She looked at Chandee and then back at my privates. She repeated this robotically two more times.

I was the second to recover. As soon as I saw Yein looking back and forth, I snatched my hands to cover myself. Finally, Yein reacted, clapped her hands to her mouth, and ran out of the room, leaving the door open. I looked at Chandee helplessly and then went to close the door.

Chandee jumped out of the bed and snatched up the bathrobe she had discarded on the floor near her father's desk. Hastily, she pulled it on and put her index finger to her lips to motion for silence. She then urgently pointed at the sofa bed and left without saying a word. I figured she was going to try to find Yein to head off any escalation in the situation. I remained there in frozen nakedness after she left, filled with embarrassment and confusion. Finally, I looked at my watch, and observed that it was 4:30 a.m.

I thought about it for a few seconds and decided to leave. It crossed my mind that Yein might be mad and awaken her parents to tell what she saw in here. Should this occur, I considered it prudent that I be absent in that conflict. My presence would only aggravate the situation, and they would be able to resolve things better without me there. All in all, I was not a member of the family, Mr. Xiang's assertions to the contrary notwithstanding.

After the conversation I had with Chandee previously concerning her father's customary punishments, I didn't think it either smart or savvy to wait there for him, who might at that moment forget about our Western customs and revert to the old wood cabinet and retrieve a bamboo stick. That was the best scenario; the worst would be pulling out a ninja sword and cutting my head off in order to restore the lost honor of both daughters—one who saw me completely naked and the other for lying in bed with me.

The Deadly Deals
Blame Yourself

When you are in a really miserable situation, you start to look around and think about who you might blame for it. You might be desperate to find someone on which to pin the responsibility for the bad circumstance and become angry. You will then start to plot revenge. In your rage at what has happened to you, as well as what is going on around you, you might not be thinking about it clearly.

I advise you to take a cold shower, pause, and reflect before you pull the trigger. Make absolutely certain that the one you think culpable for your negative experience, economical disaster, or other miseries, is not anyone you can blame. It may be yourself—the result of your own bad decisions.

Remember: one sunny, beautiful day, you might wake up and go to throw your support behind the wrong person. That person is the one who possibly brought all this misery to you, but you are the one who put the power in his hands. Then—only then—you come to the realization that there's only one person to blame, and that is yourself.

Dr. Julio Antonio del Marmol

Dr. Julio Antonio del Marmol

Chapter 9: The Evil Picture and the Devil's Daughter

I dressed hurriedly and rushed to put into motion what I had learned in intelligence training: when in doubt, stop. If outgunned, retreat and then regroup. By getting out of there, I would be able to later assess the situation with a cooler head.

Silently, I left Chandee's house. I reached the parking area and drove off. Until that moment, I was unable to breathe freely. Once I was out of there, I sighed in relief.

I drove to the Vedado and entered the Hilton to have an early breakfast. I handed the keys to the valet and entered the lobby. I walked over to the coffee shop at the right of the building, sat down, and ordered a large orange juice, a fruit salad, and a quiche Lorraine. As I ate, I reflected on what had happened not just recently but also in the last forty-eight hours. I realized that the only pleasant moments were those spent with Chandee in Rio Cristal. The rest were completely chaotic and full of tension and violence, not counting the long hours of uncertainty I had endured in Fidel's office. I had started to believe that I would be leaving in handcuffs and taken straight to the firing wall. I wondered why it had to happen. It was like bad karma had been following me all week.

I breathed deeply as I ate. I concentrated on the beautiful instrumental music playing over the speakers. I

The Deadly Deals

remembered the face of Yein standing in front of me, her eyes focused down at my privates, and I wondered what she was doing there, especially at that hour of the morning. As far as she'd known, I'd been sleeping.

I smiled as it occurred to me that the beautiful Yein was only a couple of years younger than Chandee, making her about my own age. It was entirely possible that she had a crush on me herself, and had come into my room to attempt to cuddle with me. I could have been wrong, but that is the only explanation I could come up with at that moment.

I later found out that the excuse she had given her sister was that she had gone to the bathroom and had gotten lost. In that moment, however, I realized that, if I were right in my thinking, Yein would never let her parents know what had happened, because she would have a lot to explain herself concerning her presence in my room in the middle of the night.

After I finished my breakfast, I told the waitress to hold my table, as I needed to go make a phone call. I walked over to the phone bank. I knew Mima had the habit of waking early, and so I called home. As I expected, Mima answered in a few seconds.

"Mima, it's me. Did I wake you?"

"No, no, my son," her voice replied. "I've been very worried about you. Are you OK?"

I asked after everybody in the family and then let her know that I was going to be gone for a week. "I have an invitation to stay at the beach at Varadero."

She repeatedly told me to be very careful in the ocean and not to go swimming alone, even if it were with someone my own age. After each injunction, I affirmed that I would follow all of her recommendations. By the end of the conversation, she sounded more relaxed and thanked me for the call.

"Rush back home, OK?" she said. "I miss you."

We said goodbye and I next dialed Chopin's number. I checked my watch and saw it was 6:45. I thought it might be a little early but remembered what I had told him the previous day about expecting my call in the morning. The phone rang several times. I almost hung up, thinking no one would answer. As I started to do so, I heard Chia's sleepy voice on the other end.

"Who is calling so early?"

I smiled. "I'm sorry, did I wake you up? I'm leaving the city in a little while, and I agreed to call Chopin before I did."

She said, apologetically, "I'm sorry. Is that you, Commandantico?"

"Yes."

"Oh! I'm sorry, I'm so sorry. Between one thing and another, I didn't sleep at all last night. Chopin returned from one of the musical parties at the FOCSA Building only a few hours before, and you know what happened the night before."

"Well, you've had short sleep two nights in a row—you have every right to be cranky. With me, even a single night does the trick for me."

"I'm sorry, I didn't mean to be rude."

"Don't worry," I said, "you've got nothing to apologize for."

"Thank you. Chopin is right here by me. It's a great pleasure to speak to you, and I'm really happy to find out from Chopin that everything that happened the other

The Deadly Deals

night ended very well."

"Thank you," I replied.

"Here's Chopin," she said, and I heard the receiver being handed over.

His voice, in spite of his own short sleep, was cheerful as always. "Commandantico, it's Chopin here," he said with a hearty laugh, "I'm standing by the canon, ready to fire! Where do you want me to aim it?"

I smiled as I replied, "What about the Hilton at 23rd and L Street in La Rampa? I'm waiting for you right here, and I invite you to breakfast with me. The only thing you have to bring is your mouth."

He laughed again. "What about my stomach?"

"Of course," I replied, "claro, chico, if you don't bring your stomach, where are you going to store the food?"

A little while later, the good black man entered the coffee shop and came to my table. I was finishing a coco glace, a dessert of very rich coconut ice cream served in a half coconut shell with zigzagging lines of chocolate fudge and chocolate medallions around the rim. While most of the coconut meat had been removed, chunks near the bottom remained. Adults could also choose the option of topping it with a drizzle of Grand Marnier.

We greeted each other, and Chopin sat down. He ordered a cafe con leche with a baguette, butter, and a Spanish omelet. We spoke at length for a while, and I related in full detail what had happened with Che, Fidel, and Piñeiro. I pulled out a couple of carefully wrapped duck eggs. I described to him how to prepare them and what the importance of the plan was in order to curb through intimidation the oppression of the G-2 and other branches of this regime as well as the CDR, who existed to spy on their neighbors and create division and strife within their neighborhoods.

After Chopin finished his breakfast and I answered all the questions he had, he said, "Brother, you've got to excuse me, but I need to order a coco glace. That really caught my eye when I got here and saw the pleasure it gave you to eat. I couldn't wait to finish my breakfast so that I could order one."

As he ate his coco glace, he relished the taste. He then asked me, "What did you think of the little present I left in the trunk of your car?"

I raised my eyebrows in surprise. "Yes, yes—what the hell is that? It looked like paintings or canvas, or—"

"Shh," he said to interrupt me, holding the small spoon in his hand to his lips. I sat back, wondering at his air of mystery but waited for his explanation. He had almost finished his dessert, enjoying his last spoonful of coconut. He placed the spoon on the side of the plate and wiped his mouth with his napkin.

"I left that for you the other night because it's your cut of the loot. That was the job we did while you kept Piñeiro busy in the toilets." He grinned sarcastically as he wiped at his nose. "These are the most valuable paintings they were preparing to sell at the exhibition. They could not auction them, though, because they could not find them. The organizer for that program is still going crazy. One of my contacts inside the job is one of the individuals who put the canvases in the frames. Whatever they don't sell, they remove from the frames, and roll them up with the painting face inside to protect it, and then put them in tubes to preserve them. We took sixteen paintings, and he dropped the tubes into the trash, thanks to the commotion

Piñeiro and his men were making when they surrounded the area and tore up the plumbing and concrete to sift through the sewage with the sanitation workers they brought in.

"Even though the organizers realized they were missing the works they were supposed to show the next day, they didn't want to create an even bigger convulsion than Piñeiro had already instigated. As there was a possibility that the paintings had been forgotten in a warehouse, they kept it quiet. They didn't want to appear negligent."

He nodded appreciatively. "They're probably still looking for them. I guarantee you that some head will roll over this. Some of them will lose their beautiful positions and end up in Guanacabibe, breaking rocks for their carelessness. Of course, they're going to try to delay as best they can the delivery of this bad news to the main honchos in the government."

He leaned back. "However, as soon as Fidel learns about this, the shit will hit the fan. You be very sure to put them in a safe place, because they're worth millions of dollars." He looked at me and repeated with emphasis, "Dollars. Not worthless Cuban pesos that Fidel and his brother are replacing with their pictures..."

"Why sixteen?" I asked.

"Because the boxes with the tubes came that way: in groups of ten, sixteens, and twenty cylinders. My contact didn't have the time to open them one by one and select them. He simply grabbed the whole box and put it in with the discarded empty tubes, and took it out with the rest of the trash in the dumpster. I then retrieved it from there after Piñeiro and his men left. I distributed them the way I found them, due to circumstances, more prudently: five for me, five for you, and six for my contact, who got the extra as he had assumed the entire risk for the operation."

I shook my head discontentedly and raised my eyebrow. "Don't take me wrong, OK? First of all, I didn't do anything to deserve this. Second, what are we going to do with these valuable paintings? In order to sell these, you need an expert and contact with knowledge of art. I don't know anybody in my circle, do you in yours?"

He shook his head. "Nope. I don't have the slightest idea. Let me explain something to you. I know you're young, but you're very intelligent, and I want you to understand why we did this. Hear me out, and you'll understand the reason and purpose behind it all. This opportunity arrived to us the night before last. It's not something we planned. My contact told me he had this opportunity, and I gave him the green light so that we wouldn't pass by the ability to take away something so valuable from these people. A chance like this will probably never happen again. Even if we got them all together and burned them in the backyard of somebody's house, we will help not only our compatriots here in Cuba, but everyone around the world. These murderers plan terrorist attacks every day with the money they make from the things they steal. The less money they have, the fewer resources they have to do bad things to people and spread their cancer of misery and pain wherever they get into power.

"Let me give you an example. In Africa, for instance, they're going to use the dollars they get from this art auction to go to Mexico and buy machetes. They'll then give them to some tribe in, let's say, Congo, as gifts. Then they'll go and buy some firearms, which they give to a rival tribe that is on the government's side. It makes no difference if these people have religious or territorial disputes. The results are the same: the ones with the machetes die at the hands of the ones to whom they gave firearms. They wipe out their enemies and their Socialist friends take the power in that country. Then they can suck the natural resources of that region for as long as they can keep their friends in that country in power."

He straightened in his chair and shook his head. "It makes no difference whether we can sell these valuable paintings or not. The reason we did this was simply to remove that treasure from the hands of these malicious murderers. The less money they can generate, the less damage they can do not only to us but to all of humanity."

I nodded in comprehension and smiled.

Chopin returned the smile and said, "I knew that you would understand everything." He threw his hands up. "To hell with those paintings and the millions, if it comes to that. If it weren't for you and the commotion you created in the Palace, we could never have pulled this off. That's why I consider five of those paintings belong to you—you can do with them whatever the hell you want. Just imagine it: if they're worth millions now, how much will they be worth in twenty, thirty, or fifty years? Maybe one of these paintings will be enough for one or two of our grandchildren to live very happy lives, free of any money problems. They could come to be worth billions. Even though they don't serve any purpose now for us, at least we have the great satisfaction that we took them out of the hands of these thieves and murderers."

I got up from my seat. "Really, really good job, Chopin. I'm impressed. Thank you for your great intentions to me personally. I assure you I will put them in a place where none of these thugs will ever get their hands on them. As the old saying goes: 'The thief that robs another thief is rewarded a hundred years of pardon in Heaven and forgiveness for his sins.'" I pulled my wallet out to pay for the breakfast.

Chopin walked over to me with his arms open. "I know you understand all this. Can I hug you?"

"Sure," I replied. He gave me a vast bear hug, holding me close. I said, "OK, that's enough. I think you're hugging me too long."

He immediately released me. "I'm sorry!"

I playfully punched his arm. "It's OK, I was just joking with you."

"Aw, man!" he said in protest, "You're always freaking me out with your jokes about homosexual nonsense!"

I walked over and patted him on the shoulder. "It's OK, man."

"Well, I guess I earned my breakfast, hey?"

I looked at him seriously this time. "You more than earned the breakfast—you earned a token of gratitude, and that is very difficult to repay, I assure you."

Chopin smiled in pleasure and shook his head. "No, no, no—you don't owe me anything, Commandantico. Absolutely nothing."

I smiled and said, "Very well. Anyway, I thank you from the bottom of my heart, brother."

He continued to smile as he shook his head and rolled his eyes in joking surrender. He nodded then, and we said goodbye at the hotel exit after we retrieved our cars from the valet. We left in different directions.

I looked for the signs to direct me to Varadero Beach as I thought about the valuable paintings I had in the trunk of my car. I hadn't been expecting this, and thought that there was no doubt that whatever Chopin and his contact were able to do would be great accomplishment. It certainly took a lot of guts to plan it, let alone actually pull it off. Fidel and his band of delinquents would be considerably stressed out by it, and it should remain the great mystery for them to try and determine who had pulled that job. It would keep them occupied with worry for quite some time and so rob them of precious time from their latest schemes.

I also thought that if I continued to accumulate objects of such value like these paintings and the diamonds and currencies of other countries I had found in Che's portfolio, my riches would be greater than those of Sir Francis Drake, one of the wealthiest pirates in the Caribbean.

The entrance to the luxury resort of Varadero Beach

I grinned broadly as I remembered the words of Mima. Whenever she saw me smile or laugh without a reason, she would say, "The one who laughs by himself is the one is remembering his mischievous adventures."

I realized how much truth was behind the old sayings that we were used to hearing on a daily basis. Involved in my thoughts, the time flew by so rapidly that I was surprised to see that I was entering the world-famous Varadero Beach, with its sands the color of refined white sugar. It was like walking on velvet to stroll in the sun along these sands. I pulled in at a gas station and greeted the attendant. I handed him the keys with instructions to fill the tank and run a full service check on the car.

I walked towards the telephone booths, taking from my uniform shirt pocket Tanya's card that she had given to me at the Tropicana. I dialed the number on the card, and a few seconds later Tanya's voice answered.

"Hello," I said, "this is the Commandantico, Julio Antonio del Marmol. May I please speak to Tanya?"

"This is she," she replied happily. "How are you doing?"

"Thank you for asking, very well."

"OK, I will see you in Varadero, OK? Are you going to make it tonight?" she asked doubtfully.

I smiled and said, "I'm already here. Don't worry, it's OK. We'll see each other tonight."

"No, no, no!" she protested. "Don't worry about it. If you're already in Varadero, it's good."

"Yes, I just got here a few minutes ago."

"Well, you are very good and punctual. You have a paper and pencil? I want to give you my address. Maggie has been there in the beach house since yesterday. You can go there and meet her. I've already told her about you, and she's expecting you."

I took my little phone book and pen out of my pocket to write down the address. When I finished, she said, "She loves to paint and is going to school for that. Sometimes she'll leave the house for hours when she finds inspiration and doesn't return until after dark. If by any chance you don't find her in the house, you will find the key under the planter on the left side of the steps to the pool. The house has two levels and multiple rooms. There's plenty to choose from. Whatever you like best—they're all comfortable and spacious."

"Very well, thank you very much."

"No," she protested, "by no means. Thank you for remembering what you promised me. I really appreciate it. Maggie needs somebody like you at this moment. She's going through a lot. I'll tell you later in confidence when I get there. Be kind and gentle with her. Sometimes, she can be a pain in the neck and a little rude. OK?"

"Don't worry," I answered confidently. "I can handle anybody."

"I'll bet you can. We'll see each other tonight, OK? We'll have dinner together, like a nice little family."

"Very well," I replied. "We'll see each other later. Drive carefully, OK?"

"Thank you," she said. "You're so sweet."

We hung up and I returned to the attendant to pay for the gasoline and service. I gave him a generous tip, as he had even cleaned the wheels. I drove off, following the directions Tanya had given me.

I drove for a while and entered a secluded neighborhood with beautiful, expensive, luxurious residences. I found the number I was looking for, and stopped the Mercedes before what could only be described as a mansion. I entered the key code into the intercom security system by the gate: 3322#.

The enormous gates swung open slowly. I waited a few seconds for them to completely open, and then started up the long driveway that wound along the beautiful gardens, lined on both sides by coconut trees and beautiful flowers.

I rolled my window down to enjoy the scenery. The entire estate looked like a botanical garden and appeared to be continually maintained. The fragrance of several different types of flowers filled my car, making me forget for a few precious minutes the dangerous moments I had endured over the past few days.

I drove towards the end of the driveway, parking on the left side after I passed by the front door. The grand entry before the enormous front door served a double purpose as a kind of garage as well as protecting the house from the sun and rain. I parked so that I wouldn't obstruct a future visitor, next to a small red convertible MG.

Maggie's MG

I saw a beautiful basket of ready-to-eat mangoes sitting in the passenger seat, the brilliant colors of yellow and red indicating their ripeness. I reached over the window and picked one up and smelled it. I remembered a joke about a guy who took a mango off the tree of the owner's house.

The owner yelled through the front window of the house, "You smell it, you put it down at no cost. You put your teeth in it, you have to pay me for it!"

I put the mango back into the basket, just in case someone was watching me through the window. The smell was enough for me, since my stomach was still full from the breakfast I had just eaten, and the mangoes didn't belong to me, anyway.

I walked through the gardens to the swimming pool. I looked under the planter by the swimming pool steps where Tanya had directed me to find the spare key. It took me a little searching, as the previous user had placed it to the side of the planter, rather than under it.

I returned to the house and opened the front door. I stood there in awe at the luxury of the place. I thought to myself that if this is what Tanya thought of as a vacation home, I didn't want to see the house she normally lived in. I upgraded my earlier opinion; it wasn't a common residence or even a mansion—this was a palace, with exquisite decorations and exotic mortar architecture. To be fair, the walls and design looked more like something Picasso would have done, with a white background and accents of navy blue and soft peach.

I walked through the whole place for a while, curiously exploring the house. I decided upon a room downstairs near the door, just in case I had to leave quickly. It was something I had to consider constantly. Besides its proximity to a possible escape route, this room had enormous crystal sliding doors and a breathtaking view of all the trees, flowers, and the sparkling waterfall that splashed into a fountain out on the patio. It was not a beach front property; the house was across the street from such a house.

I went into the bathroom and washed my face. While there, I looked through the contents of the medicine cabinet. I found a small bottle of violet water. I splashed a little bit of that on my face, and walked over to the bed. I decided to lie down for a few minutes and rest from the long evening I had last night. The few minutes turned into hours. My body was utterly exhausted, and it could not resist the temptation of the silence of the environment and the soft sheets and pillow which smelled so sweet and clean. I was mesmerized by it and fell asleep.

When I woke up, I looked at my watch and saw that it was 3:30 in the afternoon. I shot up as I realized I had nearly slept the entire day away. I went to the bathroom to answer nature's call. I washed my hands and left the room, marking it as mine by leaving one of my t-shirts on the bed.

I went outside and walked along the driveway and the front gardens all the way to the front gate. I saw a small door with a sidewalk that functioned as a personal entrance to enter or leave the palace. I followed the sidewalk, which connected with another one built of smoothed volcanic rocks to give the appearance of an untamed naturalistic setting. It was not only a practical way to walk between the houses to the beach, but the design was also built to prevent the beach sand coming onto the street from the sidewalks. The extremely fine sand was easily picked up and blown by the wind, and it functioned as a retaining wall to maintain the cleanliness of that aristocratic neighborhood.

I walked for a while and removed my boots and socks when I reached the sand. I put my socks inside my boots, tied my boots together by the laces, and hung them around my neck. I passed by a group of youngsters with a folding Ping-Pong table set up in the sand. Others had a large portable net erected over the sand and were playing volleyball.

We greeted each other when I came within a short distance from them. After I passed them, I continued walking across the dunes a little way from where the kids had been gathered. The dunes provided an elevation above the normal plane of the natural ground, a little above sea level. As I got closer, I could see something multi-colored shining in the hot, late afternoon sun.

As I drew nearer, I realized it was a stainless steel easel with a recently painted canvas. Sticking in the sand next to it were a few towels lying open and a couple of leather boxes hanging on a folding multicolored canvas chair. From the back of the chair hung a pair of very powerful binoculars. Tubes of paint and an assortment of brushes of varying sizes lay in a large jar that appeared to be an empty coconut.

Area Maggie preferred to use while painting

I reached the place and halted. I was frozen in surprise as my eyes looked on the canvas. The painting was nearly finished. It was an exact replica of the nightmare I'd had not too long ago of Che presiding over a diabolical ritual during which men and women were decapitated. I touched the image of the fire pit in the middle, and saw that some of the red paint from the fire came off on my finger. I looked closely at the painting and saw the exact image of my nanny, Majito. In the picture, she was chopping off the head of the demonic image that, from the angles of the nose, looked like Che. It utterly disturbed me. I could not understand how someone could have painted this, and I stood there in confusion for several minutes. It was like someone had been inside my head, watching my nightmares.

Alternatively, the painter must have had precisely the same nightmare I had. There could be no other explanation.

I craned my neck, looking for the owner of the painting and equipment there. I could not see a single soul anywhere within my range of vision. The sun had started to dip towards the horizon. I looked in the distance, and saw the group of young kids I had previously passed gathering their stuff together. Some of them started to walk towards the more built-up area of the beach. The ones left behind rushed to pick up their stuff. It looked like their intention was to follow the others as soon as they had their things together.

I continued looking around but still could not see anyone. I removed the boots from around my neck, letting them rest near the easel. I removed my shirt and weapons belt and put them down on one of the towels next to my boots.

I walked near the painting again, scrutinizing it closely. I looked into the eyes of that evil person that so resembled Che. I could not help but feel goose bumps creep all over my body from my stomach to the back of my neck. The hairs on my neck stood on end. I trembled slightly as a cold sweat broke out on my forehead and upper lip. I tore my eyes off of those of that horrific face and raised my head once more. This time, I looked for an observation point which would be more pleasant to my eyes and mind. I looked out over the ocean and the horizon where the sky met the sea.

Something caught my eye in the distance—something dark against the radiant disc of the sun against the horizon. I shielded my eyes with my hand, and saw something moving. Using my left arm to block the sun, I strained to see more clearly the dark image moving around in the water, but I could not make anything out. In a flash, I remembered the binoculars. I walked over to the chair and picked them up. I adjusted them for my eyes and held them up. I saw a young girl about my age with pale skin, dressed in a long-sleeved black evening gown—not something one usually wore to the beach, much less in the water. She wore a black straw hat as well. She tried to hold the hat with both her hands to avoid having it snatched off her head by the wind and blown away. Her long hair, red as blood, flew behind her neck. She was waist deep in the water, and she continued with difficulty walking to the deeper water of the ocean.

She stopped and turned slightly. I increased the magnification, and I could make out her face. She looked like she was trying to wipe tears from her face with her left hand. She clutched at her hat with her right hand until her left hand had done its job. Just as she was about to switch hands so that she could wipe the right side of her face, the wind snatched the hat off her head, behind her. She turned around and took some short steps back to take the hat out of the water. The tide, however, was coming in, and so the hat washed further and further ashore. She changed her mind and turned back to walk towards the deeper water.

I had a very bad feeling about this. It made no sense that she would dress this way in the first place and then abandon the hat in the second. I took off my pants and dropped them on the sand near the rest of my stuff, and I ran towards the beach in my underwear with the binoculars held to my eyes.

When I got to the beach, I stopped to catch my breath. At the border of the water, I looked through the binoculars once more and could now see that the young girl had nothing good on her mind. The water was now chest high, and she let herself fall into the water. The motion seemed extremely strange. It seemed like she didn't want to continue living, as she wasn't even holding her nose pinched closed.

She disappeared between the waves. This was sufficient for me to act. I tossed the binoculars aside into the sand. I started to run into the water, jumping over the small wavelets in my attempt to cover the distance more quickly. I ran towards where I had seen her disappear and saw in the distance the floating black hat.

I passed by the hat and snatched it with my hand. I looked around everywhere in the water, but could see no traces of the body. I held my breath and dove down, but could see nothing near the bottom, even though the water was extremely clear. I came back up and cleared my vision with the back of my hand. I caught my breath, continually scanning the area. I dove down again, several times. Worry began to grow in my mind that one of the ocean currents had swept her completely out to sea. The water was now chin high on me, indicating that she was probably taller than I was.

I turned around, ready to give up and begin the walk back towards the beach. I took only a few steps with my hands spread out to maintain my balance in that deep water.

Suddenly, the body of the young woman sprang up in the waves, almost by my side. She was unconscious, and I held her face out of the water as I rushed to give her mouth-to-mouth. Her face was deathly pale. My attempts were made difficult by the waves surging around us, so I dragged her to shore. I tried to give her air once more, raising her arms up and down like I had been taught in emergency first aid. Nothing seemed to work. She was limp and completely lifeless.

I was about to give up, and I reached inside my shirt to clutch my holy medallion of the Virgin de la Caridad del Cobre. I said in a soft whisper as I held it, "Please, Lady of Charity—help me. Don't let this young girl die. She's too young to go."

I rolled her body to the right after giving several strong puffs of breath into her mouth. I braced my knees against her back and grasped her by the upper chest with one hand and around the waist with the other. I began to force her back against my knees repeatedly. My uncle had once told me that, when all else fails, to push against the lungs to try and force the water out of them. Even if they are clinically dead, the heart will start pumping once more, and they could be rescued. It was a desperate last attempt, but it bore results.

The woman started to cough and vomit water and pieces of food. She gasped, coughed, and hyperventilated as she started breathing again. I took the medallion and kissed it. I said, "Thank you, Lady, for listening to my plea."

I held her neck against my elbow, still rolled on her side as she continued coughing. I was covered in her vomit. She opened her eyes and saw me. Instead of thanking me, she make a disgusted face. She screamed at me, "What the hell is that?"

I smiled and said, "Just your vomit. It was the food in your stomach. I'll clean it off in a moment. You have to thank God and Our Lady of Cuba." I held up my medallion. "You were dead for quite a while."

She looked angry at my words. She yelled, "Who the devil are you? Who asked you to save me and bring me out of the water, bringing me back to this filthy world?"

She tried abruptly to get up, but immediately collapsed again. She raised her right hand to her forehead in obvious distress. There was something wrong there. "My head—everything is spinning. My head feels like it's going to explode." She leaned over to the other side, and I let her go. She vomited once more, this time away from me and towards the sun.

She looked at me once more, this time more spitefully. She cleaned her mouth with the sleeve of her dress and asked, "Who the hell are you?"

I looked at her with a smile. "I don't know what your problem is. I don't believe you are in the best frame of mind talk about what your problems are now—to me or anybody. But I can tell you one thing: I don't like it very much and am not accustomed to anybody treating me discourteously and with bad manners, especially without a reason. You should be thanking me and changing that stupid attitude you have. But because you've been dead and come back to life, I will forgive you this time. And I'll answer your question, even though you didn't ask me very politely. My name is Julio Antonio del Marmol, though my friends all over the island know me as the Commandantico."

When she heard that, she rolled her eyes and put both hands to her face. "Oh, my God! This is the last thing I need today. How is it possible? This is the last straw!"

I looked at her in surprise and confusion. I looked at her in puzzlement, not understanding what she was saying. Her coughing grew stronger, a choking sound. After she stopped, she collected herself. "I'm Maggie, and you're supposed to be the guest of Tanya. We've been waiting for you to be my company for a week. You are the greatest friend of that rapist of young girls."

I looked at her in even greater surprise and utter incomprehension as to what she was referring to. Maggie looked at me and shook her head. Perhaps she understood my confusion, as my face clearly showed that I didn't know what she was talking about. She was about to say something but was interrupted by another coughing fit. She recovered herself enough to rise up from my arms and sit down. She was still weak and dizzy, so she clung to my arm as she sat up. She looked at me venomously and spat, "El Che!" She took her left hand to her forehead, trying to keep her equilibrium by holding on to my shoulder. She looked at me intensely in my eyes. "That degenerate, your friend, raped my mother. After he got her pregnant, he abandoned her and left her to her luck."

I looked at her in surprise. "Che raped Tanya and abandoned her?"

She looked at me in astonishment. "No! No, Tanya's not my mother! My mother was Maruca. Tanya is my aunt, my mother's sister. You understand? My mother died a few years ago, and my aunt brought me to live with her. My mother died in Pinar del Rio. She blew her head off, dishonored, humiliated, and full of shame, because your great friend, Che, abandoned her and never lived up to his promise to marry her at the beginning of the Revolution. My mother served them for years as a contact between the mountains and the city in the guerrilla war. She served as the link between the Revolutionary groups in the city and those in the mountains when she was about my age. They used her, all these bastards, because the soldiers of the tyrant would never suspect a girl her age was working with the rebels. On top of using her, that bastard raped her."

I remained silent, thinking of the story she had just blurted out to me. She was regaining her strength, and sat down by herself on the sand. I stood up and moved into the water to rinse my arm of the vomit. I looked at her from my position as I washed.

My God, I thought. She does indeed look like Che around the nose and eyes.

I said to her then, "If everything you just told me is true, and your father is Che, who told you all of this? You must have been very young when all this happened."

Her voice lost none of its aggressiveness or rudeness. "First of all, did you fall out of the crib or something when you were small? Or maybe you were born a little before your time and are retarded?" She didn't wait for an answer and continued, "How old do you think I am now?

I looked at her angrily and didn't even reply. I noticed particles of her vomit in my long hair and so started to rinse them off in the ocean as well. I focused on washing myself clean.

Since I didn't answer her, she continued speaking. "I'm thirteen years old. My mother killed herself two years ago. That made me eleven years old, which makes me old enough to remember anything she and my stepfather, Papá Aldames, told me about this dishonorable piece of crap friend of yours."

She raised both hands high above her head and said in a voice of increasing agitation. "Please, will you do me a favor and never call him my father again? I only want to forget that he is my father and get that out of my head. Everybody persists in forcing me to keep that in my memory."

She looked at the ocean with tears in her eyes. "That is why I was doing what you saw me doing—to see if the ocean and the salt water would take me to another world where I don't have to live with those horrible, damned memories and be sad and sour every minute I'm living, hating the fact that I'm the daughter of that despised murderer. If it weren't for him, my mother would still be alive and with me today."

I looked at her in a blend of compassion and pity. I was still angered by the way she had been talking to me. I thought that she should only know how true her words and the reality about her father were. If she did, she probably would have tried to kill herself a long time before.

But the compassion that was naturally a part of my

character manifested, and I could not help but feel bad for her. That young woman was so damaged psychologically that she wanted to end her life even when she had everything she could ever want within reach.

I returned to her side and looked at her silently for a few minutes as I thought what she said about Mr. Aldames being her stepfather. It occurred to me that she might not even know he was dead. It was also a strange coincidence that life provided, because after all, it was possible that Che had had something to do with his murder. Now everything made sense as the final links in the chain fell into place. I now knew why Fausto had led that faked robbery by himself.

I tried to cheer her up. "For good or for bad, in life we can pick our friends and whoever we want to associate with on a daily basis. But it is outside of our natural power to pick our family, especially our parents. That means that we have no alternative but to accept them the way they are. We do have the choice to reject them, but what we cannot do is erase them. No matter how hard we try, we will only find our attempts frustrated, because they are a very tangible reality that we cannot avoid. They will be in our face until the last day of our existence, to use your own words, in this filthy world."

I raised both of my hands high. "I'm going to ask you for a small favor. When you refer to Che, I would really, really appreciate if you would stop using that ironic tone of voice and calling him my friend. Even though we work together once in a while and we move in the same circles, friendship is something really sacred, something you cannot measure with thermometers, something you cannot find every day. Sometimes, it can happen that your best friend today is your worst enemy tomorrow, the one who takes you by your hand to the firing squad, puts the blindfold over your eyes and whispers, 'I'm not the one who denounced you, my friend.'"

Maggie looked at me in utter surprise. I looked into her exotic eyes. They had an undefined coloration, somewhere between blue, green and a little white. I had only seen eyes like that in vampire movies or on some actor impersonating the devil.

I continued in a serious tone, gesturing to my face and raising my eyebrows as I held her gaze. I pointed at my temple, still a little angered at the way she had addressed me. "As far as I can remember, my mother never left me unattended when I was a little baby, and as far as I've been told, I never fell out of any bed or crib. To my knowledge, the IQ tests they gave me in school rated me a lot higher than everyone else, including the most intelligent people I knew in school. With respect, if you don't want me to remind you that you're the exact picture of your father, I will be really indebted to you if you never—hear me well—never repeat those stupidities to me in the future. Do you understand me, or do you want me to repeat it to you? Maybe you swallowed too much salt water." I pointed at the top of my skull. "Or maybe you have a little leak in your penthouse.

She looked at me a little stung and angry for a moment and then burst into hysterical laughter. It made me smile. "I don't know what you find so funny, but at any rate I'm really glad to remove that funeral mask you were wearing. By the way, you should laugh more frequently. Not only is it healthy, but you look a lot prettier when you laugh."

Maggie shook her head. "My God, a charmer, too." She

didn't lose her smile, however. "I'm sorry. It was not my intention to offend you. Now I understand why you completely conquered the heart of my aunt and why she wanted so badly for me to get to know you."

She held her hand out to me. "But you haven't kissed my hand yet. Could you please help me up? My head's still spinning as the carousel horses run around my head. Between the dizziness and the migraine, I don't know if I can keep my feet."

I smiled at her. "Of course, you're a tough girl. All you need is a little time, and you'll fully recover. By the way, we never had the opportunity to introduce ourselves properly. That's why I never kissed your hand. First, I had to pull you out of the ocean by your hair like a caveman." My tone was jocular, since that wasn't really how it had happened. "Then I had to give you mouth-to-mouth respiration, and your breath was not precisely the best. I don't know if you had been eating garlic or onions. And then, to top it all off, when you regained consciousness, you baptized me with your vomit." I said all of this as I carefully helped her to her feet. I smirked. "Sweetie, this is not a normal introduction that we had—it was a tremendous one!"

She smiled once more even as she raised a hand to her forehead. "Don't make me laugh any more. My head's going to explode like a firecracker."

I looked at her mockingly. "Then don't smile. That's not a problem at all—everything is resolved. Where is the problem? I don't think I've said anything that would motivate that smile. In the circles you're accustomed to move in, I don't think you smile or laugh very much. You have a piggy bank of laughter and smiles that you've been accumulating, so when somebody makes you do either, you'll be laughing and smiling for two weeks!"

Assisted by me, we started to walk back towards the sand dunes. After a few steps, I asked her to pause so that I could bend over and pick up the binoculars I had dropped there. She looked at me in surprise. "These look like my binoculars."

"Look like!" I said in mock surprise. "How did they get over here?"

"You brought them here?"

"Of course," I replied. "How else do you think I was able to find you, dressed in black at sunset in the ocean? The only thing worse than that would have been if this had happened a couple of hours later in the pitch black. Thank God you brought them, or I would not have been able to see you, and you would most certainly be dead now."

"Yes," she replied. We continued to walk in the sand. She asked, "Will you please not tell Aunt Tanya anything about what happened?"

I looked at her in surprise. "What happened?"

"What just happened this afternoon."

"What just happened this afternoon?" I asked innocently. "I don't remember anything at all."

She smiled and nodded. She squeezed the arm that supported her as we walked in gratitude. "Thank you. Thank you twice over—once for your discretion and once for saving my life." She smirked. "From what my Aunt Tanya told me, you save my father's life not too long ago. Now you save my life. Is this not a strange coincidence? When my aunt told me you'd done that, the first thing that crossed my mind was what an idiot you were not to let him die. He deserves to die a thousand times, and it still won't repay what he's done on this earth. That's why when you told me who you are I might have conducted myself rudely to you. My aunt had said that if I didn't remember you to look for you on TV next to Fidel. I told her I don't watch any of that bullshit and had no idea who you are or what you looked like. But I'm very upset with you because you saved the life of the man who destroyed the lives of both my mother and me."

I shook my head. "Really, life has strange coincidences and ironies. The last thing that ever crossed my mind when I made that trip to Santa Clara with Che was that I would go through the horrible ordeal of seeing those young people dying the way they did when they tried to kill him. Even less that I would be sitting by Che and that, by a pure instinct of preservation and the nobility that's in my character, I would shove him down out of the reach of the bullets. I didn't even think about my own life at that moment—I was thinking more of my friend or my neighbor and that I had to save his life. It was only pure coincidence."

I stopped for a moment. We had arrived where she had set her easel up. I put my left hand to my chin and squeezed it. "Do you know something? From that day, I've asked myself a thousand times if the situation were reversed, if Che would have done the same and put himself at risk to save my life, or if he would have saved himself first and yelled at me to duck as soon as he knew for sure that he was safe."

Maggie looked at me. Without hesitation, she said, "I assure you that the last is the way he would act. He will always think of himself first and others later. Look at what he did to my mother, after all the things she did for him."

I shook my head. "Well, maybe one day I will find out his true character. I'm still trying to figure that out."

The Deadly Deals

I didn't want to be too agreeable to her. I didn't know how far she could actually be trusted. Blood is thicker than water, and for all I knew she, like her father, might decide to put me in a compromising position if I said something inappropriate.

Maggie let go of my arm, displeased at my last words. She obviously didn't like it when people disagreed with her, especially on the topic of her father.

She began to gather her things. "I can assure you of one thing," she said pointedly. "One of these days, you're going to discover how deceived you are if you think for even a moment that he'll do for you what you did for him before. I say to you, dream on! Believe me, I know every one of these people. They all have the same personality. They are egotistical and selfish. They think only of themselves and the rest of the world *al carajo*[9]." Her tone grew to full resentment and anger.

I silently continued to help her gather her things in an orderly manner. When we were finished, we began the walk back home.

---

[9] Can go fuck themselves.

Chapter 10: The Bisexual Encounter

After a while, Maggie began to feel bad because I was bearing most of the burden of carrying her things. She tried to take a few more items from me, but I didn't let her.

"I don't want to have to pick you up from the floor because you're still dizzy," I told her. "That will be double the work for me, since I'll have to carry your stuff and you at the same time. Don't worry about me, I'll be fine."

I looked at her seriously. "Will you let me give you some advice? You should look for a local doctor tomorrow. You don't have to tell your aunt anything. Get yourself checked out if you continue to feel those symptoms. The lack of oxygen to your brain could create some severe complications to your health later on. If you need money, I have it. Enough, at any rate, to help you take care of this. But I think that would be the most prudent thing to do."

She looked at me in gratitude. "You know, it's very hard to be mad at you for very long. You're not only a charmer, but you've got a very good heart. I can see that in you. But thank you, I'm feeling a lot better, and the headache is much diminished now. You see? You told me I'm tough, and I think I'm starting to believe it myself." She raised her right hand and suddenly took the easel and paints off of my shoulder before I could react.

"You're sneaky," I said.

The Deadly Deals

We reached the gate and she entered the security code. We entered the grounds and walked through the garden. The security lights were on, further illuminating the garden. If it looked beautiful by day, it was now breathtaking. It looked like a painting. The colored lights gave a look of elegance to the place.

We finally arrived at the cars. Maggie put the paints and supplies into the MG, helping me remove the burden from my shoulder. After she raised the convertible's top to shut the car completely, she put the basket of mangoes on the ground. She picked the basket up and offered one to me. "You want one?"

I smiled. "I nearly took one this afternoon."

"Why didn't you, silly?"

"I'd had a large breakfast, so I wasn't really hungry. Actually, I wound up sleeping all day. When I got here, I fell asleep, and so I missed lunch entirely. When I got up, I went to the beach where I saw all the drama."

"Oh, my God, you must be famished!" she exclaimed. "Here, take a mango now."

"No, no," I replied. "If I eat a mango now, I won't be able to eat dinner. Thank you anyway."

She pulled a cover out of the trunk of the MG. She began to put it over the car, and I assisted in getting it covered. She looked at the Mercedes. "Is this your car?"

"No. According to Fidel, it's the car of the people. In reality, though, I took it from the immense collection of cars Che has in his house in Cojimar. He loaned it to me. My car is a Volga, and it's in Pinar del Rio."

She shook her head in discontent. She held out her right hand. "Well, if this beautiful Mercedes belongs to the people, you can give me the keys, since I'm part of the people. Is that not true?"

I smiled and reached into my pocket. I pulled out the keys to the car and handed them to her. "There you go. I don't care—you can take it right now. After all, it all stays in the family."

She shook her finger at me. "I told you," she said warningly.

"Of course, *chica*. It stays in the family."

She gave me a little push as she shook her head. "All these people are full of shit. The worst part of it all is that my own family, my own aunt, is also full of shit, like all the rest of them, right up to the neck. But I love her very much. She's the only thing I have left. Between my nightmares and the bullshit I hear these imbeciles say every day—because they think they're so smart and the rest of us are morons—can anybody ask why I want to leave it?"

As she spoke, she was leaning against the MG, resting both of her hands on her head. She turned and kicked one of the wheels and screamed in frustration. "I'm so sick and tired of all this bullshit!"

I silently watched her neurotic reaction. I thought that she had the exact same neuroses as her father. The objects of her hatred and frustration, however, were completely different. Che's was focused at the established society in general. Maggie's, I had no doubt at all, were directed at her father and everything he represented.

This was the most extraordinary irony, beyond anything I could imagine, standing in front of me. I could never have found it had I searched for it. Maggie was the daughter of Che and the niece of Tanya, who was one of the most sophisticated spies—and probably assassins—on Che's team, by his own admission. If I slipped, this vacation could cost me my very life.

Another possibility was that this paranoid, suicidal girl could be another hook to catch the dangerous spy that every member of Castro's governmental circles was searching for.

I had to change the subject, so I asked her, "Did you paint that canvas on the easel?"

"Of course. Did you see any ghosts around it while I was in the ocean?"

I pointed my finger at her. "Be nice, OK?"

She smiled.

"I've got a question for you, please. Where did you get your inspiration, if you don't mind telling me?"

She tapped her head with her fingers on her forehead. "From here. That is the nightmare I was telling you about that's been persecuting me for as long as I can remember."

I looked at her gravely, but remained silent.

"What? Why are you looking at me that way? Talk to me."

I asked myself without replying to her how it could be possible. I asked once more, "Who is the man with the hood who is getting his head cut off by the black lady?"

She squinted at me inquiringly in a way that gave me chills.

"Who do you think he is?" she asked.

"I don't know," I replied. "It looked like the character we see in movies that represents Lucifer."

She nodded her head. "Yes, he is, but he came into the world with multiple faces. The face I see him with in my nightmares is the one of the one that's supposed to be my father, your frie...." Her voice trailed off as she remembered what I had asked her not to do.

She put her hand on her mouth. "I'm sorry. 'El Che.' That is the way I see him in my nightmares, and that is how I interpreted it when I painted it."

This time, I was the one who looked deeply and intensely into her eyes.

"There you go again. You keep looking at me that way. Why do you look at me so?"

I rubbed the fingers of my left hand over my forehead. I took my beret off and stepped in close to her. I didn't want anyone around us to hear what I was going to say. I cleared my throat. I said very quietly, "You might not believe what I'm going to tell you, and it will sound strange to you—as strange and unbelievable as it was to me to hear you say a little while ago that the painting is a reflection of what you see in your nightmares."

She looked at me with full attention, her gaze burning with curiosity.

"Not too long ago, I was wounded, and the wounds got infected. I had a high fever from it, and I had the most horrible nightmare I've ever had in my life. The nightmare I had, and the characters you painted—they are identical. To be more precise, the black lady you painted there," I pointed at the covered car. "Her face is exactly the same as the woman who raised me since the day I was born. If you think this is crazy and want to convince yourself that what I'm saying is true, I can prove it to you. I can take you to her so that you can meet her in person."

Maggie looked at me in shock and stepped back from me. She rubbed her face with both hands and looked at me in awed surprise. "Who are you? How can you have the same nightmare I have? Please tell me Aunt Tanya didn't put you to this in connivance with my psychiatrist. This is not logical. Please, tell me the truth behind all of this."

"I'm telling you the truth."

"How many times have you had that nightmare?"

"As I told you before, just once."

"Have you told anyone about this nightmare?"

I shook my head. "No, no. I don't remember if I said anything to the lady who was taking care of me while I was sick. Why?"

She put her hand to her head in genuine confusion. "I have never, never told anyone about my nightmares."

She lifted both sleeves to show me her arms. They bore several scar marks where it appeared she had try to cut her veins. "Every time I have this nightmare, the next day I have these destructive feelings and the desire to end my life. The sadness that grows in me second by second, minute by minute, hour by hour, concludes with the determination to destroy myself. After it goes around my head many times, I arrive at the conclusion that my life has no value and that there's no point to continue living."

I looked at her, my compassion and pity welling once more. She saw my look and raised her hand. "Please don't look at me the way you did on the beach. That makes me feel worse."

I raised both of my hands to ward off further protest. "That's not my intention. It's only a natural reaction from my feelings."

She raised her right arm and shook her head. "Don't worry. I know I'm not all together in my head. In my lucid moments, like now, I understand the misery I have in my blood is from the genes of two crazies. My father, a paranoid schizophrenic and Heaven only knows how many other psychological problems he might have. And my mother—even though I loved her with all my heart in life and will continue to love her all my life—there is no doubt she had a loose screw in her head to do what she did, without thinking for a single moment of me or anyone else. She saw nothing except her pain, frustration, and shame when she blew her head off and to hell with the rest of us.

"The most curious thing in the whole puzzle and what's driving me crazy is where you come in and what role you're playing."

As she spoke, she squeezed her chin with her left hand while simultaneously stroking her wet, long, red hair with her right. "Last night, I had the latest of those destructive nightmares. Like I told you before, I never mentioned this to anyone, not even my psychiatrists, the ones my Aunt Tanya has forced me to continually visit after my first suicide attempt. Today, almost to the hour and minute, is one year since that attempt."

She shook her head as she reflected on that. She shivered. "I feel so cold."

"Of course," I said. "The dress you're wearing is made of light gauze, and it's thoroughly soaked." I removed my uniform shirt, leaving my t shirt on. I offered it to her. She smiled and accepted it.

"Thank you very much," she said gratefully. "The night is getting very cold."

I said nothing but nodded in agreement as I returned her smile.

"You're not going to get along very well with Che for too long. You're truly a gentleman, and you have deep family roots and strong moral values. He has not even a drop of either."

She paused, so I replied, "Thank you. My mother has

repeatedly said that a man who doesn't look with respect, love, and care for a woman is not a dignified man. We all owe our existence on this earth to women. My mother has also told me that this is enough motive to find it in our hearts to forgive a woman, even when she makes the worst mistakes and has the strongest character flaws."

She smiled broadly this time. "Your mother is a great person, and probably a wonderful woman. That explains how you are the way you are. Let me clarify something to you: I have to thank you, and for that you should be proud. Until this day, I have never associated with men and have generally hated everyone." She clasped her index finger to her thumb and kissed it. "I swear this on my mother's memory, may she rest in peace. You are the first man who doesn't make me feel awkward or displeased to interact with and maintain a decent, lengthy conversation. I have never been able to spend more than a few minutes with any man before I want to send him to hell. Usually, I want to do that within the first five minutes."

By now, both hands were clenched and her jaw was taut with anger.

I stepped back, my eyebrows raised, and I held my hands up placatingly. "Thank you, but please don't get mad. Remember, we're all different. No two drops of water are identical."

She looked me straight in the eyes. "I don't even know myself why I've been telling you all these personal things about me when we've only just met. I have to confess to you the truth: when my aunt told me you were supposed to come over and spend the week with us, I said to myself, 'Oh, my God! This is the last thing I need, for this conceited Commandantico to come over here and ruin my vacation.'"

She paused and smiled. "I believe now, in this very short time I've been talking to you, that you are a very good energy, the light of compassion, and you came into my life not only to save it but also to perhaps beautify my experience. You stopped me because I was consumed with dark, destructive energy. Maybe you will transform me into something better."

I looked at her seriously. I shook my head. "Don't be so hard on yourself. We all have negative feelings. We all may do destructive things to ourselves and keep dark secrets that can be good or bad for someone else, depending on how they interpret them. That doesn't make you a bad person."

Maggie shook her head in disagreement. "I can't agree with you. You don't have any idea of the things I have done in my short existence. I cannot blame you, since you don't really know me yet, and you have a good heart. You see the good in people."

She leaned back to rest her head on the roof of the MG. Her long hair parted along her neck and shoulder. She looked up at the star-filled sky and pointed as if searching for a particular star. Still in this position, she said, "Life has very strange turnings."

Her arm stopped. "I got you! This morning, when I was almost finished with the painting about my nightmares, I had a very powerful feeling that I could die at any moment. It was like a sense of ultimate accomplishment, and my work here was done—like when a witness has finished his testimony and has exposed his agonies. I felt liberated, because I finally felt a bravery I never had before. That canvas was my testimony to my own feelings and suffering, the depiction of how I had been victimized, perhaps by my own psychological problems.

"It is strange how, after you pulled me out of the water and resuscitated me, you probably gave to my soul a new reason to live. Now that I've gotten to know you a little bit, I see a normal person such as yourself still exists. It is only now that I see the light at the end of the tunnel that I realize the possibilities for me and this world full of lies and hypocrisy."

She smiled and pointed again. "You know what? I haven't found my star in a long, long time. And tonight, I found it within seconds. It's like she's been hiding from me, because I was too much in the dark."

She raised her head from the car and held out her hand to me. She asked, "Could you please be my friend?"

"Of course! For me, it will be a great pleasure." I took her hand in mine.

"Well, this is our formal introduction. Nice to meet you, my name is Magdalena Caridad Aldames, commonly known as Maggie."

"Beautiful name, Maggie." I took out my medallion. "You see? I carry you with me all the time. My name is Julio Antonio del Marmol, commonly known as the Commandantico."

We both smiled.

She said, "My step-father gave me his name, which not only brought honor back to my mother but also kept me from being a bastard. I'm very grateful to him, since he cared nothing for the social stigma of bringing into his house a woman with the baggage my mother carried."

I said nothing but nodded my agreement. I bowed slightly over her hand and kissed it.

She pursed her lips as she smiled in satisfaction. "Oh,

how beautiful!" she exclaimed. "May I give you a hug? I not only want to thank you for all you did for me today, saving my life—remember, though, that's our secret—but also to ask your forgiveness and overlook my rudeness."

I opened my arms. "Please! You were forgiven a long time ago." We exchanged a bear hug. At that moment, we were lit by a pair of powerful headlights as a car drove up the driveway.

The car parked under the great entry, and we heard Tanya's pleasant voice laughing in genuine pleasure. She called out to us, "What a beautiful couple you guys make! Do it again, I want to take a picture to send to Che!"

Maggie's expression grew sour as she rolled her eyes in embarrassment and discontent. "Do you mind?" she asked me.

I smiled. "No, not at all. Don't worry about it."'

Tanya proceeded to take several pictures, until Maggie irritably shook her head and raised her hands. She protested, "It's OK, you've got enough pictures. Don't get any ideas. I was only thanking him for his kindness and gentility that he's demonstrated all day. He brought all my painting supplies from the beach all the way here."

Tanya hugged her with a big smile. "Don't worry, honey. I love that you guys get along so well. That is the best surprise I've had for a long time, to come and see you guys hugging each other. I saw it in my mind, I predicted it, when I invited him to come stay with us." She began to tease gently, "Don't you remember, protesting how it was going to ruin your vacation, and 'Oh, my God,' and all that? Well, is your vacation ruined?"'

As they hugged, I could see Maggie's face, and she rolled her eyes in exasperation. She released Maggie, and

The Deadly Deals

Tanya came over to me, that broad smile never leaving her face. She hugged me and said in my ear, "You don't know how grateful I am to have you here with us, and you don't know what it means to me to see Maggie so happy. Thank you." She kissed me on my neck just below my ear.

When we parted, I said, "Thank you for inviting me to your house."

She shook her head. "You're so polite! Why don't you guys help me to get all this exquisite gourmet food I've brought for dinner from one of the best kitchens in Havana?"

We both started to unload Tanya's Jaguar XK-E sports car, bottle green in color. She had not been not kidding. The food was still on the metal trays from some restaurant at which she must have had great influence, since such service seldom left those establishments.

We helped her bring everything into the kitchen. She said, "Why don't you guys go take showers? You smell like the ocean and something else. I'm sorry, but I'm very sensitive to odors. Maybe it's because you were in the sun."

I smiled knowingly. "If you only knew," I teased her.

"I don't want to know," she said. "Go take your showers. I'll see you in the dining room. I'm going to go take a shower myself."

The food smelled exquisite, especially to me, as I had not eaten anything since breakfast that day. I couldn't wait to open one of those dish covers. I had no idea what was on the trays, but it smelled so good that I dreamed of it while I showered. I hurried through it, threw my clothes on, and nearly ran to the dining room.

Unfortunately, neither Tanya nor Maggie had shown up

yet. I could hear water running through the walls. It sounded like one of the bathtubs had been filled and was now draining. I decided to kill some time and not drive myself crazy at the thought of that food by going outside and walking around the gardens.

To my surprise, a car I had not seen before pulled up the drive. It was a beautiful, hard-topped convertible Ford Fairlane—virtually brand-new of canary yellow and white. The top was down, so I leaned over the rolled-up window to look at the interior more clearly. A small, Soviet PPD-34/38 machine gun—what we nicknamed a *pepecha*—lay in the passenger's seat. Next to it was a military hat bearing a captain's insignia.

I continued to walk through the beautiful gardens towards the front gate to check my surroundings. I noticed across the street from the house a 1957 black Ford four-door sedan with two men sitting inside smoking cigarettes. They had all the signs of being G-2. I wondered what they were doing there, unless Tanya had a personal security detail.

I heard Maggie's voice behind me, calling me from the house. I turned and waved at her. She saw me and returned my wave, then beckoned me to come in, as we were now ready to eat. I walked back to the door while she waited, holding the door open and smiling. Once I was next to her, she affectionately took my arm, walking into the living room as if we were a couple.

We walked into the dining room, where the table was already laid. Tanya was there, and a tall, muscular man with a pencil mustache, dark hair, and very pale skin stood next to her. He wore the uniform of an Army captain. He stood up as we walked in, and Tanya introduced us. "This is Captain Andres Acuña. He is the chief of the G-2 station here in Varadero Beach, and a great friend of mine."

Captain Acuña held out his hand to me with a broad grin. "A great pleasure to meet you. You can call me Andres," he said in a friendly manner.

"The pleasure is mine," I replied. "My name is Julio Antonio del Marmol."

He pointed at the stars on my shoulder. "Yes, the Commandantico is very well known. I've seen you multiple times on TV with Fidel, Che, and all the other leaders of the Revolution. You might not remember, but on one occasion we shared the platform in the Plaza."

I looked at him blankly.

"I was sitting by Commander Piñeiro."

I knew now why I didn't remember him. He raised his hand with a self-deprecating expression. "Of course, there were so many people there that day that it's possible you don't remember."

I smiled and raised my eyebrows. "Yes, yes, I clearly remember your face now. I recall you actually had a beautiful, tall, blonde lady as a companion."

He raised his eyebrows and glanced at Tanya and Maggie uncomfortably.

He stammered a little. "You have a good memory! That tall blonde is my wife, but we're in the process of getting a divorce for incompatibility of character."

An awkward silence followed that for a few seconds. It appeared that particular subject had been discussed with Tanya before.

Andres tried to change the subject. He turned to Maggie. "Well, Maggie, how are you enjoying the art school?"

Maggie shrugged noncommittally. She said sarcastically, "Well, it could be a lot better if the professors there let us study for a longer period and didn't take us to so much 'voluntary work.' Before I graduate as a painter, I'll be a master at digging potatoes."

Andres smiled. "Well, this is part of what you have to offer in order to pay back to the people, because they're the ones providing that free education. Before, it used to be a privilege that only the very wealthy could receive."

Maggie rolled her eyes incredulously. "Yes, yes, of course! But not to the extreme of spending seven hours in the fields digging potatoes or whatever else and only two studying painting each day. At that pace, when I come to graduate as a painter, I won't be able to paint standing on my legs—I'll be in a wheelchair."'

Andres smiled again. "Well, well—don't exaggerate so much. I can't believe it's actually that bad."

Tanya shot Maggie a look that could kill as she served food to Andres and myself. She shook her head slightly in warning. Maggie returned the look rebelliously. Her attitude was discourteous, especially before the local G-2 head and an honored guest. Maggie threw her arms up without any discretion. She asked Tanya, "What are you looking at me like that for? Isn't what I said what's been happening in reality? Why can't we even speak the truth in this country anymore without somebody rolling their eyes at you? What happened to free expression? Or is it already dead, suffocated by this government 'of the people?'"

Tanya rapped the table. "Enough is enough, Magdalena! Control yourself, and stop with these stupidities. Andres only asked you about your studies and your school. You don't have to make a drama and a political march, creating a display of your hysterical, personal frustrations! That is not the way I've taught you."

Maggie looked at her with eyes filled with tears. She bit her lip but remained silent.

Tanya opened the trays and continued to serve the food. She directed her comments to Andres and me. "I implore you guys to forgive Maggie. She's been very nervous lately, with her studies and school, and she doesn't realize that her words could be offensive to others. Sometimes, she crosses the line in letting her own opinions and ideas take control of her, and she says things that are out of order."

I shook my head and said before Andres could say anything, "I don't think that anything Maggie said is offensive or out of order. She only limited herself to expressing her personal opinions of the way the directors, school administrators, and staff run the school. Perhaps she exaggerated a little bit about how they assign voluntary work for them on a daily basis. But if not and what she says is the literal truth, and I don't have a reason to believe that she has cause to lie to us, in my personal opinion, I agree with her. That would be wrong and a huge error on the part of the school. If they take so many hours to work in agriculture and wind up burning all their energy doing this extremely hard labor all day long, how well will they be able to concentrate the rest of the day and dedicate serious time to what they're really there to learn? That should be the priority the school should be giving. I don't see any reason for her to lie to us."

A brief silence followed. Andres stroked his chin with his hand, contemplating my words. After a few seconds, he said, "What you just said makes a lot of sense."

Tanya interrupted abruptly as she served herself a plate of the food. "I don't believe the director or the people running that school would make decisions by themselves that don't come from above at the highest levels."

This time, I was the one who interrupted by raising my right arm. "I'm sorry, Tanya, but I have to disagree with you. You don't know what I discovered not too long ago, shoulder to shoulder with Che and Fidel. We discovered that one of the big leaders in our intelligence, only seeking personal favors, created false testimonies, accumulated false evidence, and connived to destroy the reputation of a very high and important figure in our government. It was only for his personal satisfaction and vindictive character in order to earn brownie points with the Commander-in-Chief."

I leaned back in the chair, crossed my legs, and squeezed my forehead. I smiled in great satisfaction. I looked at Maggie and pointed at my chest. "But I destroyed his game, and he left Fidel's office like a dog who had been kicked in the rear end, with his tail between his legs. If there's something I don't like, it's abusers, bullies, and extremists."

I smiled secretly, knowing that I really wasn't a very high and important figure in the government. I had mentioned no names, so it was appropriate in this case, I thought, to exaggerate a little bit in order to intimidate these two and head off any more humiliating of Maggie. She had merely been speaking contrary to the government's well-publicized propaganda extolling free education.

All three of them looked at me in stunned surprise. Maggie looked at me gratefully. She tried to smile at me, but her distress only permitted a sad half-smile. Captain

Andres looked at me and asked curiously, "When did this happen? Not too long ago?"

"Two nights ago," I said. Then I looked at Maggie and said, "I would love, Maggie, for you to give me the address for your school. The first occasion I'm with Che and Fidel, I would like to ask them about this and see if this is the normal procedure for education in that particular school. It could be some extremist exploiting the youth while trying to gain some personal merit in order to advance his career within the bureaucracy that's recently been forming within our government."

I knew for a fact that she was being truthful with us and that this was how the government simultaneously indoctrinated the kids to their way of thinking and spread propaganda to the rest of the world about Cuba's free education system and the scholarships available to anyone who wanted to come to the island to study. The reality was that there was no education in Cuba. True, they didn't charge for admission or books, but it was also true that the debt was never discharged, as such graduates wound up working for the government for the rest of their lives on minimal pay.

Maggie nodded at me. She spoke ironically, directing her words more towards Tanya than to me. "Thank you, Julio Antonio, for your courtesy and fairness and for giving me the benefit of the doubt. You don't take me for a schizophrenic idiot and an adolescent full of personal frustration without any manners at all just because I tried to answer a question a guest just asked me."

Tanya interrupted her once more, this time condescendingly. "It's OK, Maggie. I understand." She held out her arm. "Would you please give me your plate,

Maggie, so that I can serve you?"

Maggie looked her straight in the eyes. "No apology for all the previous insults?"

Tanya rolled her eyes in exasperation. Perhaps it was because she had guests present, but she apologized. "OK, Maggie, I'm sorry. Could you please pass me your plate before the food gets cold?"

Maggie's pale face grew red at the supercilious tone. She didn't care to be treated like a spoiled brat and a foolish teenager. Maggie took her napkin, stood up, and dropped it onto her empty plate. In a courteous tone, she said to all of us, "With the permission of all of you, I've lost my appetite, and I don't feel very well. I'm sorry, but I'm going to retire to my room and go to sleep. I think that will be better for everyone present. I had a rotten, lousy day and am very agitated." She turned around.

Tanya, this time adopting a loving tone, said, "Maggie, please, don't go to sleep now. Going to bed hungry is not good for your condition."

Maggie spun around at that. She placed a hand on her chest. "My condition? Is that what you said? My condition? Now that I won't be present, why don't you tell them the latest diagnosis my psychiatrist gave me, so you can keep our guests very informed of my medical records and my emotional problems?"

She stormed out of the room. She continued speaking, but as she grew distant, her voice faded to an incoherent mumbling.

Tanya stood up and excused herself. "I'll be back in a second. Please, start to eat. Don't let the food get cold and allow Maggie to spoil this beautiful meal."

She left and followed Maggie, leaving Captain Andres

The Deadly Deals

and me looking at each other. He eyed the food. He pointed to the plate. "What do you think? Can we start?"

I smiled and gestured around the table. "You heard her—of course you can start. These are just small details in a family dispute."

He started to eat, but I limited myself to taking a few sips from the glass of orange juice Tanya had served me.

A few minutes later, Tanya returned. She looked at my plate and noticed that it was still full, in contrast to that of Andres, who had made a significant dent in his serving. She asked, "What, you don't like my food? You haven't touched your plate."

I smiled and picked up the rolled up napkin. I started to unroll it and pull out my silverware. "Of course I like your food. I was only waiting for you. I love your selection: beef wellington is one of my favorite dishes. You've also got sautéed mushrooms, rice pilaf, spinach soufflé—who cannot like such refined food? I only had the courtesy to wait for you."

She looked at me and smiled. She looked at Andres and his nearly-finished plate. Andres looked at the two of us, speechless. He mumbled, "Well, you told us to go ahead and start. In truth, the food smelled so good that it was very hard for me to contradict you."

Tanya smiled. "Oh, no, no—please! I told you to eat. You did the right thing."

Andres said, "Beef Wellington, eh? That is what this exquisite dish is called?"

Tanya nodded. "Yes."

She looked at me in embarrassment at the vulgarity and poor manners Andres was displaying at the table. To excuse his ignorance to a certain extent, she said, "Well, we unfortunately didn't all have the opportunity to have these culinary experiences in the capitalist society in which we used to live. Only a few had the privilege to enjoy such gourmet food. They didn't even have enough to buy a *frita* in the street or a steak sandwich."

I looked at her and limited myself to simply nodding my head. I thought about how these communists blamed the capitalists for everything. The reality was that the communist society in which we now lived, apparently everything was the same, since some people weren't even interested in educating themselves. Two years after the new society was established, and Captain Andres, the chief of the G-2 in one of the most internationally famous tourist spots in Cuba, could not be bothered to visit the number of elegant restaurants in the area, learn what beef Wellington was, or even know how to properly hold a knife and fork. He would probably never learn, because he wasn't interested in the first place. I remembered the words of my maternal grandfather: you can lead a horse to water, but you can't make him drink.

After we finished that luxurious meal, she served us a wonderful dessert of very ripe plantation bananas soaked in caramelized sugar, coated in cinnamon, that were then sliced in half with three scoops of ice cream and sweet almond bread sticks on the side of the plate. This dessert rounded out that meal with a golden ribbon, rating it as a meal fit for royalty. I complimented her for the food as only to be expected from a person of her class. She thanked me and then prepared a plate and put it on a tray.

She said, "Could I ask you a favor? Could you please take this to Maggie and persuade her to eat this before she goes to sleep? She's taken a very strong medication to help her rest, and she shouldn't take it on an empty stomach. If it doesn't bother you to get involved in our family affairs."

I said, "You must be kidding—I'm a member of the family already. It will be a pleasure for me."

I took the tray in my hands and excused myself. "We'll talk later, OK? I'll put in my best effort to get Maggie to eat this delicious meal."

I walked to her room. I heard Elvis Presley singing "Love Me Tender" playing at an almost imperceptible volume inside the room. Balancing the tray in one hand against the wall, I knocked on the door. The music stopped and Maggie's voice called, "Who is it?"

"It's me, Julio Antonio."

"Oh, OK. Wait for me one second, OK?" It took longer than I expected, but the door finally opened. Her face was red, and her breathing was agitated, as if she had been running or exercising hard. She nervously greeted me, her leg holding the door partially shut. She was wearing a nearly transparent dress of fine mesh weave. "Hey, what do you have there?"

I smiled. "Your Aunt Tanya gave me a new job in the house as the waiter. She assigned me to bring you the food, Your Highness."

Maggie shook her head as she half-smiled. "Please, take that food to my aunt and tell her that she should bring it herself, and bring a very, very solid apology for her humiliation and insults in front of her guests."

I smiled once more. "Let me correct what I said before. That was just a joke, OK? I'm not employed here, and I'm not getting a paycheck. As a guest, I don't want to mix myself into a family dispute between you and your aunt. I would really appreciate it if you would be nice and take this tray into your room. That way, you don't give me the embarrassment of returning it to your aunt. I can assure you of one thing: you're missing a great and exquisite meal. It would be a real pity to throw it away. If you decide not to eat it, why don't you do me a great favor and flush it down your toilet? That way, I don't have to bring it back, we finish the evening with a better disposition, and I won't be in this embarrassing situation of being the go-between for you guys."

From inside the room, I heard a feminine voice. "Maggie, I'm very hungry. I haven't eaten anything all day. If you don't mind, I'll eat it. You don't have to throw it away or return it."

Another female voice, deeper and husky, said, "Oh! I would love to eat it, too. Why throw it away?"

Maggie rolled her eyes. Her left arm had been against the doorjamb, while the other was behind the door. Clearly, she hadn't had any intention of letting me in. She turned slightly to speak to them. "Very well, guys. For just a plate of food, you've already blown your cover. Have you forgotten that you're not supposed to be here, or have you had an attack of amnesia?"

Both girls laughed.

The first said, "For God's sake, Maggie. Don't be so improper. Let him come in. After all the good things you said about him, I'm sure he won't say anything to your aunt about what he sees here."

Maggie turned back to me and shook her head. She clearly wasn't convinced, but opened the door. She grabbed me with one hand and pulled me inside, closing the door behind me. It was nearly dark in the room, but I immediately saw in what light there was that Maggie's two friends were half-naked. They were sitting on top of a tiger rug which lay over the marble floor next to Maggie's bed. It was a real tiger's fur, head and all. They both grinned broadly, and beckoned me to come over to them. I walked slowly in their direction. They quickly removed the tray from my hands. Both girls were older than Maggie, perhaps sixteen or seventeen years of age. Their bodies, however, were fully mature. They looked like models or dancers. I later realized that both of them were part of the dance crew at the Tropicana.

One of them was tall and dark-skinned, with refined European nose and lips. Her hair was artificially colored white and cut very short, more like a man's cut. Her eyes were honey colored. Her features were blended of European and Asian descent. She held out her hand and said, "I'm Shela."

"Julio Antonio," I replied.

The other one also extended her hand. She was tall, as well, with beautiful long, wavy black hair. Her skin was extremely pale, even white, with blue eyes and large, exotic lips. "I'm Gladis." She looked at my pistol curiously. "That pistol is for real?"

Before I could answer, Maggie said, "What kind of question is that? Of course it's real, and it kills for real. You want him to shoot you to find out?"

Gladis laughed nervously. She didn't like what Maggie had said but didn't dare to contradict her. Clearly, Maggie ran the show here. She said, "Maggie, chill out, or I'm going to give you a painful bite—not like the one I gave you before."

Maggie shook her head and rolled her eyes. "Remember what I told you, OK?" She pointed at me. She was clearly embarrassed.

I looked straight at Maggie after this exchange. My eyes had fully adjusted to the darkness, and for the first time I realized that she was completely naked under her net dress. I couldn't help it—as soon as I realized her nakedness, in my embarrassment, I looked up at the mosquito netting near the ceiling. She sat down on the rug next to her friends. As she sat, I was given a full color picture of her privates, and I snatched my eyes away hastily once more. She realized this, and thoroughly enjoying my discomfiture, rather than covering herself, she spread her legs even more. Shela and Gladis opened the containers on the tray. Every time they tried some of the food, their expressions reflected their complete satisfaction.

Gladis shifted over to make a space for me. "Come here," she beckoned. "Come here, Julio Antonio—sit down here with us. We can share this lovely meal that Maggie wanted to throw away for the sake of her pride."

I raised my right hand high while I touched my stomach with my left. "No, thank you—I've already eaten, and very well. I'm quite full. But Maggie should eat something. It's not good to go to bed with an empty stomach."

Shela and Gladis looked at me, and then at each other. They burst out laughing. When they regained their composure, Shela said, "Honey, Maggie's already gone to bed with an empty stomach. And she had no problems, eh, Maggie?"

Maggie shook her head discontentedly at the jokes her two friends were enjoying in front of me. She was very uncomfortable with this, because apparently she didn't want me to know what her sexual preference was. To ease her past this, I said, "Well, since my mission is accomplished, I'll leave you ladies to it. It's been a great pleasure to meet you guys."

Gladis pouted. "Are you leaving already? Why don't you stay with us a little longer?"

Shela cut a piece of beef wellington and held it to Maggie's mouth. Maggie took the offered piece and began to chew.

I was not only feeling out of place but also very uncomfortable. I started to walk towards the door. Maggie followed me to the door. She took my arm and said, "Thank you very much for bringing my food. Please, forgive my friends. They are a little existentialist, but they are good people, good friends. Please don't tell my aunt you saw them in here. She wants to isolate me from everyone. I think you're the only person that she really wanted me to meet and has been pushing for being my friend. Nobody was ever good enough for me before."

"That is a sign of love," I replied. "It can be a little possessive, but the reason she would like me to be around you is because she has the perception that I'm Che's great friend after saving his life. However, Tanya looks like a good person; remember, she's your blood. Family is the only thing that very rarely fails us."

She nodded.

Before I left, I said, "You don't have anything to worry about from me. Whatever I saw or heard I will never repeat. I only repeat something if absolutely necessary to punish someone for something done to me, somebody I love, or somebody I care for—otherwise, my lips are completely sealed with a key I don't give to anyone."

"Thank you," she replied.

"You're welcome. You have a good night, OK?"

"You, too. See you tomorrow," she said.

I walked through the corridor towards my room. Tanya was sitting in the parlor, drinking coffee with Andres. I greeted them both. As soon as she saw me, she asked, "Did you get her to eat something?"

I smiled. "I assure you that tomorrow you will find that tray completely empty in the kitchen."

She smiled and kissed my cheek. "Thank you very much. Maggie is a rebel."

"Well," I said, "she's got more than enough crazy genes in her body to act a little oddly sometimes. You have to forgive her. She's a good girl. Good night to you both."

The Deadly Deals

The Annoying Zeroes

    There are those annoying ones who enjoy pushing our buttons and make everyone angry while they look for a reason to fight with you—but they never do anything good for anyone. They are always ready to argue about anything on any topic without a positive solution for anything they argue for. In order to not downgrade ourselves by using derogatory language, I have decided for myself to call them, simply and concisely, zeroes in our lives.

    Like wasps in our eyes in our journey through life, you cannot avoid them buzzing around in your face, telling you what they are worth, which is really nothing. During our daily struggles, always here and there you will find one or more of these zeroes, no matter what or where you go in life to the right or the left. That is the reason you should not lose your class or lower yourself to their level. Always remember that you are dealing with a zero, and simply don't call them a nasty word. What else can you expect? You're really dealing with a royal asshole, after all; but let's still call them a zero in benefit to ourselves, and you don't lose your class after all.

    Dr. Julio Antonio del Marmol

Dr. Julio Antonio del Marmol

Chapter 11: Tanya's Attempt to Cover Up

Tanya wished me a good night in return. Andres was taking a drink of his coffee and so was unable to reply.

I went to my room and lay on the bed without removing my clothes. I looked at the ceiling and started to think about all the strange things that had occurred during this hectic day. As I lay there, I asked myself if what had happened with Maggie was part of the new species of men and women Che and Fidel wanted to create—what they called 'the man of the future.' The new socialist structure the Revolution's leaders had imposed on the island had been constructed without a care for the feelings of any of the others who had helped form it. The tropical communism's concept of humanity was the homo cubanis, without any moral or religious restrictions or adherence to any of the rules of the old capitalist society. They chanted in their communist anthems, "No Caesar, no bourgeois, and no God." Perhaps, in their hatred of the free market system, they made the mistake of playing a dangerous game of Russian roulette in engineering a socialist structure which they thought would only destroy the old bourgeois capitalist system that they so despised.

In conclusion, after two years, the Revolution had created a new human being that, rather than having anything good, had the appearance of a new creature—a fictitious Frankenstein monster a hundred times worse than the old version of humanity the capitalist system had offered to us.

After meditating on this at length, I raised myself up from the bed. I thought that enough time had passed for everyone to be asleep. I went to my travel bag and switched to the black jogging suit I was going to use whenever I embarked on an adventure in which I wanted to avoid being identified. I used a long black baseball cap to cover my face. I left my uniform and pistol, taking with me only the commando knife, which I concealed inside my waistband.

I crept out of my room by the back sliding door, across the garden, and around the border of the swimming pool. I reached the Mercedes and opened the other travel bag which contained the duck eggs. I tucked a few into the top of my jogging suit and a few more into my pants. As I did so, I looked at the convertible owned by Andres. It was still parked in the same place, and I smiled. It wasn't just Maggie having sex tonight. It appeared her Aunt Tanya had asked the young officer to spend the night.

I walked to the front gates and looked around, carefully concealing myself against one of the columns. I saw what appeared to be Andres' escort still across the street in the same car. Clearly, they weren't going to budge if he was staying overnight at the house. The car was even in the same position.

I decided to walk away and explore the perimeter of the property to locate a different exit. I didn't want to be seen by those guys in case I encountered trouble, and I didn't want to jump the high wall because of the eggs in my pockets. I finally found a rear exit near the border of the wall. It appeared to be a runoff for excess rainwater, fed by a series of ditches along the walls of the property. They came together to empty into this drain, which appeared to lead to the street sewers behind the property. I tried to lift the small gate, but I noticed it was locked shut on the side. I examined the lock, and returned to the Mercedes. I took the tire iron out and returned to the small gate. I stuck the bar under the lock and pulled with all my might. One of the prongs on the gate snapped. I liked that, as it appeared that the lock was still intact, and should anyone investigate further, the rust would make the damage look like the natural result of corrosion.

I went back to my car, carefully cleaned the iron, and returned it to the kit from which I had taken it. I headed back to the patio and very carefully opened the gate. I slid under and closed it after me. There was a metal ladder inside, and I descended into the sewer. I walked to the next junction for the street and cautiously lifted the manhole cover to see if the coast was clear. I slipped out and replaced it.

I walked down the street through an empty lot and came to the corner. I saw the Ford in the distance and Andres' bodyguard still lounging inside in front of Tanya's residence. I walked away, to put some distance between them and myself. I took in the numerous mansions in the area. The majority of the cars in the driveways were Volgas and Soviet jeeps, which clearly marked that these expensive places were now possessed by the government elites. One mansion had two flagpoles—one flying the Spanish flag while the other displayed the Cuban flag. I assumed that this belonged to a high diplomatic attaché of the Spanish government, as there were also several

The Deadly Deals

security guards all around the place.

Beach where the Ministry of the Interior confronted the young kids, breaking up their beach party

A large fire on the beach caught my attention. I followed the light to see what was going on. As I drew closer, I heard North American rock and roll music playing loudly. I was not surprised, because the only people hanging around these private beaches were foreigners, and that was the kind of music being played elsewhere in the world. These large resort areas had fewer and fewer Cuban nationals, even though the Revolutionary government had, in the beginning, criticized the bourgeoisie for being the only ones who could enjoy such places. Now, the Cuban bourgeoisie had been replaced by the foreign bourgeoisie who brought in the precious dollars the government so badly needed to finance their internationalist ventures around the world which spread their demagogy of freeing the world from the shackles of the capitalist.

The sound of barking dogs mixed in with the music. I saw marked police cars and heard people arguing. There was a gunshot, and I rushed to see what was happening.

Dr. Julio Antonio del Marmol

About a hundred young teenagers surrounded a small group of policemen. The police had tried to remove a portable record player. The situation had escalated to the arrest of several of the youths, who were seated in handcuffs in the back seat of the police car. The others had started to argue and were resisting the confiscation of the portable player. One of the officers had hit a kid with his baton. The kid then smashed a beer bottle over the policeman's head, and he had retaliated by shooting the aggressor in the stomach. The kid collapsed in the arms of the others. This was unusual in such a distinctive international resort. A young girl cried at the police, "Murderers! Why did you have to shoot him? He didn't do anything to cause that!"

I had by now blended in with the crowd. The situation was escalating. One policeman loosed his grip on the leash of one of the agitated dogs, giving it enough slack to bite one of the kids. The Department of Technical Investigation, another repressive arm of the government, arrived with several buses, probably with the intention of making a massive arrest. I had seen this before as an intimidation tactic with a large group of teenagers. All these kids were doing was having a bonfire on the beach and listening to rock and roll music. The Revolution had been telling them that they could do whatever they wanted without social restraints and that promiscuity was the new era. Now, however, out of the blue, they want to prohibit to these same youngsters from listening to North American music or even chewing gum. Burning fires on the beach was now considered an abuse of the freedom the government had allowed to them.

I noticed someone in the DTI cars surrounded by several

The Deadly Deals

bodyguards. I recognized him as the Minister of the Interior, Commander Ramiro Valdés. He not only headed the DTI in that position, but also the G-2, and so he was ultimately Piñerio's boss. I knew at once that this conflict had to have started in the early hours of the evening, long before I had arrived. It had by now deteriorated to the point they feared an international scandal.

All that could be seen were foreigners; the group had grown in spectators, and it was still growing. Some of the tourists were taking pictures, and one group was even filming it as it happened. I could see Valdés start to issue orders to some of his underlings, who then passed the orders to the police and the regular DTI agents who were still arriving in cars.

A couple of the agents walked over to the tourists who were taking pictures and to the film crew, trying to get them to stop. Two men and women of Mexican origin argued that they could take whatever pictures and film they wished. They had been authorized by the government's Culture Department and were there filming a documentary about life in Cuba. After displaying their badges and identification, the police had no alternative but to go back and report to Valdés what had happened. Valdés had to let the Mexicans continue to film. He was clearly nervous and wished to avoid making the situation worse by creating even more commotion.

More tourists and neighbors arrived to observe the situation, which continued to further spiral into arguments between the police, DTI agents, and the teens, who still resisted having the record player confiscated. The loud music continued to play, and an ambulance arrived for the young man who had been shot and the police officer with the injured head. Paramedics attended to the kids who had been bitten by the dogs.

Very carefully, I slid around the edge of the crowd to avoid being recognized by Ramiro. I heard him say to one of his men, "Call the fire department and put that goddamned fire down. Then separate them so that they dissolve, handcuff them, and put them in the goddamned buses. This has been going on too long already. Who is the moron who shot that kid? You don't do that in public!"

"Commander," one of the men said, "that was before we got here. That was the local police. The fire department is already on its way here; we called them a long time ago."

"Very well. Let me talk to these *Elvispresleyanos*[10] bourgeoisie parasites, see if I can calm them down so that they listen to reason."

Followed by a small group of guards, he yelled out, "Will you please, somebody, turn off that goddamned music, or at least turn it down? I want to talk to you guys. I am the Minister of the Interior, Commander Ramiro Valdés, and I don't want any more people taken out of here in ambulances."

The argument between the youth and police stopped momentarily. Only the dogs could be heard occasionally barking, though the music continued at the same volume. Ramiro ignored it and yelled, "I repeat: I'm here to try and avoid anyone else getting hurt. But you are disturbing the peace. It's now very late, too late to make all this noise,

---

[10] The communist government would use the term *Elvispresleyannos* as a derogatory name for teens who liked to listen to American music, especially rock and roll. Even chewing gum was considered subversive, as it had been banned.

especially with that music that only the worms and Counterrevolutionaries in this country listen to." He raised his hand arrogantly. "Will you please turn that goddamned music off? That way I don't have to scream to talk to you guys!"

A few seconds passed, and the music turned off. One of the youths said, "We had this music going at seven o'clock this evening when one of these assholes came and tried to take it from us. We're entitled to listen to whatever music we want!"

More cars from the police and the DTI continued to arrive. There were also G-2 arriving at the scene of this now-political show. Ramiro still screamed at the top of his lungs, "Whatever happened is what happened. Now, I'm asking you to quiet down, disperse, and go home!"

He raised both hands to point at the sky. "You guys have exhausted our patience! One police officer with his head cut open and one of you with a bullet in the stomach. You see these buses? You have five minutes to disperse, or you will be sent to labor camps with the social scourges, worms, and Counterrevolutionaries. Do you want us to do that? The decision is now in your hands."

He pointed at the ambulances, one departing and two others arriving. "I repeat: I don't want anyone to have to leave in those ambulances."

Everyone remained silent, intimidated by his aggressive tone and the powerful threat he had just made. Some of them began to pick up belongings, turn around, and unhappily disperse.

One of the young girls snatched up the record player, but a police officer started to take it. "No!" she yelled, "This doesn't belong to you, it belongs to me!"

This reignited once more the bad situation. Ramiro had already turned and started to walk towards the cars. But the girl's shout caught the attention of the others who had started to disperse. She had started to wrestle with the two officers who were attempting to remove the record player. One of the dogs bit her in the leg. She screamed in pain, and the situation returned to the same point at which it had started earlier.

One of the police struck out with his baton, and the youth regrouped. They started to throw bottles and whatever else they could get their hands on at the officer holding the dog and the policemen who were attempting to take the player. The fire department arrived, and Ramiro ordered them to start spraying the kids with the hose. The cold spray forced the multitude to break up in the direction of the beach.

This time, the police, DTI, G-2, and fire department formed a cordon and forced them back along the beach. The youngsters had no alternative than to retreat. As they moved away from the cars, the spectators moved a little behind them to see what was going on as the kids continued to scream and throw things.

I used the opportunity to discretely separate from the crowd. Making sure that nobody could see me, I baptized the cars of Ramiro Valdés and two of his high officers with the eggs. I put eggs on all the DTI and G-2 cars I could find. When I ran out of eggs, I pulled out my commando knife and started to slash the tires of the remaining cars. I didn't stop, as the commotion created a distraction which gave me the perfect opportunity. Without wasting a single second, I continued to puncture the tires of each vehicle I could see, including the fire department trucks. The only ones I spared were the two ambulances, thinking that they were only there as a humanitarian gesture to provide medical services to whoever needed it. That made them, in my mind, a neutral party in that conflict.

They had already backed the kids to the edge of the water. Some of them even jumped into the ocean to avoid the high pressure cold water. They had run out of bottles and rocks to defend themselves. Some tried to run to the side, but they were unable to leave.

Suddenly, the water ceased, as the tanks in the pumper trucks ran out. The fire department had not, in their haste, hooked up to the city supply. This gave the kids their chance, as they outnumbered the aggressors. They screamed at the top of their lungs as they surged forward like some Viking force. With a chorus of frightened yelps, the dogs tore free from their handlers and ran for their lives in front of the charging crowd. The police, DTI, G-2, and firemen were overrun, knocking all the men over, making even Ramiro eat sand. They dropped to the ground with their arms over their heads protectively as the teens ran right over them. The tables were turned as the defenders suddenly took to the offensive. The men lying in the sand looked like worms wriggling in the ground, ironically resembling the nickname they liked to call their enemies.

I was on my knees stabbing the last tire of one of the fire trucks. One of the firemen at the top of the truck shouted, "Hey! What the hell are you doing?" He jumped from the top of the truck onto the sand, an ax in his hand. He charged towards me in an attempt to defend his truck.

I switched the knife from my left hand to my right and adopted a defensive stance, preparing to fight with him. It was a moonless night, and I was in the shadow of the truck, his back towards the beach. I heard the shout of the crowd heading our way. He turned to look and saw the tsunami of human bodies running our way, completely bull-rushing the few remaining police like a truck runs over cans in the street. He tossed his ax into the truck and climbed a utility ladder to get up and out of the way of that mass of people to avoid the same fate of the police.

I reacted quickly and ran away from the entire scene. As I ran, I carefully maneuvered towards my right so that I could return to the spot I had entered the beach from. I heard shots behind me, but I had no idea if they were shots in the air or towards the crowd. It might be an attempt to rein in the stampede. I heard them shouting for people to stop. A few arrests were made but not many. They realized they didn't have the ability to transport everyone. As I ran back to Tanya's place, I smiled as I imagined the sadistic Ramiro's face when he got to his car and found all four tires slashed and the precious gift I had left: the egg a la chocolate.

Unfortunately, my eggs had been limited. If not, I would have done exactly what Chandee had done to Che's Oldsmobile. When she had told me about that, it gave me such great satisfaction that it was almost a physical relief to leave that crap all over that despised sadist's car. He was responsible for the deaths of so many good Cubans.

After I ran for a while, I halted to catch my breath and calm down. There was no longer a reason for me to run, so I walked at a normal pace, filled with a great sense of satisfaction. I had achieved more than I had hoped for, and it was very pleasing to give to these corrupt government bullies a taste of their own medicine. They were used like trained attack dogs on our own people, and they were unused to being the victims of the same tactics of harassment.

I thought also that this night had brought to me the immense pleasure of creating a great inconvenience to the plans of Ramiro Valdés after what I had done to all of his cars. I had the tranquility of knowing that I had nothing compromising on me at that moment, so I decided to enter by the front gate of the mansion instead of enduring the unpleasantness of my previous route through the sewers.

To my surprise, as I neared the gates to the property, I saw the Ford sedan was gone. I retrieved the front door key and tried it in the lock of the small pedestrian gate. It worked, much to my relief, since I had not wanted to use the key code to open the vast gate which allowed cars access to the driveway. As I walked inside, I noticed that Andres' Ford Fairlane was also no longer there.

I looked at my watch, and saw the time was 2:30 a.m. I smiled and thought that Andres had the wisdom to return home and sleep the rest of the night by his beautiful blonde wife and so avoid raising any suspicions in her about his infidelity and maintain the peace in his house.

As I walked by Maggie's MG, I raised the cover a little bit to look into the passenger side window. I wanted to see if her painting was still inside. To my surprise, the car was completely emptied of all the things Maggie had previously deposited inside—no brushes, paints, easel, or the painting. She must have come out to bring everything into her room.

I checked everywhere, including the pockets behind the seat, the bench behind, and the floor. As I was searching, I heard the front door of the house open behind me. I dropped the cover at once and looked for a place to conceal myself on the other side of the car in the bushes by the house. I stepped back a couple of paces before I realized that the cover was stuck on the rear antenna. As I hid in the bushes, I heard a couple of voices speaking very softly to avoid the sound carrying. It was Maggie and her two friends, coming in my direction.

They came up to the MG and together they took the cover off of the car. To my relief, no one noticed the antenna, possibly attributing any disturbance to the wind. Maggie rolled up the cover and opened the trunk to drop it back there. As she did, I saw Shela grab Maggie by the waist in a very masculine way. She gave Maggie a long, passionate kiss, which Maggie returned.

They parted, and Shela walked to the opposite side of the car. Gladis walked over to Maggie. Maggie opened the driver's side door, and without waiting for her lips to dry from Shela's kiss, grabbed Gladis to give a kiss of the same level of passion. This time, however, Gladis was not content with only a kiss. She caressed and fondled one of Maggie's small breasts. With her other hand, Gladis clasped Maggie close to her. She tried to take advantage of this dessert, since she was the last to sample the sweets.

The three of them crammed inside the MG, Maggie behind the wheel as Shela and Gladis shared the passenger seat. They drove down towards the gate. I followed the car with my eyes until I saw that it indeed had left the premises and the large gates had closed behind them. Only then did I leave my hiding place. I walked around the gardens to the pool and entered the house by the back door of my room.

I washed my hands and face and then changed into another jogging suit. After my run in the tropical night, I needed a new suit. I removed my hat and put it along with my sweaty jogging suit into the travel bag.

I left my room and walked through the house to Maggie's room. The door was locked, but it wasn't a difficult matter. After a few seconds, I had the latch pulled to one side, and was able to open the door. I looked around for the painting. There was a detail I wanted to check for in that diabolical picture—something I thought I had seen but might have been my imagination.

After searching fruitlessly for a while, I looked in a small linen closet. Wrapped in a couple of towels was the painting. Maggie must have wanted to avoid the possibility of Tanya discovering it and confronting her about the demonic depiction on the canvas and growing more concerned about Maggie's mental health. Maggie might then be compelled to do something she said she had only done with me: relate the recurring nightmare and so reveal fully where she was coming from emotionally. She might have also been concerned about Tanya relating to Che his demonic depiction in the painting, given how close her aunt was to him. Evidently, the nightmares were so disturbing that she didn't like the simple act of remembering them whenever she spoke of them to someone and so hadn't even related them to her doctors.

I removed the painting from the closet and draped it over the drawers of a vanity opposite the bathroom sink. There was a vast wall-to-wall mirror on the wall behind the sink. I didn't see the reflection of the painting, so closely was I concentrating on deciphering the demons and rituals portrayed in it. Eventually, I could see that I hadn't been imagining things. Almost like a watermark behind the whole thing was the image of a kid around my age. What caught my attention immediately was that the kid was dressed in clothing that closely resembled my uniform. There was something on the image's head that didn't look like hair—it more closely resembled the beret that I customarily wore when in uniform. I stepped back in amazement. I stroked my chin and asked myself in confusion, "What does this signify? What kind of coincidence is this?"

Like a flash of lightning in the sky, it shot into my mind that the only person on this earth who might be able to decipher this and had the good will to tell me the truth would be Doña Carmen, the healer and medium, who was my late friend Daniel's grandmother.

It raised another question, however: how could I take it out of the house without Maggie's missing it? Knowing her, she probably looked at it several times a day and so would notice its absence at once. Based on the conversation we'd had, she would have no doubt that it was I who had taken it, especially as I had told her in detail the previous day about how I had endured the exact same nightmare. Perhaps I could ask her to loan it to me and explain what I wanted to do with it. Since we had hit it off so well, perhaps she would permit me to take it with me for a few days.

As I was thinking about all of this, I raised my head. Something caught my eye. To my surprise, when I turned around and looked at the vast mirror behind me, the painting's reflection looked significantly different: superimposed behind all the images on the painting I saw the Devil's face. I whirled and looked directly at the painting, but the face was no longer there. When I looked back in the mirror, and Lucifer's image was there once more. He was holding a cross in his hand with the body of Christ still nailed on it, and with both hands he was holding this crucifix over the fire as if he were about to drop the whole thing into it.

However, each time I viewed it with the naked eye, the image wasn't there. I wondered if even Maggie knew she had done this and was aware of this incredible optical illusion within the morbid and surrealistic painting she had created. If that nightmare produced in her such a deep and abiding terror, why would she paint it? She now had given it physical form and it could now live in posterity. At the very least, it gave physical life to something which previously had only been a product of her mind.

I nodded my head. I said softly, "Perhaps that was her reason for painting it. In setting these horrific images onto canvas, she might hope to get them out of her brain forever." I smiled. "Maybe that was the reason she told me that she felt like a big weight had been taken off her shoulders when she finished it." I wondered if she had, in fact accomplished that removal—I certainly wished with all my heart that she could find a way to banish those nightmares forever.

I heard a noise which jerked me out of my reverie. It sounded like someone was trying to open the door with a key. Very quickly, I wrapped the painting back up and replaced it where I had found it. I turned the lights off, and opened the door to the same linen cupboard the painting was concealed in. I squatted down on my heels and left the door open a slight crack so that I could see who was entering.

I heard someone walking around, opening and closing drawers of the dresser by Maggie's bed. A few minutes passed, and I could see in the dim light coming in from outside a completely naked body in front of me. The lights went back on, and I saw that it was Maggie. She walked in front of the mirror in the bathroom. For several seconds, she examined her body. She felt her right breast with her left hand, examining a small bruise there. It looked like it was a hickey, and she shook her head unhappily. She took a few steps to sit down on the toilet, and she left my field of view. I heard her urinate.

The door to the bedroom opened again, and Tanya's voice asked, "Maggie! Maggie, are you here? Are you awake?"

Maggie stood up, once again entering my view. She wiped herself with some toilet paper and leaned down to flush the toilet. She replied, "Yes, I'm here. I'm awake and in the bathroom. What do you want?" Her tone was unfriendly and aggressive.

Tanya replied sweetly, "I just wanted to ask your forgiveness and apologize to you. I want to make peace with you. I cannot sleep when we're so mad at each other."

Maggie shook her head with an expression of discontent on her face. I shifted my position slightly, bracing myself lightly against the shelf above me. It wasn't a fixed shelf, and so it tipped. Something heavy wrapped in towels fell down onto my legs. At the precise moment this noise was made, Maggie had started the faucet to wash her hands. I was petrified, wondering if she had heard that soft thud. I looked at her, but she was washing her hands with no indication that she had heard anything. I carefully breathed a sigh of relief.

Maggie dried her hands and turned off the light. I groped in the darkness to explore the object which had landed in my lap. I heard the sound of liquid sloshing slightly in a glass bottle—perhaps a bottle of liquor. Even though the light in the bedroom was on, my position was such that it did not provide a great deal of illumination—just a tiny bit which was reflected from the bathroom mirror. I carefully tried to open the closet door a little more so that I could see what it was in my lap while at the same time hear more clearly her conversation with her aunt.

Tanya was trying to apologize to Maggie without admitting any responsibility on her own part. Maggie, with her rebel spirit, was not about to let her get off so easily and was demanding a legitimate apology that didn't involve Tanya shifting half of the blame onto the younger woman's shoulders.

As they argued, I unwrapped the long bath towel in my lap. Inside it was a glass jar like the kind used for pickles or olives. I completely uncovered the jar, placing the towel on the floor next to me. I lifted the jar up. There were objects floating inside the liquid within the jar. In that dim light, however, I could not discern what it was that was floating inside. At the same time, I thanked God that it had landed in my lap instead of the marble floor. The sound of the glass breaking would certainly have given away my hiding place nor been camouflaged by the sound of running water in the bathroom sink.

With my knee, I nudged the door a little more open. I raised the jar once more, and was astonished at what I saw. It looked like they were cut off human penises and tongues. I looked more closely, and realized that my eyes had not been deceiving me. I could even see veins and pieces of cartilage hanging from the stumps. It was clear that the amputations had been performed with a dull instrument. A feeling of horror gripped my body as I remembered Maggie's words earlier when she told me that I didn't even know what kind of horrible things she had done.

I covered my privates with my hand as I made a face of revulsion. I carefully wrapped the jar back up, trying not to make a sound, and replaced it on the shelf from which it had fallen. After I had done this, a feeling of confusion and terror swept through me as I recollected once more Maggie's words: I don't know what part you have to play in this nightmare.

A cold sweat rolled down my forehead, and I mopped my face with the back of my hand. I didn't know if it was my nerves or the smallness of that closet, but it seemed to shrink in size and the temperature seemed to increase. I had to wonder what those body parts were doing in Maggie's bathroom.

In the meantime, it appeared that Tanya and Maggie had reached an agreement. The tone of their voices had grown more familial and friendly, calmer. Maggie certainly had lost the abrasiveness in her voice.

I decided to leave my hiding place at this point to get near to the bathroom door so that I could listen better. Now that their conversation was being carried on in more normal tones, it had grown inaudible. As I left, I explored a little more. I saw another closet near the door to the bathroom. Several bathrobes hung inside—in case I had to run and hide, I would not have to return to the tiny closet with its macabre contents.

Suddenly, Maggie's voice regained its rebellious tone as she screamed, "I told you a million times! I'm not a little girl anymore. I've also told you that you have to let me decide what is good or bad for me, because I will never learn to be independent and on my own one day if I don't make my own mistakes! You know how much I love my stepfather. How dare you hide his death from me—because you think it's the best thing for me? I never had any father but him! This is unbelievable, Aunt Tanya! You tried to push on me this rapist piece of crap man who's never even recognized me as his daughter, knowing that the only father who actually raised and protected me was Papá Aldames. It's certainly something I never had from your dear friend! How dare you keep this news from me for all these weeks?"

Tanya replied, "Precisely because of that is why I never told you. It happened right in the middle of the worst nervous crisis you've ever had, when you cut the head and other things off of the man who delivered us drinking water to our home in Nautico." I nervously covered my privates once more with one hand, while the other caressed my neck.

Maggie shouted even louder, "Why don't you yell that even louder, so that everyone will hear you? Better yet, why don't you put it in the most important newspaper in Havana? Do you have an empty head, or have you forgotten that we have guests in this house? Since, however, you're saying that, why not make it complete? That prick tried to rape me! Don't tell only half the story, give them the whole story!"

Tanya tried to calm her down. In a kindly tone, she said, "Maggie, calm down, please. We both know that many women get raped in the world, but they don't decapitate the rapist nor cut off his sexual organs. By the way, Mr. Aldames is already dead and buried. I didn't tell you that because you were going through a crisis at that moment. I was protecting you. I don't know if you can understand that, but I did it for your own good. If you want, when we return from our vacation, I will give you some money, and if it will give you any peace, I'll go with you so that we can buy a floral arrangement to leave on his grave."

Maggie got hysterical at that. "Everything you want to fix with goddamned money! This time, it's too late! I should have been there at his funeral when it happened, just like he was at my mother's funeral, while I was going through my pain. Because of you, I failed him by not being there when he needed me the most, in his last minutes! You just told me he didn't die instantly. How could you not think of that before? How could you not realize it would break my heart?" She began to cry hysterically. "How can I live with that on my conscience?"

Apparently Tanya moved to console her, because Maggie screamed, "Don't touch me! Get away from me! Leave me in peace!"

In a loving tone, Tanya said, "I know the pain you're feeling at this moment, Maggie. It's completely natural. I know you loved him; but after all, he was not your real father. Your real father is Ernesto Guevara, and he wants to get close to you so he can try to help you. Don't let this great opportunity he's offering you pass you by. Remember, he has all the influence and power in this world to give you a happy life."

Maggie screamed at the top of her lungs, "I don't want anything to do with that Nazi-loving communist assassin! His hands are filled with innocent blood! Mine are blood-soaked, too, but the blood on my hands are from murderers and rapists like him!"

The Deadly Deals

Tanya grew angry now, and her tone became more intense. "Communist, yes—but where did you get that idea that Che's a Nazi lover? Have you gone crazy? What is wrong with you?"

Maggie's tone lost its hysteria and changed to one of cynicism. "Don't pretend with me to be an innocent, OK? I'm living in the same house with you, and I've heard with these two ears not too long ago in our home about the papers in his wallet that my mother stole from him before she killed herself. Those papers contained a photo ID card from the Nazi Party that he was a member of in his youth in Argentina. I heard him tell you that they were in a safe in Papá's office. To use his own words, it was your 'damn sister' who had those compromising documents. She told him before she died that she was going to ruin him. Sometimes I wonder whether my mother killed herself, or if he sent someone to kill her!"

Tanya's tone was defensive. "You must have heard wrong. Why the hell would Che have any relationship with the Nazis? On the contrary, he's a Communist."

Maggie said ironically, "That's not all that I heard. I also heard that those friends of his used the money they sent from Argentina to consolidate Hitler's power in Germany. Sometimes I wonder why the house was torn apart when my mother died. They said it was because she went crazy, but it always looked to me like someone was looking for something."

Everything clicked together in my mind. I knew that they hadn't found what they were looking for and must have killed her anyway. Maggie screamed once more, "From what you just told me, the exact same thing just happened with Aldames. It wasn't a robbery—it was a very well-planned murder, organized at the very highest level: that of your partner, Che!"

Tanya replied loudly in a voice which sounded demoralized, "You are crazy! You don't want people to say that you're talking like an idiot. Now, not only did Che kill your mother, but he killed Aldames as well, all to recover a photo ID of his membership in a political group...."

Maggie interrupted, "The Nationalist Liberation Alliance was the name of the group. They even had a bird as a logo that looked like the Nazi eagle."

"Maggie, Maggie, Maggie," Tanya said, "even if this is true, how is this detrimental to Che? All it shows is that, before he was a Communist, he sympathized with some kind of Nazi organization in Argentina. What relevance does that have today? We all change political ideas. What difference does it make now? Really, Maggie—your psychiatrists are one hundred percent on the ball. You're not only a schizophrenic, but you're also delusional."

Maggie replied, "It's very possible that I'm both. But what I've heard from the mouths of both you and Che does not change my mental state. I would love to see the headlines not only in Cuba, but all around the world: 'Commander Ernesto Guevara—Ex-Nazi Supporter and Hitler Associate.' That won't sit very well with the political image he wants to establish internationally."

Tanya yelled, "Do not dare to speak of this to anyone! Anyone you tell this to, you sentence to death!" Her tone was menacing now. "Watch out, young lady, because you could end up like that man in our house with his head cut off and your tongue up your ass!"

Maggie yelled back, "You and Che don't scare me—not a single one of you. I know how to defend myself. And before that happens, I will cut you both into pieces! I would prefer a thousand times over being a delusional schizophrenic to being a salaried murderer, like the rest of you, for a house in Varadero and another one in Havana's exclusive Nautico district, with a new Jaguar at the door! You're merely an associate to the rapist and murderer of your own sister, a murderer of boys, women, and men all over the globe. Oh, and let us not forget the occasional tumble you take in bed with the father of your own niece!"

I heard the sound of a loud smack, and Maggie screamed in pain. "You going crazy, *carajo*? Who are you, to raise your hand to me? That's it! That's it!" I heard the sound of drawers opening. "I'm getting the fuck out of here. I don't ever want to see you again—you get out of my room right now, or I'll cut you to pieces! I'm sick of all this bullshit and humiliation!"

I heard Tanya in a calm voice say, "I'm sorry, Maggie, I'm sorry. You just manage to drive me out of my head sometimes."

The sound of drawers opening and closing continued to sound, as if Maggie were looking for something but was unable to find it.

Tanya must have tried to hold or embrace her, because Maggie yelled again, "Stay away, or I'll cut you into pieces!"

Tanya screamed in pain. "What are you doing with that razor? I've prohibited you from having any cutting tools with you!" The sound of rapid footsteps told me that Maggie must have run after her with the razor. "My God, Maggie, have you gone crazy? You're going to hurt someone with that!"

"Get out of here! Get out, or I'll decapitate you like you do to your enemies and make you disappear."

The door opened quickly and slammed shut once more. The drawers continued to open and close. I heard footsteps walking in my direction. There was no time to get into the closet, so I ducked into the shower and hid behind the curtain. It was very fortunate that I did so, because the first thing she did was go to that closet.

She violently yanked all the bathrobes out, nearly ripping the hangers through the fabric as she did so. She left and threw the robes on the bed, returning a few seconds later to retrieve the painting from the linen closet. A few more seconds later, she got the jar.

Around the corner of the curtain, I could see what she was doing. Her face was red with fury, and her eyes continually wept tears, as she repeatedly wiped at them with her hand. She paused in front of the mirror and said to her reflection, "Father, they will pay. Even if you're dead like my aunt says, I promise to you that they will not impugn you the way they did my mother. This I swear." She kissed her thumb to her reflection. She bit her bottom lip and shook her head.

"Pricks," she muttered.

She turned the lights off, and a few minutes later I heard the door to her room open and close. I remained where I was, because I knew she would not be able to carry all of that in a single trip. I didn't regret my decision, because it wasn't long before she returned. She made two more trips, and then came once more into the bathroom to use the toilet once more. She washed her face in one of the sinks.

Finally, she left. I waited for fifteen minutes. When I heard no further noise, I left my hiding place. Slowly, I entered the bedroom to make sure she had nothing left there. Only then did I open the door and quickly got out of

The Deadly Deals

there. Trying not to make any noise, I went straight to my room. To my surprise, wrapped in the same towel as before with a note attached, I saw the painting on my door. I brought them quickly inside my room and closed the door.

I read the note: "Thank you for coming to meet me. Thank you for all your gentleness and the pleasant time you gave me, as well as all the other things that you and I know I have to thank you for. I will hold you in my heart always as the great friend and brother I never had.

"Unfortunately, I have to cut short my vacation and change my plans. But I don't want this to ruin your vacation here. I leave you this painting as a present. Maybe you can find a logical reason in all these irrational things. If you don't want it, please destroy it, but don't tell anyone where it came from or mention my name. As you can see, the painting is not signed.

"Thank you for all you did for me, and I'm sorry I didn't say goodbye in person, but I didn't want to wake you up. I left very early in the morning. Don't believe a single word my aunt tells you. She is a sophisticated spy for your 'friend,' Che. She is in his service and will do anything, even kill for him and all the delinquents around him. They've taken this beautiful Revolution from my mother and from us. Your friend to death, Maggie. Love, peace, and friendship.

"P.S. Be careful with my aunt. She is extremely dangerous, perhaps even more dangerous than Che. Please destroy this note as soon as you read it and flush it down the toilet. I trust you, and I thank you again for everything. Your dark friend, Maggie."

I picked up the picture and took it out to the trunk of the Mercedes in the exact same way she had wrapped it.

As I did so, I saw that the MG was gone. I felt a tremendous release that Maggie had departed. There was no doubt in my mind that she was not completely together mentally. I didn't need to be a psychiatrist to know that.

However, after hearing the conversation between her and Tanya, I made up my mind that I preferred to be in her company on a deserted island or anywhere than to be in the companionship of her Aunt Tanya. No matter what her problems were, Maggie had more principles and human values than her hypocritical aunt. After that conversation, Tanya was to me a photocopy of Che. It was probably why they got along so well.

At that moment, I realized that while sitting inside that small closet I had already decided to cut short my mini-vacation. The motive behind her aunt's invitation was, in truth, that I associate with her rebellious niece.

She had come to the realization, perhaps recently, of Maggie's sexual preference. Since Tanya didn't embrace that, she probably wanted me to attract her to desiring men over women. She might even have felt guilty, to a certain point, for being in part responsible for isolating her niece from all the young men of Maggie's age simply because none of them met Tanya's standards. She had only brought Maggie to the Tropicana as a way to bring her into her lifestyle. As a result, Maggie had only associated from a very early age with Tanya's fellow dancers, who had a tendency towards a homosexual lifestyle.

Maggie had probably seen men kissing each other as well as women kissing each other, and had grown up as thinking of it as perfectly normal. Since her aunt had never made a derogatory comment about it in her presence, it must then have gained the force of approval. Maggie now found it completely strange as a young adult that her aunt would recriminate her for being a lesbian herself and attempt to separate her from her friends, the same people who had been around her all her life. Given this, the purpose of my visit must therefore have been nullified, now that Maggie had abandoned her vacation to return to Havana.

I realized that, after a single day there and sweating my rear off in the early morning hours in that closet, there was a very real possibility of losing my manhood, my tongue, or even my head, and that image did not sit very well in my mind. At that moment, I didn't have a single one of my weapons on me, not even my poison ring, and so would have been defenseless had I been discovered and assaulted. I sweated bullets as I imagined those two women tying me up and mutilating my body. It briefly crossed my mind that Tanya's reason for inviting me there was only because she, in a conspiracy with Che, wanted to get rid of me.

I returned to the house and my room, composing a note to Tanya in my mind, giving some excuse as to my departure that I could leave at the door to her room. Certainly the most prudent action for me was to get out of there as soon as possible. As I was gathering my things together, I realized that not everything that had happened was bad. In a single day, I had achieved four things of great importance for my work.

First, I had given a kick in the backside to Ramiro Valdés—one of Piñeiro's partners in crime, one of the worst schemers in Castro's government. I had managed to humiliate him, watching him roll around in the sand like the worm he liked to characterize his enemies as. It gave me joy to see him eat the dirt he deserved. That I hadn't even planned it only added sauce to my pleasure.

Second, I had gotten to know the true personality and feelings of one of my worst enemies, as well as elements of his dark and nefarious past. Che's previous association with the Nazis as a youth could come in handy at some point. Che's first political steps directed him to ally with the worst international criminals, who were responsible for the wholesale slaughter of Jews in their concentration camps around Europe. It said a lot about his ambitions and lack of morality. Che only dreamed of power, and in that dream he had initially embraced the Nazi flag. When he saw that it wasn't going to go well, he only switched to another flag bent on world domination: the Soviet flag, converting himself into an international spy in service to the KGB.

Third, I finally had discovered who really was the dark hand behind the murder of Mr. Aldames. I had been having doubts for so long as to why it had happened. Neither Tanya nor Maggie knew that I had physically been a witness to the execution of that honest man. Now, from their argument, I knew the reason. I had come to the conclusion that, without any doubt, Che had commanded this in order to erase an inconvenient portion of his past. He had sent his most trustworthy man, Fausto, who also was one of the most dangerous assassins he had on the payroll. Fausto was only sent on special missions of extreme importance because of his efficiency in destroying evidence. If his Soviet masters, especially, discovered Che's previous Nazi sympathies, his future would become most uncertain. I shook my head in distress as I remembered the details of that terrible day in Mr. Aldames' office. It was engraved in my memory and will be for the rest of my life. Perhaps destiny put me there that day to be the sole witness of that criminal act so that it would not go unpunished.

All the pieces of the puzzle were now in my possession. I had to credit Maggie for helping me reach the conclusion that Che was behind it all, even though she had not been there herself.

Fourth was the picture. I had actually managed to obtain that from Maggie without stealing it. I now was free to take it to Doña Carmen and get an answer to all the crazy nonsense I could not comprehend in that portrait.

I sat down at the desk and wrote a note to Tanya. After I finished, I packed my travel bags in preparation to leave. I wanted to make sure I left everything as clean as I had found it and was putting the finishing touches on the bed when the door behind me opened, surprising me. I had not locked it, anticipating an immediate departure. Entering the room with a tray of breakfast in her hands, a large smile on her face, and wearing a completely transparent bathrobe was Tanya. She said, "Good morning." She looked at my bags lying on the floor in surprise. "What's the matter? Are you leaving?"

I shamefacedly pulled the note out of my shirt pocket and handed it to her: "Thank you for all the great attention and courtesies. I didn't want to wake you up, so I wrote you this note. Truthfully, I couldn't sleep very well last night. All night I dreamed I heard voices and fights between two people. Apparently they never reached any agreement, and I kept waking up all night. I got out of bed and was going to go to the Mercedes. When I opened my door, I found a note from Maggie on it. She told me in her note that she was going back to the house in the capital. So I decided it would be better if I left, too. After all, the only reason you brought me over here was to be your niece's companion."

Tanya turned and set the tray down on the dresser. She turned back to face me and stepped to me. She hugged me and kissed my cheek. "Oh, no, no, no. I didn't only invite you for Maggie. Of course, I want you to be her friend, but you're also a very good person. I know we'll have a great time with you here. You'll bring a little of your good personality and happiness to us, which would make for us a great vacation together."

She paused. She leaned away, but kept hold of my arms. "Don't let Maggie and her psychoses and schizophrenia ruin both your vacation and mine. After I spoke with Che before coming out here, he said you really deserve to have a week's vacation. He asked me to treat you with all the respect and honor you deserve. He said you are a great friend, loyal, and you give the best of your service to the Revolution."

I replied with a small smile. "Thank you." I was a little uncomfortable with the close proximity to her with that translucent gown.

I picked up my travel bags once more. "I really appreciate all your attention and hospitality, and thank you for making that breakfast so early in the morning for me, but you must forgive me. I'm not hungry. Maggie offered me some mangoes last night and I ate them just this morning. I was even dreaming of them last night, since I didn't want to spoil my appetite for that wonderful dinner with you guys by eating them when she first offered them to me."

The Deadly Deals

"Don't worry," she said. "If you're full, I'll save the breakfast for myself. By the way, what you thought you heard in your dreams was no dream. It was me and Maggie—we argued pretty badly and loudly early this morning. I'm sorry we disturbed you and didn't let you sleep in peace. Unfortunately, Maggie gets worse the older she gets. She's becoming very irresponsible and spoiled. Actually, she scared me this morning. She actually pulled a razor blade on me. I don't think I'm going to be able to live with her for much longer. At the same time, I fear that if I let her go, she might end up mixed up with the Counterrevolutionaries. Her hatred for her father blinds her to the point of blaming him even for the death of my sister. Che had nothing to do with that—my sister was another schizophrenic. Maggie is a replica of her in that regard. I don't know if you are aware of it, but she's tried to kill herself a couple of times. I won't be surprised to discover that one of these days she does exactly what her mother did, and blows her brains out."

Tanya paused and looked me directly in the eyes. "Do you mind if I read the note Maggie left for you?"

I replied very seriously. "I'm very sorry. I did what she told me to do in the note: after I read it, I tore it into pieces and flushed it down the toilet."

Tanya shook her head gravely, not too pleased. Her expression grew sad. "If she put nothing compromising in that note, why would she ask you to do such a thing?"

I shook my head. "I didn't understand it myself, either, when I read it at the end of her note. But as a disciplined and loyal soldier, I learned in the past years to comply with orders and not argue about them. Out of loyalty to the great friendship we were cultivating over the few hours, I complied with her wishes immediately."

Tanya shook her head and smiled cynically as she scratched her cheek absently. "Even if she didn't ask you to destroy the note but only not to show it to me, you would be doing the same, wouldn't you?"

I grew deadly serious at that. "Yes, ma'am. And I think that's something nobody should have to be ashamed of and should all admire in somebody, even though it bothers us a little, just because it's not exactly what we wanted to hear. But whoever is not loyal to their friends cannot ever be loyal to us."

Tanya said, "Of course, but we should have priorities with certain people. Especially in this case, when I was the one to invite you to my house."

She paused and looked at me. My attitude did not change as I continued to look her in the eyes gravely. An awkward silence ensued as neither of us spoke for a few seconds.

Finally, she half-smiled and said, "Well, your attitude makes me feel a lot better. Taking into consideration that you are Che's friend, even if Maggie wrote something about him that could be detrimental to his political career and damage his reputation, I know for a fact that you will not repeat that to anybody. Will you?"

I stared her in the eyes and replied, "I don't think I've earned the trust of Che, Fidel, Raul, Camilo, and many others because I was prone to tell one what the other has been saying whenever they were not getting along with each other one hundred percent."

This time, Tanya's smile was genuine. She put her hand on my shoulder and said, "You know what? It's really a pity that you've decided to leave. But if that's what you want, I cannot stop you."

She sighed. "Even though you're very young, when I listen to you I can close my eyes and ignore your age and have a great and magnificent time with you as a companion. Now that Maggie's left, it means you and me only in this house. Andres had to go to the middle of the island for a few weeks for a military exercise. I will be very lonely in this big house for the rest of the week. But if you decide to leave, like I said before—I cannot hold you. In my life, I've never met a mature man with your qualities."

I smiled and said, "Thank you very much. I really have to go, but I appreciate your comments. They mean a lot to me coming from somebody who has the absolute trust of Che—and a beautiful, desirable woman with a great personality like yours. From the bottom of my heart, I hope you find a way to enjoy the rest of your vacation."

I pulled my book out of my pocket and wrote my phone number on it. "This is my home number in Pinar del Rio—for you and Maggie only."

She smiled and hugged me again.

On my way out, I said, "Don't worry—Maggie will be back in a few days, once she's got over her anger, probably asking for forgiveness."

Tanya rolled her eyes. "I doubt it. Maybe, when she comes back, she won't find me here. I'm very mad with her, and I'm sick and tired of her neuroses."

I showed her the key to the house. "Do you want me to put this back where I found it?"

"Yes, yes. Oh, and if you want to come back here and bring somebody, this is your house. Don't lose the code for the gate."

"Thank you very much. You are very generous and

polite."

She waved that off dismissively. "You have a good trip back to the capital. I'm sorry for all the inconvenience you had here."

I smiled. "What inconvenience? I didn't have any."

I left the house, closing the door behind me. I put the travel bags in the trunk, went over to the pool, and left the key under the planter. I got into the car, put some paper napkins in my lap, and unwrapped some of the mangoes I had in a bag. I ate my breakfast as I drove off.

With a satisfied smile on my face as I ate, I thought that nothing in this world, even if I died of hunger, would make me even consider touching the breakfast that Tanya had brought to me after I what I had overheard in that bedroom in the early morning hours. I knew that Tanya was capable of doing anything to protect Che. If it even remotely crossed her mind that Maggie had made any confession to me about what she wanted to hide from Che, I could have wound up being another victim of coincidence, only because I happened to be in that house that day. Maggie had sympathized with me, which she normally didn't do with anyone. Even though that was what Tanya had initially been looking for, the irony was that the series of events that unfolded could have turned that instead to a death sentence for me. It had crossed my mind even as Maggie had recited the headline she had pictured about Che.

This concludes the fourth part of Rites of Passage of a Master Spy. Julio Antonio's trials and adventures continue in Volume V, Evil Rituals. For even further adventures of the Lightning, visit our website, www.cuban-lightning.com.

Photo Credits

p. 19 1959 Buick La Sabre
Photo by Nimmerya at https://commons.wikimedia.org/wiki/File:1959_Buick_Elektra_225_Riviera_Sedan_side.JPG

p. 22 1957 Oldsmobile
Photo by dave_7 at https://commons.wikimedia.org/wiki/File:1959_Oldsmobile_(1261625198).jpg

p. 124 Some of Che's "Amazons"—dancers at the Tropicana
Photo by Bgabel at https://commons.wikimedia.org/wiki/File:Cub_h_tropicana.jpg

p. 138 The Hotel Riviera
Open domain per https://commons.wikimedia.org/wiki/File:Hotel_Riviera-Havana.JPG

p. 191 Arzate, in his cover passing out pamphlets in New Orleans

Open domain per https://commons.wikimedia.org/wiki/Lee_Harvey_Oswald#/media/File:Pizzo_Exh_B-Oswald_leaflets_FPFC-WH_Vol21_139.jpg

p. 227 The entrance to the luxury resort of Varadero Beach

Photo credit AlejandroLinaresGarcia at https://commons.wikimedia.org/wiki/File:VaraderoBeach05.JPG

p. 230 Maggie's MG

Photo credit Jaguar from cs at https://commons.wikimedia.org/wiki/File:Mg_B.JPG

p. 233 Area Maggie preferred to use while painting

Photo credit Gardenparty at https://commons.wikimedia.org/wiki/File:Varadero_beach_20.jpg

p. 279 Beach where the Ministry of the Interior confronted the young kids, breaking up their beach party

Photo credit AlejandroLinaresGarcia at https://commons.wikimedia.org/wiki/File:VaraderoBeach31.JPG

The Deadly Deals

Other Works

Cuba: Russian Roulette of the World
The Cuban Lightning: The Zipper

Rites of Passage of a Master Spy saga
Cuba: The Truth, the Lies, and the Coverups
The Havana Conspiracies
The Dark Face of Marxism

Forthcoming
The Evil Rituals
JFK: The Unwrapped Enigma

www.ingramcontent.com/pod-product-compliance
Lightning Source LLC
Chambersburg PA
CBHW031308150426
43191CB00005B/134